ECHOES of GLORY

Time-Life Books also publishes a series of books that chronicles in full the events of the American Civil War, 1861-1865. The titles are:

BROTHER AGAINST BROTHER *The War Begins*
FIRST BLOOD *Fort Sumter to Bull Run*
THE BLOCKADE *Runners and Raiders*
THE ROAD TO SHILOH *Early Battles in the West*
FORWARD TO RICHMOND *McClellan's Peninsular Campaign*
DECOYING THE YANKS *Jackson's Valley Campaign*
CONFEDERATE ORDEAL *The Southern Home Front*
LEE TAKES COMMAND *From Seven Days to Second Bull Run*
THE COASTAL WAR *Chesapeake Bay to Rio Grande*
TENTING TONIGHT *The Soldier's Life*
THE BLOODIEST DAY *The Battle of Antietam*
WAR ON THE MISSISSIPPI *Grant's Vicksburg Campaign*
REBELS RESURGENT *Fredericksburg to Chancellorsville*
TWENTY MILLION YANKEES *The Northern Home Front*
GETTYSBURG *The Confederate High Tide*
THE STRUGGLE FOR TENNESSEE *Tupelo to Stones River*
THE FIGHT FOR CHATTANOOGA *Chickamauga to Missionary Ridge*
SPIES, SCOUTS AND RAIDERS *Irregular Operations*
THE BATTLES FOR ATLANTA *Sherman Moves East*
THE KILLING GROUND *Wilderness to Cold Harbor*
SHERMAN'S MARCH *Atlanta to the Sea*
DEATH IN THE TRENCHES *Grant at Petersburg*
WAR ON THE FRONTIER *The Trans-Mississippi West*
THE SHENANDOAH IN FLAMES *The Valley Campaign of 1864*
PURSUIT TO APPOMATTOX *The Last Battles*
THE ASSASSINATION *The Death of the President*
THE NATION REUNITED *War's Aftermath*
MASTER INDEX *An Illustrated Guide*

For information on and a full description of the Time-Life
Books series listed above, please call 1-800-621-7026 or write:
Reader Information
Time-Life Customer Service
P.O. Box 85568
Richmond, Virginia 23285-5568

Echoes of Glory is a three-volume set. The other titles are:

Arms and Equipment of the Confederacy
Illustrated Atlas of the Civil War

ECHOES of GLORY

ARMS AND EQUIPMENT OF

THE UNION

By the Editors of Time-Life Books

TIME-LIFE BOOKS · ALEXANDRIA · VIRGINIA

Time-Life Books is a division of Time Life Inc.

TIME LIFE INC.
PRESIDENT and CEO: George Artandi

TIME-LIFE BOOKS
PRESIDENT: John D. Hall
PUBLISHER/MANAGING EDITOR: Neil Kagan
Vice President, Director of Finance: Christopher Hearing
Vice President, Book Production: Marjann Caldwell
Director of Operations: Eileen Bradley
Director of Photography and Research: John Conrad Weiser
Director of Editorial Administration: Barbara Levitt
Chief Librarian: Louise D. Forstall

Published by Time-Life in conjunction with
Borders Press, a division of Borders, Inc.
311 Maynard, Ann Arbor, Michigan 48104

Tally Hall Press is a trademark of Borders Properties, Inc.

Printed in 1996. © MCMXCI Time-Life Books.
Second printing. Printed in U.S.A.

Published simultaneously in Canada.
School and library distribution by Silver Burdett
Company, Morristown, New Jersey 07960.

TIME-LIFE is a trademark of Time Warner Inc. U.S.A.

Library of Congress Cataloging in Publication Data
Arms and equipment of the union / by the editors of
  Time-Life Books.
      p.   cm. — (Echoes of glory)
  Includes bibliographical references and index.
  ISBN 0-8094-8854-X (trade)
  ISBN 0-8094-8855-8 (lib. bdg.)
  1. United States. Army—Firearms. 2. United States.
Army—Equipment. 3. United States—History—
Civil War, 1861-1865—Equipment and supplies.
I. Time-Life Books. II. Series.
UD383.A75 1991 973.7'41—dc20 91-2277 CIP

ECHOES OF GLORY
Editor: Henry Woodhead
Administrator: Jane Edwin
Art Director: Herbert H. Quarmby
Deputy Editors: Harris J. Andrews, Kirk E. Denkler

Editorial Staff for Arms and Equipment
of the Union
Picture Editor: Kristin Baker Hanneman
Writers: Marfé Ferguson Delano, Barbara C. Mallen
Assistant Editor/Research: Quentin Gaines Story
Senior Copy Coordinator: Anne Farr
Editorial Assistant: Jayne A. L. Dover

Special Contributors: Carolee Belkin Walker (copy);
Kenneth C. Danforth, Stephen G. Hyslop, Kimberly A.
Kostyal, M. Linda Lee, Brian C. Pohanka, Jennifer J.
Veech (text); Anne K. DuVivier (art); Gail V. Feinberg
(pictures); Roy Nanovic (index)

Correspondents: Elisabeth Kraemer-Singh (Bonn),
Christine Hinze (London), Christina Lieberman (New
York), Maria Vincenze Aloisi (Paris), Ann Natanson
(Rome)

Photographs by Larry Sherer

Consultants and Special Contributors:

Earl J. Coates, a historian and museum curator for the U.S.
Department of Defense, has studied Civil War arms and
equipment for the past 30 years, specializing in supply
operations. He has written numerous articles on the subject and is the coauthor of An Introduction to Civil War
Small Arms. He is a member of the Company of Military
Historians and the North-South Skirmish Association,
which he serves as deputy commander.

Mark Elrod is a historian and musicologist with an in-
terest in 19th-century America. He organized and
equipped the Federal City Cornet Band of Washington,
D.C., a re-creation of a mid-19th-century United States
military band. A fellow in the Company of Military Historians, he has coauthored A Pictorial History of Civil
War Era Musical Instruments and Military Bands.

Col. John R. Elting, USA (Ret.), former associate professor
at West Point, has written or edited some 20 books,
including Swords around a Throne, The Superstrategists,
and American Army Life, as well as Battles for Scandi-
navia in the Time-Life Books World War II series. He was
chief consultant to the Time-Life series The Civil War.

Les Jensen, museum curator with the U.S. Department of
the Army, specializes in Civil War artifacts. A fellow of the
Company of Military Historians and a contributor to The
Image of War series, he is also a consultant for numerous
Civil War publications and museums and author of the
32d Virginia Infantry volume in the Virginia Regimental
Histories Series. He was for eight years the curator of
collections of the Museum of the Confederacy in Richmond, Virginia.

Michael McAfee specializes in military uniforms and has
been curator of uniforms and history at the West Point
Museum since 1970. A fellow of the company of Military
Historians, he coedited with Col. John Elting Long Endure: The Civil War Years and collaborated with Frederick Todd on American Military Equipage. He is the
author of Artillery of the American Revolution, 1775-
1783, and has written numerous articles for Military
Images Magazine.

Howard Michael Madaus, curator of the history section
of the Milwaukee Public Museum since 1968, is a noted
authority on Civil War flags and firearms. In addition to
supervising exhibits of military equipment, he is the author of two books, The Battle Flags of the Confederate
Army of Tennessee and The Warner Collector's Guide to
American Longarms. He has also published numerous
articles relating to military equipage in such journals as
Military Collector & Historian and The Flag Bulletin.

Chris Nelson, a former journalist, has been a Civil War
collector and reenactor for more than 30 years. He is
a member of the Company of Military Historians, a
contributing editor to Military Images Magazine, and
the coauthor of Photographs of American Civil War
Cavalry.

Contents

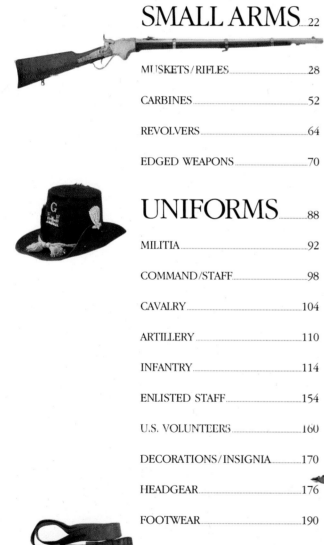

6

A Federal brigade commanded by General Winfield Scott Hancock *(on brown horse at left)* repulses a Confederate attack at Williamsburg in May of

1862. The action, for which Hancock earned the sobriquet "The Superb," was painted by Julian Scott.

Brotherhood of Arms

Men of the 78th Pennsylvania Infantry doffed their hats for this group portrait taken atop Lookout Mountain, Tennessee. The regiment served at Chattanooga from December 1863 until May 1864, when it marched into Georgia. Caught in the open at Pickett's Mill on May 27, the Pennsylvanians held for four hours and suffered 49 casualties before being ordered to withdraw.

It was the sixth of April 1862, and 20,000 Federal soldiers from Major General Don Carlos Buell's Army of the Ohio were marching toward the distant sounds of battle. The Civil War was nearly a year old, but most of Buell's midwesterners had yet to hear a shot fired in anger. Now they would finally "see the elephant"—the soldier's euphemism for combat that conjured up the awe rural Americans experienced when a traveling circus and its exotic menagerie came to town. The largest engagement of the War to date was under way, a massive bloodletting on a four-mile-wide front between Pittsburg Landing and a humble log parsonage called Shiloh Church.

In the shuffling column of blue-clad troops marched a 19-year-old Indiana store clerk named Lindley B. Moore. The private had signed up with Company F of the 30th Indiana Volunteer Infantry as a musician six months earlier, and during an uneventful tour of duty in Kentucky and Tennessee he had found war to be a mighty dull affair. His company "was all of good material," Moore remembered, "but without experience." Most of the men thought that the fight up ahead would not amount to much, and some "offered odds that we would go home without smelling burnt powder."

But when the firing grew in intensity to a dull roar, even the skeptical became silent and apprehensive. The men picked up their pace, possessed of what Moore called "that indefinable feeling which seems to precede great battles—a feeling at that time so new to us that we did not recognize it."

It was dark and raining by the time the Union troops passed through the Tennessee River town of Savannah and boarded steamboats to take them the last few miles to the battlefield. Moore and his comrades had to push their way through ambulance wagons and throngs of stretcher-bearers bringing back the wounded. Regimental bands tried to inspire the jittery reinforcements with patriotic airs, but Moore thought the music seemed "a little out of place."

The Indianans found an even more chaotic state of affairs when they disembarked at Pittsburg Landing. Moore would never forget the sight of raindrops splashing on the pale faces of the dead, and the vacant stares of muddy, powder-smeared survivors—"a scene calculated to make a profound impression on an imaginative boy but lately loosed from his mother's apron strings."

Dawn of April 7 found Moore and the 30th Indiana ready to play their part in the second day of the Battle of Shiloh. The men stripped off their knapsacks and moved forward through thick woods, struggling to preserve their alignment. The officers' brusque commands, combined with the jostling and cursing, reminded Moore of the familiar frustrations of battalion drill. He decided they were "fooling away time."

There was still no enemy in sight when orders came to halt. Then further instructions were shouted: "Load at will" and "Fix bayonets." Moore likened the clink of bayonets on hundreds of musket barrels to "a noise like the dumping of a cartload of railroad spikes." At the colonel's command the colorbearers unfurled the regimental flags, but since there was no wind, the banners "drooped rather despondingly about the staffs."

The men of the 30th Indiana had barely resumed their advance when the war exploded all around them. A Federal brigade came tumbling back in confusion, pursued by Confederates whose high-pitched rebel yell rose eerily above the crash of musketry. "I was nearly stunned by the volley which blazed from the woods in front," Moore recalled, "a noise surpassing anything I had ever imagined." The Yankees returned fire, and soon the line was shrouded in a thick cloud of sulfurous smoke.

Moore loaded and fired as fast as he could as bullets scythed through the ranks around him. His colonel was shot twice, and the major went down. "Men were falling in every direction, or hobbling, wounded, to the rear." At one point the regiment began to break, then reformed alongside its colors. Moore caught a glimpse of the brigade commander, bleeding from a severe wound but bravely flourishing the flag of an Illinois unit.

"By the time we had looked after the wounded a little, we realized that we were very tired, very hungry, and very glad that the battle of Shiloh was over."

PRIVATE LINDLEY B. MOORE
30TH INDIANA INFANTRY
REGIMENT

"All at once the men began to cheer," Moore wrote. As suddenly as it had begun, the firing ceased, and the cloud of smoke lifted to reveal gray-uniformed regiments in full retreat. Fresh Union troops came jogging into line at a double-quick, their commander cursing because they had arrived too late to share in the fighting. The 30th Indiana marched back toward the landing to replenish ammunition and reorganize its depleted ranks.

Private Moore realized that he had lost all track of time. "I thought it must be about noon," he recalled, "and my thoughts naturally turned toward dinner, but, to my astonishment, it began to grow dark. By the time we had looked after the wounded a little, we realized that we were very tired, very hungry, and very glad that the battle of Shiloh was over."

Lindley Moore had seen the elephant.

Attended by a crowd of well-wishers in Detroit, the 1st Michigan Volunteers receives its colors in May of 1861. Photographer Jex Bardwell's image is marred by a crack across the glass negative.

Government statistics reveal that the average Union soldier was 25 years old, with brown hair, blue eyes, and a light complexion; he stood five feet eight and a quarter inches tall, and weighed 143½ pounds. Like Moore, most hailed from a rural or small-town environment, although Northern armies contained a much higher percentage of urban recruits than did Southern forces. Of the two million men who served the Union, 500,000 were of foreign birth—principally German and Irish—and many units had an ethnic composition.

Although the Federal government was able to use the men and matériel of the prewar standing army, these regulars numbered fewer than 18,000 men who could fight. As was the case with their Confederate counterparts, most Northerners who flocked to the colors in 1861 were volunteers—recruited and organized under the auspices of the various states, then mustered into U.S. service. The disparity in population between North and South was reflected in the numbers of regiments that served. Whereas a Confederate state might muster 80 regiments during the course of the war, New York fielded more than 250, Pennsylvania and Ohio some 200 each. The institution of the draft in 1863, and the widespread payment of bounties as an incentive to enlist, succeeded in maintaining the strength, if not the quality, of Union forces.

Young men of the North were moved to volunteer for a number of reasons. For some, it was the patriotic belief in the sanctity of the Republic. "We are God's servants, engaged in His work," stated Lieutenant Colonel James Rice of the 44th New York. "In the loss of our country all is lost." Harvard freshman Warren Lee Goss felt compelled to join up, "or forfeit my birthright as an American."

The abolition of slavery was the primary motivation for some enlistees, while others came to detest the institution through firsthand observation in occupied Southern territory. "The time is coming when the bright light of universal liberty will burst forth," an Illinois soldier predicted, "when the clank of the slave's chains and the crack of the driver's whip and the hollow moan of the goaded man shall be heard no more forever in our land."

Most Union troops, however, were decidedly ambivalent about the issue of emancipation, even when it became a stated war aim of the Union government. Some were outright opposed to the notion; Colonel Marcus Spiegel of the 127th Ohio informed his wife, "I do not fight or want to fight for Lincoln's Negro proclamation one day longer than I can help." Although many whites doubted the ability of black men to bear arms, 166 regiments of the United States Colored Troops would play a significant role in winning the war for the Union.

Whatever their ideological motivations, the volunteers manifested a cocky self-assurance and an overriding desire to get to the war before it was over. Cyrus Boyd, a sergeant in the 15th Iowa, wrote home that he and his comrades were "having lots of fun and glory," and were "proud as peacocks" in their new uniforms. But, like many another young soldier, Boyd's enthusiasm was

A soldier of the United States Colored Infantry poses with his wife and twin daughters in this wartime portrait. Altogether, 178,892 blacks served in the Union army, and 32,369, or more than a sixth of their number, died in uniform.

soon tempered by the harsh realities of military service. Four months later, the sergeant was camped in a disease-ridden bivouac on a bank of the Mississippi River. "Mud deep and growing deeper," he wrote. "Uniforms in bad plight—feet wet and cold and patriotism down to zero."

Early Union failures on the battlefield made it clear that the war would not end easily and quickly and that only rigorous training and firm discipline would enable the Federal soldiers to translate patriotism into victory. "We found ourselves in the iron grasp of stern, unrelenting military rules," recalled one soldier. "If every man among us had been a convicted felon, the cordon of guards around the camp could not have been more strenuously maintained." Three months into the war, another thought many of his comrades "would give all they possess to get free."

In a letter home, the 83d Pennsylvania's Oliver Willcox Norton informed his parents that "the first thing in the morning is drill, then drill, then drill again. Then drill, drill, a little more drill. Then drill, and lastly, drill. Between drills we drill, and sometimes stop to eat a little and have a roll call." Norton thought the drill was "as much as I can stand." Even if he did not realize it at the time, Private Norton was inevitably evolving into the disciplined, unquestioning member of the team that a soldier was expected to be.

Civil War tactics were predicated on the mid-19th-century doctrine that emphasized massed firepower rather than marksmanship. Whether on the drill field or the battlefield, each soldier was expected to maintain elbow contact with the man on either side, while a scant 13 inches separated the front and rear ranks of a regimental line of battle. Skirmishers generally went ahead to probe the enemy positions, but would habitually fall back on the main command once battle was joined. In theory, Civil War engagements consisted of blocks of men endeavoring to smash a way through their foe with volleys of musketry, then exploiting their success at the point of the bayonet.

Each of the 10 companies in a regiment was trained to work in concert with one another—wheeling and countermarching, maneuvering from column into line and back again—while the regiment itself similarly interacted with larger brigades and divisions. The complexities of company and battalion drill were outlined in detailed but often baffling fashion in tactical manuals whose perplexing terminology and enigmatic diagrams proved the bane of a generation of American officers.

The challenge of transforming independent-minded American citizens into a well-drilled fighting machine proved the undoing of many a fledgling commander. It did not help that more than a few new officers were political appointees with scant qualifications as leaders of men. One New Yorker characterized his colonel as "an habitual drunkard" who was "so testy and muddleheaded that he is no more fit to command a regiment than a schoolboy would be." Leander Stillwell of the 61st Illinois was chagrined to discover that his captain "had no military qualities whatever" and "could barely write his name." In drill the unfortunate officer was "laughable," replacing proper commands with frantic instructions to "swing around, boys, just like a gate."

But if some officers failed to rise to the challenge, others proved surprisingly proficient in their efforts to instill discipline. James A. Beaver, a 24-year-old Pennsylvania lawyer turned colonel, was a case in point. Beaver had the advantage of having served as the commander of a militia regiment before the War, and he put the experience to good use when he took charge of the newly recruited 148th Pennsylvania. The first thing Beaver did was to inspect his troops. Believing that an orderly appearance was a prerequisite for military proficiency, the colonel fined any man with a soiled shirt, a missing button, or a dirty face. Soldiers with rusted muskets or tarnished belt buckles risked confinement in the guardhouse. Beaver was equally insistent on strict uniformity of dress; as one subordinate remembered, "A slouch hat was an abomination

In a panoramic display of military muscle, two brigades of the Federal IV Corps maneuver during training exercises near Chattanooga in the spring of 1864. Skirmishers lead waves of double-ranked infantry across the field while artillery pieces draw up to give support. The IV Corps was part of General George Thomas' Army of the Cumberland, the largest of the armies that Sherman would lead into Georgia.

in the regiment." The camp was thoroughly policed, tents realigned according to regulations, stumps uprooted, and the company streets swept with a broom.

Once he was satisfied with the look of his troops, the colonel set about drilling the men with a fanaticism that one officer thought "would have done credit to a graduate of West Point after years of active service." Company and battalion drills occupied the better part of the day, and evening classes of instruction were held for company officers, sergeants, and corporals. Although the rank and file at first despised their commander as the worst type of martinet, his severity transformed the 148th Pennsylvania into one of the best volunteer units in the Army of the Potomac.

For a Yankee regiment, a typical day in camp began at dawn, with the regimental fifes and drums—bugles in the case of cavalry and artillery—sounding the jaunty tune that signaled reveille. Tousle-haired and sleepy-eyed soldiers filed into their company streets, and the first sergeants called the roll. Breakfast was followed by sick call, at which point the regimental surgeon examined all men pleading illness. In the ceremonial ritual of guard mount, sentries were selected from each company and posted about the camp for a 24-hour detail. Next, those men not excused for sickness or detached on guard duty participated in a two-hour company drill, followed by the noon meal. In the afternoon, the regimental commander put his 10 companies through their paces in a drill that lasted two or more hours.

Following a brief period of rest during which the men were expected to clean and polish their accouterments, the companies were reassembled for another roll call and inspection. The troops then filed onto the drill field for dress parade, an elaborate and carefully choreographed ceremony that marked the end of the day's formalities. Supper was followed by "tattoo," signaling the end of the day, and then "lights out." Most soldiers were asleep by 9:00 p.m.

The spit and polish of an established camp was largely abandoned in the field; but whether in camp or on campaign, the soldiers' rations were invariably a source of complaint. The inevitable hardtack sometimes hosted weevils, what one Pennsylvanian called "a handful of 'squirmers.'" The soldiers reported, "If we had to eat in the dark, our protection then lay in breaking our cracker into a cup of boiling coffee, stir it well, and then flow enough of the coffee over to carry off most of the strangers and take the balance on faith."

Troops habitually soaked their hardtack in water, then fried it in the grease of their issue of salt pork. Edward Weightman of the 9th New York Zouaves concluded, "In whatever manner crackers are treated by fire, they are improved."

Other staples in the Federal soldier's diet were rice, hominy, and dried beans or peas, as well as dried, or desiccated, vegetables that the men labeled "desecrated." And if so inclined, the Yankees were able to spend a portion of their $13-a-month pay ($16 beginning in 1864) to buy overpriced delicacies, such as canned fruit and oysters, from traveling sutlers.

Although Union soldiers were as a rule better fed than their Confederate counterparts, they did go hungry at times. Supply wagons often proved incapable of keeping up with the troops on the front line. Following the Battle of Gettysburg, Private John Haley of the 17th Maine reported that his unit had gone without food for several days, and that some men were "nearly insane from hunger." Haley complained that "present rations are about enough to keep a chicken in fair order. We could eat a corpse and chase the mourners."

Since the Civil War was for the most part waged in Southern territory, it was only natural that Union troops sought to augment their issued rations with livestock and produce foraged from the surrounding countryside. Many Federal commanders viewed such activity as vandalism and sought to prevent it, but other officers merely looked the other way when hungry men in the ranks went foraging. "A flock of 150 sheep near our encampment came to a very sudden serving up last night," wrote Lieutenant Samuel Nichols of Massachusetts. Nichols bent the rules again when he came across 30 plump turkeys in a Virginia farmer's granary. "You may get the rest of the story from the man who formerly owned them," the lieutenant wrote home, "and who now mourns the loss of 30 turkeys, one troublesome dog, and a few sundries." Occasionally, foraging assumed a more violent character, as when Federal troops ransacked the town of Ruckersville, Mississippi, in October 1862. Perry L. Smith of the 12th Iowa reported that "houses were burnt and the devil turned loose generally." Smith's division commander punished the culprits by having them stand at attention for three hours. In rare cases, pillagers might be executed.

As the War went on and casualties mounted, a new generation of Federal commanders sanctioned the destruction of civilian property as a strategic necessity for crushing the Confederate will to wage war. "We must fight them more vindictively, or we shall be foiled at every step," wrote the Union brigade commander Strong Vincent. "We must desolate the country as we pass through it, and not leave the trace of a doubtful friend or foe behind us." Vincent, who was killed at Gettysburg, had little chance to put his theory into practice, but others did. The lawless behavior of freewheeling Yankee "bummers"—irregulars who foraged on the flanks of Sherman's army in his epic march from Atlanta to the sea—gained the undying enmity of the Southern people.

On the march, the Union fighting man stripped down to the bare essentials—knapsack or blanket roll, haversack, canteen, and cartridge box with 40 rounds of ammunition. At night he and a comrade would button their canvas

Private Billy Crump, orderly to Colonel Rutherford B. Hayes of the 23d Ohio Infantry, returns from a foraging expedition in West Virginia laden with poultry, eggs, and butter. Soldiers hungry for fresh food held a resourceful forager in high esteem. Hayes, who became president in 1877, appointed Crump his White House steward.

"Everyone drinks to excess when the opportunity offers, chews and smokes incessantly, and swears habitually."

PRIVATE EDWARD WIGHTMAN
9TH NEW YORK INFANTRY
REGIMENT

shelter halves together to form a small *tente d'abri,* in soldier parlance a "dog" or "pup" tent. Sometimes the soldiers dispensed with tents and rolled up in heavy woolen blankets or ponchos to sleep under the stars. The manners of veteran campaigners were rough, to say the least. "Deprived of the restraining influences of their home life," one soldier remembered, "they lapsed into a state of primal barbarism." A private in the IX Corps complained to his parents that "everyone drinks to excess when the opportunity offers, chews and smokes incessantly, and swears habitually." Such behavior shocked upright young men like the New York artillery captain John Howard Kitching, who informed his mother, "I have seen more open wickedness and unblushing sin, since my connection with the army, than I ever dreamed of before." In the field, Yankee soldiers were just as likely as their Rebel foes to fall prey to flies, fleas, body lice, and other vermin that swarmed over their filthy camps. Some soldiers joked that in their clothing they found lice with the letters *I.W.* tattooed on their backs—evidence that the vermin were "In for the War." Even in battle, men were conscious of being infested. In one fight, a Yankee colonel was seen waving his sword with one hand while feverishly scratching himself with the other.

Like their Southern counterparts, Union soldiers at times were as ragged as they were dirty. Supplies were far more bountiful than in Southern armies, but transportation problems and mismanagement of quartermaster stores were widespread and caused severe shortages in the field. When President Lincoln reviewed the V Corps after the Union victory at Antietam, Private Alfred Davenport of the 5th New York Zouaves gave vent to his frustrations. "Those who had overcoats were ordered to put them on to hide the rags and make him believe that they had jackets," Davenport wrote of the president's visit. "I had not had on a jacket for two months, nor a change of underclothing." In November of 1862, a Pennsylvania soldier was shocked to see men of the 4th Maine "marching and countermarching over the hard frozen ground in their bare feet, and with only a part of a leg to their pantaloons."

It was no wonder that such rugged conditions furthered the spread of illness. "The hospitals here are filled with the sick," complained a Federal surgeon at Lexington, Kentucky. "How men who tramp around all day in mud and water ankle-deep, and then lie down at night to sleep in blankets saturated with water, can preserve health is a mystery to me." In November 1862, Isaac

Soldiers in William Brooks' division of the Federal VI Corps guard the pontoon bridges at Franklin's Crossing during the Second Battle of Fredericksburg in 1863. This photograph was taken during a lull in the battle: Shortly thereafter some of these men were killed in the fighting around Salem Church.

Jackson of the 83d Ohio informed his sister that he had been ill for three weeks. "Last night I done some tall coughing," Jackson said, but "there is some who does some desperate bad coughing. You never heard the like." Malaria, typhoid, and dysentery, as well as childhood ailments such as measles, took a greater toll of the armies than battle did. Of the nearly 360,000 Union dead, some 200,000 succumbed to disease. Another 25,000 died in prison camps.

The long winter months were a time for rest and refitting, the troops constructing cozy log huts that often boasted bunk beds and fireplaces. "We pass most of these winter evenings very pleasantly," the Connecticut volunteer Charles Lynch noted, "visiting, singing, reading, telling stories, writing, studying, discussing the war, and wondering when we will go home." According to Lynch, the most popular camp song was "Home, Sweet Home."

Winter was also a time for replenishing the vacant ranks with new recruits, or in the latter part of the War, draftees. Grizzled veterans would often haze the new arrivals unmercifully, dubbing them "fresh fish," "paper collar soldiers," "mamma's darlings," or "blue cherubs." But there was also grudging respect, and pity, for the wide-eyed newcomers. "They were looked upon sadly and in a certain awe," General Joshua Chamberlain wrote, "as those that had taken on themselves a doom."

With the coming of spring, the Union armies again marched forth to confront the terrors of the battlefield. Captain Elbridge J. Copp, a battle-hardened New Hampshire man, recalled that "the fear of what was coming" often turned even veteran soldiers into shirkers: "I have seen men so overcome with fear when moving up to the front, that they fell out of the ranks, and in spite of orders and threats of their officers, laid themselves upon the ground in perfect helplessness." But most soldiers lost their fear when the firing started. "It was load and fire at will as fast as we could," wrote Private Rice Bull of New York. "The nervousness and fear we had when we began the fight passed away, and a feeling of fearlessness and rage took its place." An Iowa officer serving in Grant's Vicksburg campaign noticed that battle turned even normally quiet soldiers into "yelling, screaming madmen, wild with excitement and shaking the gleaming bayonet."

Some were able to display a studied indifference to danger. At the Battle of Fair Oaks, one-armed General Philip Kearny urged his men on with these insouciant words: "Go in gaily, boys, you'll find lovely fighting all along the line!" Lieutenant Henry Ropes of the 20th Massachusetts told his friends at home that the bullets ripping through his knapsack and overcoat during the Union assault on Fredericksburg felt merely "like fishes nibbling."

Even if a soldier came through the fight unscathed, the aftermath of battle held terrors of its own. "The dead are frightfully smashed," a Maine volunteer wrote after Gettysburg, "some split from the top of the head to the extremities, as butchers split beef." A Pennsylvanian recalled that "the stench on the battlefield was something indescribable. It would come up as in waves and when at its worst the breath would stop in the throat."

Constant danger and death gave rise to a grim fatalism that pervaded the ranks, particularly during Grant's relentless, casualty-filled drive on Richmond in the summer of 1864. The 14th New Jersey's Major Peter Vredenburgh explained to his family: "So many whom I know have been killed, that it makes it seem but a short step from this to the next world. You can have no idea with what perfect indifference everyone here regards life." A young staff officer named Washington Roebling wrote from the Cold Harbor front: "Another one of my best friends in the army has been killed. About the only comments made were 'I wonder whose turn it will be to go to the devil next,' and 'They say there are people who have died in their beds.' "

Through all their hardships and suffering, the Northern soldiers were sustained by bonds of comradeship that had been forged in fire and blood. "What wonder that men who have passed through such things together," mused General Joshua Chamberlain, "should be wrought upon by that strange power of a common suffering which so divinely passes into the power of a common love."

For the survivors, it was a bond of brotherhood that would far outlast their test in the crucible of war. Four decades after the Civil War, the Union veteran Frederick Hitchcock attempted to put into words the pride and enthusiasm he had felt as he marched alongside his comrades in an 1863 review of the Army of the Potomac: "As I gazed up and down those massive lines of living men, felt that I was one of them, and saw those battle-scarred flags kissed by the loving breeze, my blood tingled to my very fingertips, my hair seemed almost to raise straight up, and I said a thousand Confederacies can't whip us."

"So many whom I know have been killed, that it makes it seem but a short step from this to the next world. You can have no idea with what perfect indifference everyone here regards life."

MAJOR PETER VREDENBURGH
14TH NEW JERSEY INFANTRY REGIMENT

For Colonel Henry Knox Craig, the 70-year-old U.S. Army chief of ordnance, 1861 could scarcely have begun on a more troublesome note. On December 30, 1860, the Ordnance Department in Washington received a telegram announcing that the Federal arsenal at Charleston, South Carolina, had been taken over by secessionist forces. Within two weeks, arsenals at Apalachicola, Florida, and Baton Rouge, Louisiana, were seized. By February 18, the arsenals at San Antonio, Little Rock, and Augusta had also been captured.

Colonel Craig had been in the U.S. Army for 49 years and had served as chief of ordnance for the past nine. He ran his department with the sure hand that reflected years of experience. Prior to the capture of the Southern arsenals, he supervised 24 such establishments from Maine to California. Also in his charge were the two armories that manufactured nearly all of the small arms for the U.S. Army and the various militias. These two facilities, in Springfield, Massachusetts, and Harpers Ferry, Virginia, had a combined annual production of about 22,000 firearms.

In addition, Craig's department was responsible for distributing weapons to the Regular Army and to the militia of each state. Although the standing peacetime army numbered only about 16,000 men, supplying these troops was no easy task. Units were posted in every part of the nation, most of them scattered across the western frontier.

Like the Regular Army, each state militia received arms in a yearly requisition based on the population of the area it served. Most militia units were supplied with serviceable but outdated arms, although organizations with political clout often received the same new arms that were issued to regulars.

One other major duty fell to the Ordnance Department: the development, testing, and evaluation of new small arms and artillery. Small-arms technology had improved steadily since 1841, and in the 1850s it accelerated sharply, in both the private and the Federal sector. In fact, during Craig's tenure as ordnance chief, the United States had taken the lead in many aspects of arms innovation, particularly the techniques of mass production and the standardization of parts.

By 1861, nearly all military arms were still loaded through the muzzle, but a few of the more advanced breechloading arms were available. The percussion ignition system had taken the place of the venerable flintlock, but many of those vintage arms were still stored in arsenals, waiting to be altered and modernized to the percussion system.

Before 1855, rifled longarms were considered impractical for infantry use because they were slow to load; thrusting a round, solid-lead ball down the lands and grooves of the rifling was more difficult than loading a smoothbore. All this was changed by the ingenious but simple invention of Claude Minié, a captain in the French army. Minié developed an elongated soft lead projectile with a hollow, cone-shaped base. It was perfected by an American, James H. Burton, master armorer at Harpers Ferry. This bullet, known ever after as the Minié ball, was cast slightly smaller than the diameter of the rifled bore so that it slid easily past the rifling. When the gun was fired, the exploding powder caused the soft lead of the hollow base to expand into the grooves of the rifling. This gave the bullet a spin that stabilized its flight and dramatically increased its range and accuracy. The rifled arm soon became a practical weapon for all infantrymen.

An army that wanted to retain any military advantage now needed to acquire rifled arms, in addition to updating its older weapons. Methods were devised to cut rifling into existing smoothbore arms, and in 1855, the ordnance technicians at the Springfield Armory began designing a new weapon that would become the mainstay of the Civil War soldier: the .58-caliber, Model 1855 rifle musket (and slightly smaller rifle).

The output of both national armories—Springfield and Harpers Ferry—was devoted to the production of these high-quality arms. In 1861, a slight variation, the Model 1861, was introduced. The new version eliminated a complicated tape primer and substituted a simpler percussion-cap system.

The next important step was the development of breechloading shoulder arms. Operating a muzzleloader, an infantryman had to take his weapon from firing position and rest the butt on the ground in order to gain leverage to ram the bullet down the bore with a slender steel rod. When muzzleloaders were issued to men on horseback, loading became a major problem. Breechloaders, on the other hand, were relatively simple for a mounted man to operate, and they were the obvious choice for the cavalry.

The most popular breechloading shoulder arms of the decade before the War were the rifles and carbines made by the Sharps Rifle Manufacturing Company of Hartford, Connecticut. By 1861, the Sharps carbine was standard issue for the U.S. Cavalry, although it was available in only limited numbers. Tests were also being conducted on other breechloaders, including the Burnside, Merrill, Maynard, and Joslyn carbines.

The breechloaders, however, were intended only for use by the cavalry. The Ordnance Department gave no serious thought to providing breechloaders for the army's largest element, the infantry. Most Regular Army officers, including Colonel Craig, reasoned that infantrymen armed with such rapid-firing weapons would consume excessive amounts of ammunition. And the increased rate of fire, it was thought, would lead to decreased accuracy. Thus the muzzleloading rifle musket was deemed the only suitable weapon for a foot soldier.

Before the War, handguns were generally used only by cavalrymen and officers. Handgun production in the United States was dominated by the Colt Patent Firearms Manufacturing Company, located (like Sharps) in Hartford. Colt's six-shot revolver had been adopted for military use in 1847 as a sidearm for mounted troops. By 1861, other revolver makers were attempting to enter the handgun market. Remington, of Ilion, New York, and Smith & Wesson, of Springfield, Massachusetts, were the two biggest contenders, but there were at least 60 others, all clustered in New York, Pennsylvania, and New England. Their arms were rifled, and the dozen or so that were suitable for military use had an effective range of 50 to 75 yards.

By 1860, American innovations such as the Colt revolver and the Sharps carbine had received wide attention in England and Europe, as had American advances in mass production and standardization. Although most major European powers produced their own arms, the techniques for production were as varied as the quality of the products. Only in England, Austria, and Belgium were arms produced that were as good as those made in the United States.

The events of spring and summer 1861 threw the Ordnance Department into turmoil. On April 12, the Confederates attacked Fort Sumter. The nation was at war, and for Colonel Craig and his officers there could be no more business as usual. Fort Sumter surrendered on April 13. Two days later, President Lincoln called for 75,000 volunteers for three months' service to put down the rebellion. Virginia seceded on April 17, and the next day, Virginia troops seized the vital arsenal at

Harpers Ferry. The U.S. Ordnance Department had made no provision to strengthen defenses or even prepare for the possible removal of the arms and machinery there. Almost half of the government's small-arms manufacturing capability was suddenly gone.

On April 24, Colonel Craig resigned as ordnance chief because of ill health. Lieutenant Colonel James Wolfe Ripley, who succeeded him, was only three years younger than Craig, but he was energetic and experienced in all aspects of ordnance.

Initially, at least, the arms supply in the remaining Federal arsenals seemed adequate. When Ripley took command, there existed an inventory of 437,433 muskets and rifles; 4,076 carbines; and 27,192 pistols—a comfortable figure for a short war. There was, however, one serious flaw. Fewer than 40,000 of the infantry arms were of modern design. The rest were smoothbores, many of them altered from flintlock to percussion. Of these, some of more recent manufacture had been rifled and sighted to handle a .69-caliber Minié ball. Still, with most units of the state militia already armed, Ripley and the Union brass saw no reason for immediate concern. The greater need was for cavalry arms. These were the harder-to-manufacture breechloaders, all of patent design and not produced by Federal armories.

As May and June unfolded with numerous clashes of Union and Confederate volunteers, Ripley set about attempting an orderly supply of the troops. With the Harpers Ferry Arsenal in Rebel hands, he pushed the Springfield Armory to full production. On June 11 Ripley reported, "The present capacity of Springfield Armory is about 2,500 arms per month, and measures are in rapid progress to double, at least, that product." A week later, the output was estimated at 3,000 a month, and Ripley was planning to contract with four private manufacturers to produce 100,000 Model 1861 rifle muskets over the next nine months.

It was during this initial push to arm that the new ordnance chief emphatically stated his unyielding policy regarding innovations: "A great evil now especially prevalent in regard to arms for the military service is the vast variety of new inventions, some in my opinion unfit for use as military weapons and none as good as the United States musket." In an age of new firearms technology, Ripley was convinced that the older weapons, invented by his generation, were the most suitable for waging the Civil War.

On July 21, the two major volunteer armies in the field met and fought near Manassas, Virginia. The Union defeat there on the banks of Bull Run infinitely complicated the Union arms picture. By July 25, Congress had approved additional calls for volunteers, requiring 500,000 men for three years of service. Patriotic Northerners poured forth in greater numbers than expected. The shortage of arms quickly went from bad to worse.

Governors and senators wanted the best weapons for their states' sons. Political influence quickly siphoned off the rifled arms at hand. In direct competition with the Ordnance Department, Massachusetts and New York already had agents in England buying Enfield rifle muskets for their soldiers. By mid-June, New York had contracted for 20,000 Enfields and had already received enough to arm one regiment.

Complaints of the scarcity began pouring into Washington during the summer. Brigadier General Ulysses S. Grant, in Cairo, Illinois, wrote: "My cavalry are not armed. The infantry is not well armed." From Louisville, Brigadier General William T. Sherman lamented, "We are moving heaven and earth to get arms, but the supply is scant." The arsenals were all but empty, and the Springfield Armory could not keep pace with the demand. Private arms manufacturers were gearing up to produce military weapons, but it would take time before they could produce enough to have any effect on the shortage.

On July 27, Colonel George L. Schuyler was dispatched to Europe as purchasing agent for the U.S. government. Schuyler had instructions to "make such purchases of arms as you deem advisable upon the very lowest terms compatible with the earliest possible delivery." At the same time, the import firm of Herman Boker & Company of New York received the go-ahead from the government to purchase arms independently on the European market. As if this were not enough, the American minister to Belgium, Henry Sanford, was buying any and all arms he could acquire.

These official buyers soon found themselves in competition with one another, with Confederate purchasing agent Caleb Huse, and with numerous unofficial firms that were buying arms on speculation. All of them were competing with the state agents representing Massachusetts and New York.

The Confederate agent Huse had a three-month head start on his rival Schuyler and had sewn up a number of English contracts for Enfield rifles by the time the Federal representative arrived in Europe. The Union was slow to catch up. The first arms purchased by Massachusetts arrived in July. Thereafter, a steady flow of European weapons began to appear at American ports. Those not purchased outright by the Federal government were snapped up by state agents. It was nearly a year before the Ordnance Department was able to gain control over the quality and type of imports flowing to the army.

Because of the early indiscriminate buying, a flood of shoddy foreign firearms inundated the ranks of the army. Stories of rusty, misfiring, inaccurate, and unworkable arms appeared in Northern newspapers and

official battle reports. Some imported weapons were of such large caliber that the soldiers labeled them "pumpkin rollers," or "stovepipes." The recoil of such weapons packed a healthy punch. It was said that "you could tell how many muskets had been fired by counting the number of men kicked flat." The iron of some imported bayonets was so soft, the soldiers joked, that it apparently was "designed to coil round on the enemy." The bad reputation that foreign arms earned early in the War was never overcome.

In fact, several foreign firearms were highly regarded, among them the Austrian Lorenz, the Saxon rifle, and the French Lefaucheux pistol. But the British Enfield was the only foreign arm universally immune to derision. By mid-War, nearly half the Union infantry carried Enfields. They were equal in quality to Springfields and, very importantly, their caliber was nearly identical. The same ammunition could be used in both weapons.

Within a year, Lieutenant Colonel Ripley had earned the star of a brigadier general. His efforts to expand domestic production were beginning to pay off. Virtually all of the nation's private gunmakers were situated in the North, and offers to supply patent arms of dozens of different types poured into the War Department. The urgent need for breechloading cavalry carbines and pistols for the mounted troops was filled by various manufacturers offering different designs, some of which might never have gotten off the drawing board had it not been for the exigencies of war.

Patent carbines such as Smith, Starr, Gwyn & Campbell, Ballard, and Wesson all found their way into the hands of Union cavalrymen. So did revolvers by Adams, Joslyn, Savage, Whitney, and Remington. Sharps and Burnside, the carbines that had seen the most prewar use, were ordered in large numbers, as were Colt revolvers.

But Ripley remained as steadfast as Craig before him in the conviction that the single-shot, muzzleloading rifle was the proper longarm for the infantryman. When a request for breechloaders from the famous skirmisher unit, Berdan's Sharpshooters, made its way up the bureaucracy to Ripley's desk, he refused it. Only after Lincoln interceded on behalf of the marksmen did he acquiesce. During the buying spree of 1861 and 1862, several state units had been armed with non-conventional breechloaders, but always against Ripley's wishes.

Much to his credit, General Ripley was able to bring domestic arms production under control. Not all contractors met production expectations, but these were soon weeded out. By October 1863, in what turned out to be his final report, Ripley stated with justifiable pride: "As regards small arms, we may now consider ourselves perfectly independent of foreign aid. The supply from the Springfield Armory alone for the coming year is estimated at not less than 250,000, while from private parties there will probably be received at least 250,000 more."

In the meantime, two weapons had appeared that were so contrary to the elderly general's way of thinking that not even overwhelming battlefield success would lessen his opposition to them. They were the Henry and Spencer repeating rifles. These two arms were far more sophisticated than even the popular Sharps, which fired only a single shot and used a paper or linen cartridge requiring a separate percussion cap. The Henry and Spencer fired a new metallic cartridge with the primer built in, dispensing with the percussion cap. Furthermore, each contained a magazine that enabled the user to load and fire repeatedly by simply moving a lever, cocking the hammer, and pulling the trigger. The Henry was even automatically cocked as the lever was manipulated.

In Ripley's mind, these weapons presented no advantage over muzzleloading arms. In fact, they did have disadvantages. They required special ammunition that would be wasted by excited soldiers who fired it too fast. And the complexity of their mechanics meant that they were sure to malfunction. Ripley used every bureaucratic means he knew to block the inventions.

It took a visionary 32-year-old volunteer officer from Indiana named John T. Wilder to break the impasse. Wilder had entered the service in 1861 as captain of Company A, the 17th Indiana Infantry, and by December of 1862 he had risen to colonel of the regiment. Then he was given command of a brigade of four infantry regiments and a battery of light artillery. After he failed in January 1863 to intercept a raiding column of Confederate cavalry at Munfordville, Kentucky, Wilder determined to have his brigade mounted. His plan went beyond granting mere mobility to his troops, however. Simply being able to catch the Rebel horsemen was not enough; Wilder envisioned a command with sufficient firepower to whip the Southerners.

At about this time, another young man, Christopher Spencer, inventor of the Spencer rifle, was traveling through Union-held Tennessee and Kentucky, demonstrating his invention. He was confident that once the soldiers saw what his rifle could do, grassroots demand would force the Ordnance Department to order it in quantity. In March of 1863, at Murfreesboro, Tennessee, Colonel Wilder watched Spencer demonstrate his miraculous repeater and was immediately convinced that the Spencer was just the weapon he needed to arm his newly mounted infantry brigade. In a world dominated by the rifle musket, which a skilled soldier could fire three times a minute, the Spencer's capability to fire up to 14 rounds in the same span of time was phenomenal.

When Wilder failed to obtain the new rifle through normal channels, his men offered to put up their own money for the weapons. In the meantime, however, the brigade received the horses that Wilder had so fervently requested. The Ordnance Department, in a turnabout, decided that since Wilder's men were now mounted, they could be issued breechloading repeaters. On May 15, 1863, they got their Spencers.

Fate chose an otherwise obscure clash at Hoover's Gap, Tennessee, on June 24, 1863, for a test of the Spencer on the battlefield. Wilder's mounted brigade, operating out in front of the Union army, had pushed a screening force of Confederate cavalry through the gap. Wilder then took position to hold the gap until the main army arrived. Using the advantage of their repeating rifles to the fullest, his men repulsed repeated charges by Confederate infantry. From then on, they were called the Lightning Brigade.

Word of Wilder's success spread rapidly through the Union army. Meanwhile, Spencer had persuaded Lincoln himself to observe a demonstration of his weapon outside the White House. The clamor to obtain Spencers now resounded loud and clear.

On September 15, 1863, General Ripley was forced to retire, and was replaced by Lieutenant Colonel George D. Ramsey. The new ordnance chief was of the same generation as both of his predecessors and in many ways just as conservative. But there was one important difference: Ramsey believed totally in the advantage of breechloading rifles for the infantry. He also enthusiastically endorsed the repeating arms, with their metallic cartridges. Under Ramsey's guidance, the production of repeaters soon flourished.

The Spencer became the weapon of choice for Union officers. One of them, Major General James H. Wilson, reported to the chief of ordnance in January 1865: "There is no doubt that the Spencer carbine is the best firearm yet put into the hands of the soldier, both for economy of ammunition and maximum effect, physical and moral." Most Union infantrymen, however, would never get to carry a repeater. The rapid growth of the Union cavalry and its demand for Spencer carbines meant that even with stepped-up production, few repeating rifles were available for infantry use.

Even with his support of breechloaders to his credit, Ramsey's conservatism in other areas, particularly artillery, led to his replacement in September 1864 by Major Alexander B. Dyer, aged 49. Dyer, former superintendent of the Springfield Armory, progressive, dedicated, and energetic, had been one of the first proponents of magazine-fed arms. He had also been a leader in the effort to standardize the caliber of all shoulder arms in the army. In January 1865, Dyer established a board of officers to test new infantry weapons. Not a single muzzleloader was ever considered for testing.

In the decade from 1855 to 1865, small-arms technology had advanced more rapidly than in the fourscore years since the Revolution. The rifle musket enabled an infantryman to strike his enemy accurately at distances previously unheard of. Breechloaders increased his rate of fire. Magazine-fed repeating arms combined these advantages.

Many military commanders failed to grasp the efficacy of the new weapons, and so, in the end, the Civil War remained a conflict dominated by muzzleloading arms. The new breechloaders were less important in numbers than in the psychological effect they had on soldiers of both sides. The proud Union soldiers who were armed with Spencers or Henrys considered themselves invincible. Confederates who had to face them must have felt that a nation that could produce such weapons was indeed unconquerable.

In Defense of Old Glory

At the outset of the Civil War, Union Secretary of War Simon Cameron and Chief of Ordnance James Ripley believed that the Union's modest store of firearms would see Federal forces through the conflict. The number of troops necessary to quell the so-called rebellion had been estimated at 250,000. The Federal arms reserve of 437,433 rifles and muskets, when augmented by state arm stocks, should suffice—or so they reasoned.

By July 1861, however, little remained in the national arsenal but .69-caliber altered smoothbore muskets. These unwieldy arms, their Napoleonic-era flintlock ignition systems recently converted to percussion, were outdated. The Union's entire allotment of modern rifled weapons—including some 40,000 Model 1855 "Harpers Ferry" rifles and rifle muskets and Model 1841 "Mississippi" rifles—was snatched up in the first six weeks of the War. Although earmarked for the regular militia and three-year volunteers, these choice weapons quickly fell into the hands of influential politicians, who disbursed them to favored regiments. Not until mid-1861 would the Federal armory in Springfield, Massachusetts, begin turning out what came to be the Union standard, the Model 1861 Springfield rifle musket. Until then, Billy Yank would make do with his smoothbore.

U.S. MODEL 1861 SPRINGFIELD RIFLE MUSKET

The flamboyantly garbed Company F of the 114th Pennsylvania, a Zouave infantry regiment, proudly displays its Model 1861 Springfield rifle muskets in this photograph taken at Petersburg, Virginia, in August 1864. Soldiers of the 114th Pennsylvania Infantry were mustered into service in August of 1862—late enough to receive an allotment of the reliable Springfield percussion arms, whose production commenced with the War.

The Federal Arsenal's Finest

U.S. MODEL 1855 PERCUSSION RIFLE

Only a few of the more than 7,000 .58-caliber rifles originally manufactured on this pattern existed in Federal arsenals at the beginning of the War. Most were damaged or destroyed during the Confederate takeover of the armory at Harpers Ferry in April 1861. The rifle was designed to accept a saber bayonet with scabbard *(right)*.

U.S. .58-CAL. CARTRIDGE

At the start of hostilities, the finest weapons in the Federal war chest were the .58-caliber rifled arms—primarily altered Mississippis and U.S. Model 1855s. Manufactured to conform to the new standards for arms established by then-Secretary of War Jefferson Davis in July 1855, these weapons were designed to fire the quick-loading, accurate .58-caliber Minié ball. By eliminating all calibers but the .58 from its muzzleloading regulation arms, the government greatly simplified weapons production.

YANKEE WITH MODEL 1855 RIFLE MUSKET

U.S. MODEL 1841 "MISSISSIPPI" RIFLE

Originally fabricated in .54 caliber, this regulation percussion arm was rerifled to the new Federal standard of .58 caliber and refitted with a long-range sight. Nearly 5,000 of the rifles, named for a regiment of Mexican War volunteers, were altered at the Harpers Ferry Armory from 1855 to 1860.

U.S. .54-CAL. CARTRIDGE

SABER BAYONET AND SCABBARD

U.S. MODEL 1855 PERCUSSION RIFLE MUSKET, .58 CALIBER

The first rifle musket to be produced by the Federal government, this arm was also the first American weapon to shoot the Minié ball. Like its rifle counterpart, the rifle musket was outfitted with the Maynard tape priming system *(below)*. A socket bayonet could be attached to the muzzle.

SOCKET BAYONET AND SCABBARD

MAYNARD TAPE PRIMER

In the 1850s, the U.S. government fitted thousands of its arms with this automatic ignition system. Cocking the hammer fed a roll of fulminate-studded tape over the nipple; when the trigger was pulled, the hammer struck the fulminate patch, firing the gun. Moisture rendered the primer useless, however, and it was discontinued around May of 1861.

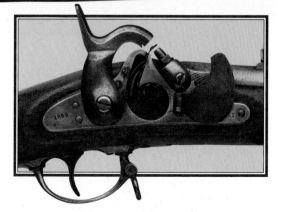

The Modernized Smoothbores

**.69-CAL. MINIÉ BALL
CARTRIDGE**

U.S. MODEL 1822 MUSKET, CONE-IN-BARREL ALTERATION

In the 1850s, the U.S. government converted thousands of its .69-caliber Model 1822 flintlock smoothbores to percussion by modifying the lock and boring a hole in the upper barrel for a percussion cone. Many of the arms, identical to the musket above, were ceded to state arsenals.

**.69-CAL. SMOOTHBORE
ROUND BALL CARTRIDGE**

U.S. MODEL 1841 RIFLE, REMINGTON ALTERATION

E. Remington & Son, a private armsmaker in Herkimer, New York, rebored 6,000 of these Mississippi rifles from .54 to .58 caliber and attached lugs for saber bayonets under a Federal government contract let early in the War. Contracts for alteration were let to other private armsmakers as well. Colt altered 10,200 Model 1841s between 1861 and 1862.

MODEL 1822 RIFLE
REMINGTON MAYNARD ALTERATION

This weapon, designed in 1816 as a flintlock musket, was altered to percussion and rifled as part of a Federal contract awarded in 1855. E. Remington & Son was tasked with forging 20,000 Maynard primer locks and forwarding them to the Frankford Arsenal in Philadelphia, which then installed the locks, rifled the .69-caliber bores, and attached long-range sights. Most of the guns were issued to early volunteers.

U.S. MODEL 1842 RIFLE
MUSKET, SIGHTED

From 1856 to 1860, the Federal armories at Harpers Ferry, Virginia, and Springfield, Massachusetts, rifled nearly 10,000 of these Model 1842 .69-caliber muskets and outfitted them with long-range sights.

SOCKET BAYONET AND SCABBARD

34

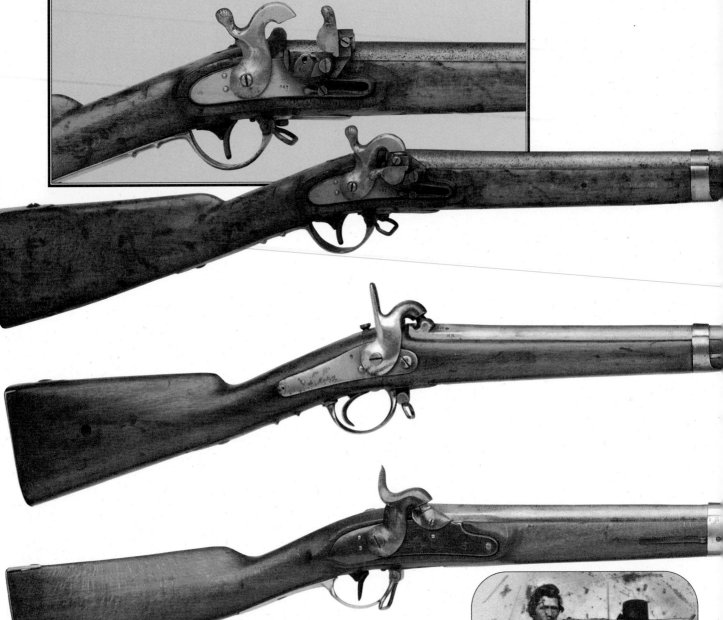

Sixteen-year-old Private Leonidas M. Jordan of Company C, 2d Ohio Infantry, poses for an early War photograph with his father, Hiram. Clutched in Private Jordan's hand is a .69-caliber Ponder rifle musket, named for John Ponder of Philadelphia, who imported 13,000 of these Belgian muskets in 1861.

AUSTRIAN MODEL 1842 TUBELOCK MUSKET

More than 25,000 of these percussion muskets were acquired early in 1861. In place of the standard percussion nipple, the .70-caliber tubelock had a latched hood over a pan *(top left)*. To prime the smoothbore, the user dropped a fulminate-packed copper tube into the pan and closed the hood, which had a firing pin inside. When the hammer hit the hood, the tube exploded, firing the gun.

FRENCH MODEL 1842 RIFLE MUSKET

Rated by the Ordnance Department as third-class—a serviceable but substandard arm—the French Model 1842 was originally manufactured as a .69-caliber smoothbore. The French later rebored many to .70 and .71 caliber and rifled them. Some 25,000 of these French weapons, imported by Herman Boker & Company of New York, a large supplier of foreign arms, were sold to the U.S. government.

PRUSSIAN MODEL 1809 MUSKET

Among the arms Prussia unloaded on the Union was the Model 1809 musket, an altered .72-caliber percussion smoothbore. Yanks armed with these guns complained that "they were not Springfields," and the government replaced them if it could.

Imported Firepower

As the Union entered the first summer of the War, its arsenals bare and domestic arms production at a trickle, the Federal government turned to the Continent for weapons. By late July, the War Department had dispatched three agents to Europe with the aim of buying up every serviceable arm the Old World could muster. Keen to sell their obsolescent arms at panic prices, the Europeans offered up every smoothbore curiosity and odd-caliber rifle they could find. The Federal agents, spurred on by Confederate competition, bought the arms with reckless abandon.

Luckily for the Union cause, of the more than one million weapons purchased, 80 percent were said to be dependable. The remaining 20 percent were, however, by one Indiana volunteer's reckoning, "the poorest excuse for guns I ever saw."

Sufficient to Pass Muster

AUSTRIAN LORENZ RIFLE

A tendency to collect fouling, or hard carbon, in its breech detracted from the otherwise fine reputation of this .54-caliber rifle, 226,000 of which were purchased from Austria by the Federal government at a cost of $2.6 million. Many of the arms were later rebored to .58 caliber to permit the use of standard-issue .58-caliber Federal ammunition.

PRIVATE WITH MODEL 1859 RIFLE

PRIVATE WITH SAXON RIFLE MUSKET

FRENCH MODEL 1859 RIFLE, BELGIAN VARIANT

Among the finest longarms imported by the Union
were the lightweight French Model 1859 and its
Belgian copies made in Liège. The U.S. Ordnance
department rated these rifles on a par with the
U.S. Model 1861 Springfield. This Liège-made
variant accepted a .61-caliber Minié ball.

SAXON MODEL 1857 RIFLE MUSKET

Known popularly as the Dresden rifle, the .58-
caliber Saxon Model 1857 was considered
unhandy but reliable by the Yankee foot soldiers
who carried it into battle. Thousands of Model
1857s were imported from Dresden, Germany, and
issued to Federal volunteers early in the War.

QUADRANGULAR BAYONET AND SCABBARD FOR THE LORENZ

Using the tool at right—a combination screwdriver, bore cleaner, and bullet extractor—Union soldiers kept their Enfields in top repair. The bullet mold *(below)* could be used to fashion new bullets.

The Best from Britain

The best of the imported Continental arms were the British-pattern Enfields—sturdy, deadly accurate weapons. Competition between Yankee and Confederate arms agents for these highly prized muzzleloaders was keen indeed. By numbers alone, the Union won the contest: Federal agents secured more than 500,000 Enfields, while Rebel agents contracted for only 400,000.

The Confederacy might have gotten more Enfields except for the government's insolvency. In 1862, the Rebel arms agent Caleb Huse made a tentative agreement with the London Armoury Company for its entire output of Enfields. Only the Confederacy's inability to pay up enabled the Northern agent to make the deal.

BRITISH MODEL 1853 ENFIELD RIFLE MUSKET

After the U.S. Model 1861, the British Enfield was the most heavily used arm of the Civil War. The .577-caliber rifle musket accepted the same Federal-regulation .58-caliber ammunition as the Springfield but was two inches shorter and a few ounces lighter.

BRITISH MODEL 1853 ENFIELD RIFLE

This .577-caliber muzzleloader, five and a quarter inches shorter than the Enfield rifle musket, was the standard arm of the British infantry during the 1860s and was imported by both the North and the South for their light infantry and rifle units. Without its hefty bayonet *(below, right)*, the rifle weighed only eight pounds seven ounces.

.577-CAL. ENFIELD CARTRIDGE

A unit of unidentified Federals pose in camp with their four-and-a-half-foot-long Enfield rifle muskets with attached socket bayonets.

SOCKET BAYONET AND SCABBARD, RIFLE MUSKET

SABER BAYONET AND SCABBARD, RIFLE

.58-CAL. CARTRIDGE AND AMMUNITION PACK

A Yankee Favorite

"We have plenty of men," wrote the Union general John Frémont in July 1861, "but absolutely no weapons." Faced with a critical arms shortage, the U.S. War Department retooled its national armory in Springfield, Massachusetts, to mass-produce a rifle musket designed on a new pattern, the Model 1861.

The Springfield would become the most popular infantry weapon of the War. Wrote one Yankee of his new Model 1861, "Our guns were issued to us, beautiful pieces, walnut stock, well oiled, the spring of the lock just stiff and just limber enough; barrel, long and glistening."

U.S. MODEL 1861 SPRINGFIELD RIFLE MUSKET

The rugged Model 1861 Springfield saw more action from 1862 through 1865 than any other Federal arm. More than 700,000 of the .58-caliber Springfields—favored over their Model 1855 predecessors for their simple construction and reliability—were manufactured during the War.

U.S. MODEL 1863 SPRINGFIELD RIFLE MUSKET

A refinement of the Model 1861, the .58-caliber Model 1863 Springfield retained the fundamental features of the original but substituted the modified barrel bands, simplified bolster (percussion chamber), redesigned hammer, and streamlined ramrod of the Special Model 1861 *(below)*.

COLT SPECIAL MODEL 1861 CONTRACT RIFLE MUSKET

The first Federal contract awarded for the wartime production of rifle muskets went to the Colt Patent Firearms Manufacturing Company of Hartford, Connecticut, on July 5, 1861. Colt agreed to deliver 25,000 arms roughly patterned on the U.S. Model 1861 that incorporated certain cost-cutting design features—including a modified rear sight and a recontoured lock plate. The mechanical parts of the Special Model 1861, which were manufactured on machinery similar to that used to make British Enfields, were not interchangeable with those of the U.S. Model 1861. Colt manufactured an additional 50,000 of these Special Model 1861s under two successive contracts at a cost to the government of $20 per gun.

IGNATZ GRESSER, 128TH PENNSYLVANIA, WITH 1861 SPRINGFIELD

Springfields by the Thousands

Even at breakneck output, the Springfield Armory's production of the Model 1861—a quarter million arms over two years—fell short of demand. The government had to let contracts with 20 private manufacturers to supply an additional 450,000.

The contract-produced Model 1861 Springfields *(right)* differed from their Federally manufactured counterparts only in respect to the name on the lock plate. Each cost the United States Treasury between $15 and $20.

The Special Model 1861 contract rifle musket *(far right, bottom)*, a close cousin to the U.S. Model 1861, was designed and first produced by Colt. It was also fabricated by three other private contractors, which added an additional 77,000 arms to Colt's wartime production of 75,000 Special Model 1861s. Each rifle produced by a contractor was examined by government ordnance inspectors. The inspector fired a proof charge to test the barrel and removed the lock and fittings to check the various components with standard gauges. If the weapon passed inspection, the barrel was struck with "VP," for viewed and proved, along with an eagle's head acceptance mark. The inspector then imprinted his initials on the stock.

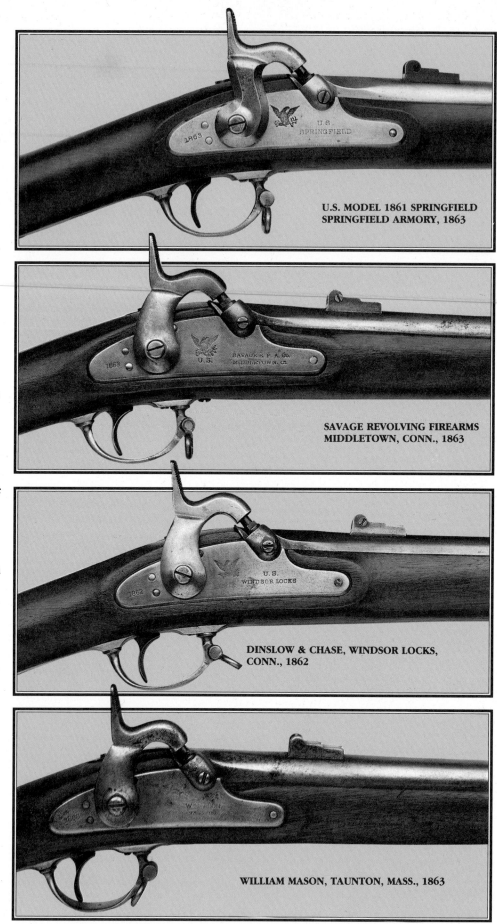

U.S. MODEL 1861 SPRINGFIELD
SPRINGFIELD ARMORY, 1863

SAVAGE REVOLVING FIREARMS
MIDDLETOWN, CONN., 1863

DINSLOW & CHASE, WINDSOR LOCKS,
CONN., 1862

WILLIAM MASON, TAUNTON, MASS., 1863

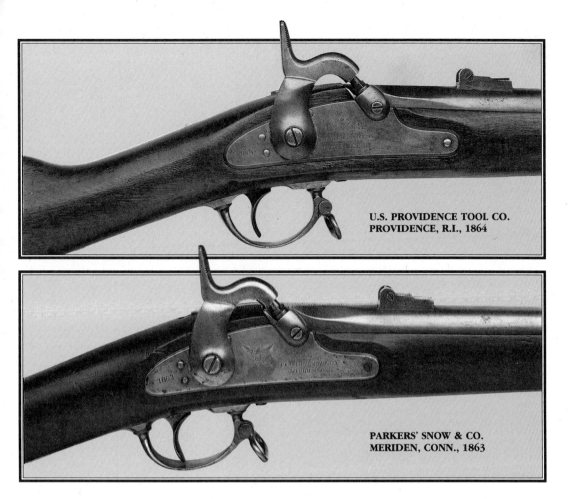

U.S. PROVIDENCE TOOL CO.
PROVIDENCE, R.I., 1864

PARKERS' SNOW & CO.
MERIDEN, CONN., 1863

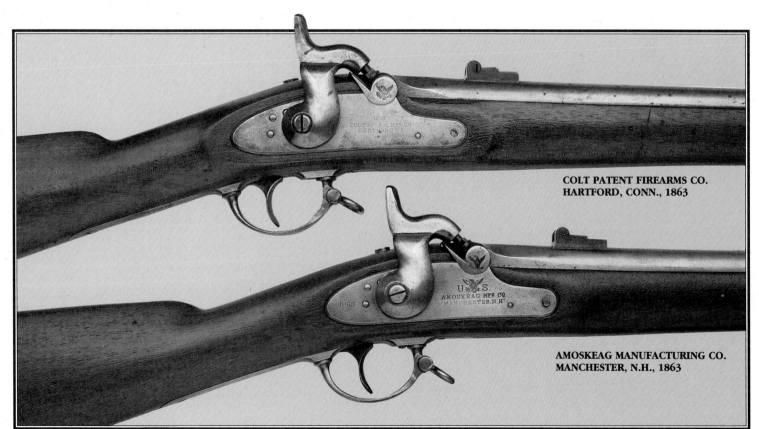

COLT PATENT FIREARMS CO.
HARTFORD, CONN., 1863

AMOSKEAG MANUFACTURING CO.
MANCHESTER, N.H., 1863

STADIA SIGHT

Holding the sight exactly at the length of the string, and level, the rifleman adjusted the sliding piece until his target filled the aperture and then read the range on the graduated scale located on the rim.

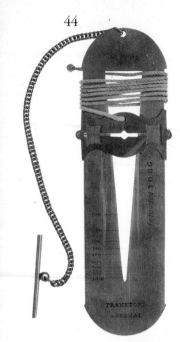

The four Hollis brothers, of Elgin County, Illinois *(from left to right, Isa, Clark, Nelson, and Francis)*, volunteers in Birge's Regiment Sharpshooters, 66th Illinois, show off their sporting arms. Most likely supplied by Horace Dimick, renowned maker of the "plains rifle," the weapons had one-inch-thick barrels that varied in caliber from .48 to .55.

Marksman's Choice

In the fall of 1861, at the urging of Hiram Berdan, an amateur target shooter from New York, the U.S. War Department mustered two regiments of expert marksmen. Designated as the 1st and 2d U.S. Sharpshooters, the regiments functioned as companies of skirmishers—crack shots who preceded Union troops into battle, harassing the enemy with sniper fire.

Initially, the government had no suitable arms for the sharpshooters; early volunteers relied on target and hunting weapons from home. It took President Lincoln's influence to get them proper breechloaders—and these were Colt rifles, not the hoped-for Sharps. For these, the men would wait until May of 1862.

DOUBLE-SET-TRIGGER SHARPS RIFLE, NEW MODEL 1859
Newly commissioned Colonel Hiram Berdan went over the head of the chief of ordnance to obtain these .52-caliber breechloaders for his sharpshooters. The rifles were equipped with double triggers—the rear for cocking the gun, the forward for hair-trigger firing.

JAMES TARGET RIFLE
Equipped with a four-power telescopic sight, this 14-pound, .45-caliber muzzleloader delivered accurate fire up to 500 yards. Two companies of Berdan's Sharpshooters used the James rifle during the siege of Yorktown in the spring of 1862.

MORGAN RIFLE, .46 CALIBER
Rifles such as this 35-pound "heavy" made by John C. Wells of Milwaukee are typical of the telescopic match rifles used by Yankee marksmen. The Morgan came with a false muzzle *(right)*, which protected the true muzzle from damage, and a rifle case *(below)*.

MORGAN RIFLE, FALSE MUZZLE

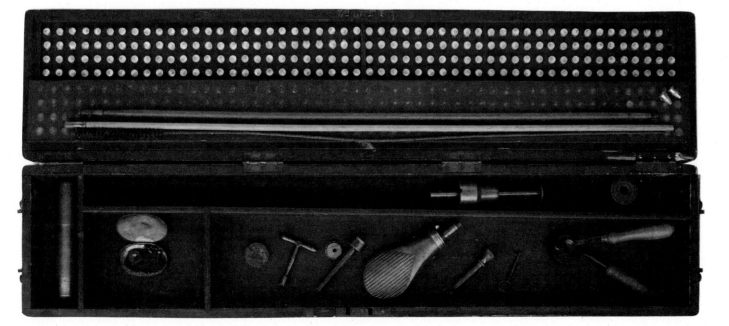

The Terror of Chickamauga

The vast majority of Union soldiers went into battle armed with single-shot muzzleloaders—slow-firing but trustworthy arms whose simple construction guaranteed easy maintenance and long use. The more advanced weapons—breechloaders and repeating rifles—were reserved for a limited number of select Federal units, such as Berdan's Sharpshooters and the 21st Ohio Infantry Regiment.

At the Battle of Chickamauga, the 535 men of the 21st Ohio used their Colt revolving rifles with devastating effect, helping to prevent a Federal rout. In five hours of fighting, they fired an astonishing 43,550 rounds with their repeaters. "My God," said a Confederate prisoner, "we thought you had a division there."

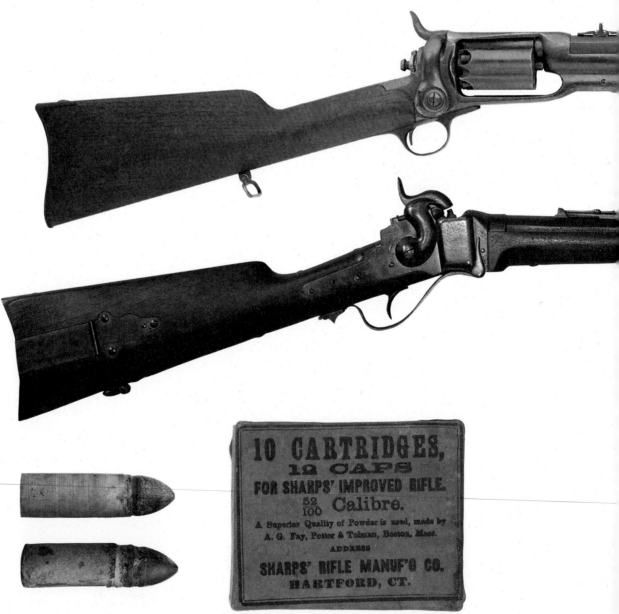

Sharps' linen or paper cartridges were combustible. After inserting one in the bore, the firer raised the breechblock, which sheared off the cartridge end, exposing the charge. The spark from the musket cap consumed the cartridge.

10 CARTRIDGES, 12 CAPS FOR SHARPS' IMPROVED RIFLE. 52/100 Calibre. A Superior Quality of Powder is used, made by A. G. Fay, Foster & Tolman, Boston, Mass. ADDRESS SHARPS' RIFLE MANUF'G CO. HARTFORD, CT.

Five infantrymen and an officer *(far left)* of the 21st Ohio pose with their rapid-fire Colt rifles. The Federal government stopped buying Colts after 1863 in favor of the faster-firing and more reliable Spencer rifle.

COLT REVOLVING RIFLE

A rifle-size version of the Colt revolver, this .56-caliber repeating breechloader was prized for its rapid action. However, it was capricious, at times discharging all five chambers at once and severing a few of the firer's fingers from his forward hand.

SHARPS NEW MODEL 1859 RIFLE

The most famous of the single-shot breech-loading rifles used during the War was the Sharps. The chosen weapon of the renowned 1st and 2d U.S. (Berdan's) Sharpshooters, the .52-caliber breechloader had a range and a rate of fire three times as great as those of a muzzleloader. The breechblock dropped when the trigger guard was lowered, exposing the bore for easy loading.

An unidentified private, most likely a member of the 6th Connecticut Veteran Volunteers, stands at attention with his Sharps rifle.

Infantryman-turned-horseman Private John Munson of Wilder's Lightning Brigade pauses at the side of the trail with his Spencer rifle.

SPENCER REPEATING RIFLE

The most sought-after breech-loader of the War was the Spencer. Capable of delivering up to 14 rounds a minute, the 47-inch-long, .52-caliber repeater held seven cartridges in a spring-fed tubular magazine that fit into a tunnel in the buttstock. Operating the lever then fed the cartridges forward one by one into the breech for firing.

HENRY REPEATING RIFLE
.44 CALIBER

Described by one Rebel as "that tarnation Yankee rifle they load on Sunday and shoot all week," the Henry carried 15 rounds in its magazine. A lever action simultaneously cocked the rifle, ejected the spent case, and put a fresh cartridge in the chamber.

The powder in the Henry's copper-cased cartridges, like the Spencer's, was impervious to moisture. The primer was in the cartridge's rim, eliminating the need for percussion caps.

50 CARTRIDGES
FOR
HENRY'S REPEATING RIFLE,
MANUFACTURED BY THE
NEW HAVEN ARMS CO.
NEW HAVEN, CONN.
No. 44—100.

The Awesome Repeating Rifles

Few Federal infantry regiments were lucky enough to receive the revolutionary repeaters that made their appearance during the final two years of the War. These were the magazine-fed, metallic-cartridge-firing Spencers and Henrys, whose lightning action terrorized Rebel regiments.

One awe-struck Confederate taken in May 1864 by the 1st D.C. Cavalry, a mounted regiment equipped with Henry 16-shooters, had this to say: "Your rapid firing confused our men. They thought the devil helped you and it was of no use to fight."

Despite the repeaters' tremendous popularity among the ranks, the Federal Ordnance Department purchased fewer than 15,000 Spencer and Henry rifles in all.

Posing with their mascot, troops of the 7th Illinois Infantry color guard flaunt the rapid-fire Henry rifles that saw them through the Atlanta campaign. Although the 7th Illinois was equipped with standard army-issue rifle muskets, the men of the color guard were among the more than 200 soldiers in the regiment who privately purchased the formidable Henry at $50 a gun.

SHARPS & HANKINS NAVY CARBINE
The barrel of this Navy-model breechloader was covered with a thin leather jacket to guard against rust. The front sight held the jacket in place. The weapon fired .52-caliber rimfire cartridges and was well liked by the navy, which purchased more than 6,000 of these carbines between 1862 and 1865.

SABER BAYONET AND SCABBARD FOR WHITNEY PLYMOUTH RIFLE

Seaworthy Small Arms

Federal warships plying narrow Southern
waterways faced the danger that their
big guns could do little to prevent a lightning strike by an enemy boarding party.
To guard against this risk, each warship
maintained a small arsenal of weapons for
combat at close quarters.

In times of peril, the weapons were
taken from storage and passed out to selected crewmen. Besides the cutlass—the
traditional sailor's sword for hand-to-hand

fighting—a Federal sailor might also carry
a carbine or a rifle.

During the War, naval small arms differed from infantry weapons only in that
their metal surfaces were sometimes
tinned, lacquered, or sheathed in a pro-
tective leather casing to prevent corrosion
from contact with water. When not in use,
the arms were stored in deck-top ship's
boxes or hung on racks in convenient
locations throughout the vessel.

SPENCER REPEATING NAVY RIFLE
The .52-caliber Spencer Navy rifle delivered its fire
via the same seven-cartridge magazine that made its
brother arm, the Spencer carbine *(pages 60-61),*
famous. To render the Spencer shown here seawor-
thy, its exposed metal parts were tinned; more commonly, Navy Spencers were treated with a lacquer of
beeswax, linseed oil, and boiled turpentine. The
Navy Department purchased 1,009 of the weapons.

WHITNEY PLYMOUTH NAVY RIFLE
Designed in accordance with the recommendations of Admiral John
A. Dahlgren for use aboard the U.S.S. *Plymouth,* the .69-caliber
Whitney Plymouth had a heavy 34-inch barrel with an oversize
muzzle lug for attaching a 27-inch saber bayonet *(below).* The
gun was a product of the Whitney Armory of New Haven, Connecticut.

CARBINES

Taking aim with their Sharps carbines, dismounted troopers of the 1st Maine Cavalry Regiment fire on Jeb Stuart's Cavalry Corps at Middleburg on June 19, 1863. With the use of breechloading carbines, cavalry were increasingly employed like mounted infantry.

UNION CAVALRYMAN WITH STARR CARBINE

STARR LINEN CARTRIDGE

STARR PERCUSSION CARBINE

From July 1863 to the end of the War, the U.S. government purchased 20,500 .54-caliber Starr breechloading carbines such as the one shown above. Patterned on the more famous Sharps, the Starr lacked its look-alike's sturdy reliability. According to one Federal assessment of the weapon, "The mechanism is too light and complicated. It works well enough while perfectly new but the least dirt deranges it."

SHARPS CARBINE, NEW MODEL 1859
Federal Chief of Ordnance James Ripley favored the straightforward construction of the .52-caliber Sharps carbine over the complex designs of more advanced breech-loaders. Accordingly, the Ordnance Department purchased nearly 80,000 of the carbines during the War. To load the Sharps, the user pulled the trigger guard forward *(box, above)*, lowering the breechblock and exposing the cartridge chamber.

SHARPS .52-CAL. PAPER CARTRIDGE

SHARPS .52-CAL. LINEN CARTRIDGE

Arms for Cavalrymen

The carbine—the short-barreled cousin of the rifle and musket—was the essential weapon of the cavalryman. There was a shortage of these lightweight, easily handled arms at the beginning of the War. Because of the comparatively small size of the prewar regular cavalry—only six regiments—the reserve of carbines in the national armory amounted to only a few thousand.

Fortunately for the Union, prospective manufacturers soon inundated the Ordnance Department with dozens of innovative carbine designs. The Federal government adopted no fewer than 17 different makes and models, the most advanced of which were the mass-produced magazine-fed metallic-cartridge breechloaders, such as the Spencer. Those initially purchased in the greatest numbers, however, were the simple paper-cartridge breechloaders featured here and on the next two pages.

GWYN & CAMPBELL CARBINE
These .52-caliber carbines—dubbed grape-vines for their distinctive serpentine trigger-guard levers—were issued to Federal cavalry in the Western theater between late 1862 and 1864. Troopers loaded the Gwyn & Campbell by unlatching the trigger guard *(right)*, which depressed the breechblock's forward section and unsheathed the cartridge chamber.

MERRILL CARBINE

The U.S. War Department bought 15,000 of these .54-caliber breechloading percussion arms from the Baltimore-based Merrill, Thomas & Company during the War. Never popular, the Merrill had a top-loading latch lever *(top, left)* that needed frequent repair. When drawn up and back, the lever opened the breech, which accepted a paper cartridge.

U.S. MODEL 1843 HALL CARBINE

The first breechloader adopted by the U.S. government, the .52-caliber Hall carbine was produced at Harpers Ferry from 1837 to 1843. Beginning in early 1861, the government sold 5,000 of the well-made but outdated Model 1843 as surplus, only to repurchase them at the War's outset at inflated prices.

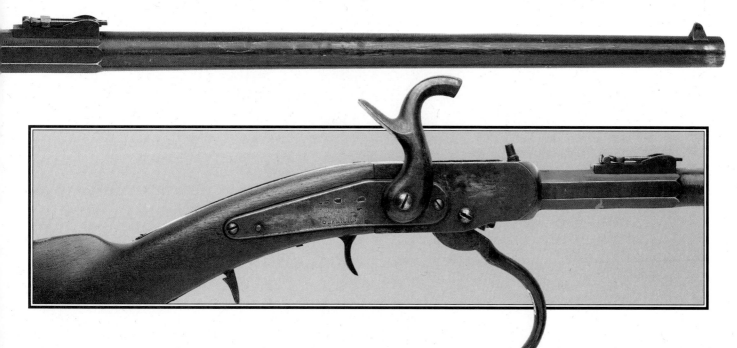

The New Breechloaders

Early in the War, Yankee ingenuity achieved unparalleled expression in the manufacture of breechloading carbines. The sudden and overwhelming demand for compact, quick-loading cavalry arms stimulated the creation of a bevy of new breechloader designs: barrels that tipped up or hinged downward, cylinders that revolved, and breechblocks that slid vertically, tilted, or swung to the side.

In many models, newly invented moistureproof brass or copper cartridges replaced the combustible paper or linen cartridges. Most of the breechloaders that took metallic cartridges still required a percussion cap for ignition, but a few—notably the Spencer *(pages 60-61)*—used rimfire cartridges. Captured rimfire arms were of no use to the Rebels, who lacked the equipment to make the cartridges.

.50-CAL. MAYNARD COPPER CARTRIDGE

Fixing a somber gaze on the camera, three Yanks sit for a photo clutching Gallagher carbines. Of 50 officers surveyed during the War, 40 rated the Gallagher as worthless.

GALLAGHER PERCUSSION CARBINE

At a cost of $30 each, Gallagher breechloaders were one of the least expensive arms of the Civil War. The U.S. government purchased nearly 18,000 of the .50-caliber weapons between 1861 and 1864. Although loading the Gallagher was easy—when unlatched, the trigger-guard lever tilted the breech up *(top)*—extracting the brass-cased cartridge after firing was a frustrating and time-consuming chore.

.50-CAL. GALLAGHER BRASS
CARTRIDGE

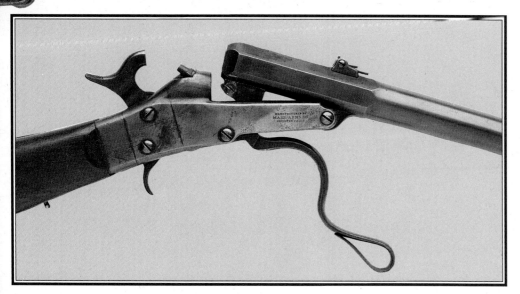

MAYNARD PERCUSSION CARBINE

The .50-caliber Maynard was one of the surest-shooting and best-liked carbines of the War. Its loading mechanism *(left)* operated like the Gallagher's, but the similarity ended there. The Maynard took a wide-based copper cartridge with a lip that made it easy to extract the spent shell after firing. In 1863 the Union contracted for 20,000 of these excellent weapons, which were delivered between June of 1864 and May of 1865. An earlier model of the carbine was used extensively by the Confederacy.

BURNSIDE PERCUSSION CARBINE

The .54-caliber Burnside—named for its inventor, Union General Ambrose Burnside—was the first metallic-cartridge breechloader adopted by the Federal government. On the whole, the Burnside was considered a reliable and accurate weapon, although field reports cited problems with the spring that held the trigger-guard loading lever *(right)* in place. When cocked forward, this spring-controlled lever was designed to lower the breech-block, opening the loading chamber. The cavalry-man then seated the conical brass cartridge *(far right),* returned the trigger guard to its horizontal position, and placed a musket cap *(far right, bottom)* on the nipple. A pull of the trigger threw the hammer forward, sparking the percussion cap and driving a flame into a hole in the base of the metallic cartridge, firing the gun. More than 50,000 Burnsides were issued during the War.

SMITH PERCUSSION CARBINE

The .50-caliber Smith was the fourth most frequently issued Union cavalry arm. It accepted a rubber-encased or foil-wrapped brass cartridge, which the trooper inserted directly into the down-hinged barrel after pressing a catch in front of the trigger *(left)*. However, the rubber cartridges were unpopular because they tended to stick in the breech when the guns got hot.

SMITH CARBINE .50-CAL. CARTRIDGE

SMITH CARBINE PLUG

SMITH CARBINE TOOL

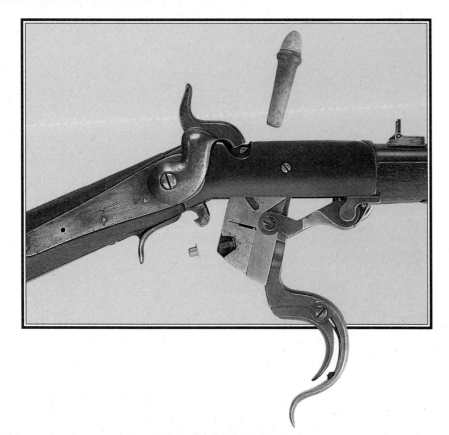

BURNSIDE CARBINE .54-CAL. CARTRIDGE

PERCUSSION CAPS

The Innovative Rimfires

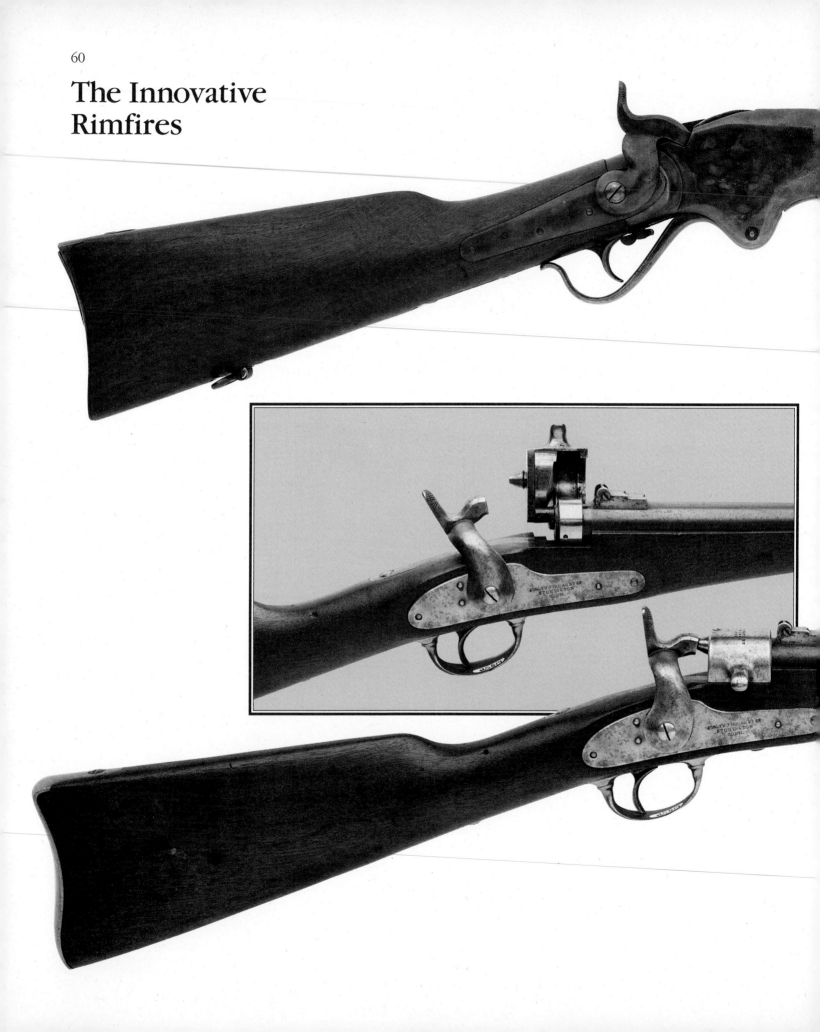

SPENCER REPEATING CARBINE

Yankee officers cited the Spencer as one of the single greatest factors in winning the War. No Confederate arm was a match for the .52-caliber Spencer, which fired seven shots from its magazine in less than 30 seconds. Because the repeaters weighed a hefty 10 pounds when loaded and took exotic primed rimfire cartridges, the conservative chief of ordnance James Ripley blocked their purchase until 1863.

.52-CAL. SPENCER CARBINE CARTRIDGE

TWO CAVALRYMEN HOLDING SPENCER CARBINES

JOSLYN RIMFIRE CARBINE, MODEL 1862

Between July 1864 and February 1865, the Joslyn Firearms Company of Stonington, Connecticut, supplied the Federal government with some 11,000 rimfire Joslyn carbines, 4,000 of which were the Model 1862 shown above. The six-pound 10-ounce weapon used a .52-caliber Spencer rimfire cartridge. To operate the Joslyn, a hook-like latch on the top of the semicylindrical breechblock *(left)* was flipped up, uncovering the firing chamber, into which the cartridge was inserted. The hammer struck a firing pin at the rear of the breech and pushed it into the rim of the cartridge, detonating the explosive material in its base.

FEDERAL CAVALRYMAN HOLDING A BALLARD CARBINE

SHARPS & HANKINS ARMY CARBINE, NEW MODEL 1862

Invented by Christian Sharps, designer of the famous Sharps carbine, the .52-caliber Sharps & Hankins carbine was the first of the rimfire breechloaders to incorporate a firing pin in the breechblock, a hammer safety mechanism, and a spring-loaded catch to extract spent cartridges from the barrel. The U.S. Ordnance Department bought 1,200 of the technologically advanced carbines in 1863. More than 6,000 of the Navy model Sharps & Hankins—which was simply the Army model with a leather-cased barrel—were ordered between 1862 and 1865 for use aboard navy vessels.

.44-CAL. BALLARD CARBINE CARTRIDGE

BALLARD CARBINE, .44 CALIBER

In 1864, the state of Kentucky purchased 4,600 of these .44-caliber Ballard carbines. The cleanly constructed rimfire single-shooters were issued to regiments such as the 13th and the 45th Kentucky Volunteer Cavalry. To ready the 17-pound, 38-inch-long carbine for firing, the trooper pushed the curved trigger-guard lever forward *(right),* freeing the breechblock from the barrel. He then dropped a .44-caliber copper rimfire cartridge into the loading chamber, returned the trigger-guard lever to its former position, and took aim.

REVOLVERS

COLT ARMY REVOLVER
Widely issued to cavalrymen, the .44-caliber Colt Army took loose powder and ball or cartridges of paper, foil, or skin. To load the percussion six-shooter, the hammer was half-cocked, freeing the cylinder. Ammunition was dropped into each chamber and tamped down with the rammer under the barrel.

CAVALRYMAN WITH TWO COLT ARMY REVOLVERS

Yankee Handguns

At a town meeting shortly after the start of the War, the citizens of Ashby, Massachusetts, agreed to provide each volunteer with a bowie knife, a Bible, 10 dollars, and a revolver.

The Federal government was less forthcoming. Handguns were issued only to cavalrymen and mounted light artillerymen; infantry volunteers who fancied sidearms had to get their own. It was not long, however, before foot soldiers and troopers who did carry handguns counted them

more of an encumbrance than an asset. "Pistols are useless," wrote Major Leonidas Scranton of the 2d Michigan Cavalry. "I have known regiments that have been in the field over two years that have never used their pistols in action. At a charge, the saber is the weapon."

The Union purchased 373,077 handguns during the War. Among revolver aficionados, the Colt and Remington models known as Army (.44 caliber) and Navy (.36 caliber) ranked as hands-down favorites.

REMINGTON ARMY REVOLVER

Because the bulk of the revolvers made by Remington were manufactured after 1860, most were in the hands of Yankees. Like the Colt, the Remington six-shooter came in two models: the .44-caliber Army *(above)* and the .36-caliber Navy. Around 115,563 Remington Armys were sold during the War.

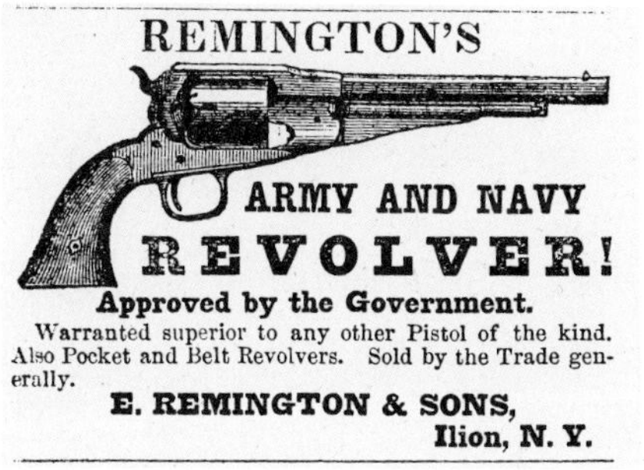

REMINGTON'S

ARMY AND NAVY REVOLVER!

Approved by the Government.

Warranted superior to any other Pistol of the kind. Also Pocket and Belt Revolvers. Sold by the Trade generally.

E. REMINGTON & SONS,
Ilion, N. Y.

COLT NAVY REVOLVER

The .36-caliber Colt Navy saw extensive service on the battlefield. Many cavalrymen, citing the Navy's greater handiness, chose it over the larger-caliber Army. Between 1851 and 1861, Colt produced more than 200,000 of the Navy six-shooters.

A Colt armory fire in February 1864 halted revolver production for more than a year.

WHITNEY NAVY REVOLVER

Some 11,000 of the .36-caliber Whitney Navy revolvers were bought by the U.S. Ordnance Department for issue to cavalrymen. New Jersey purchased an additional 800 of the six-shot handguns for its state militia. The Whitney was highly regarded, and its design was copied by a number of arms manufacturers.

JOSLYN ARMY REVOLVER

Troopers of the 5th and 6th Ohio Cavalry returned their Joslyn five-shooters to the Federal ordnance officer following the Battle of Shiloh in April 1862, complaining that the .44-caliber revolvers were unfit for military service. As a result, the Ordnance Department stopped buying the Joslyn, 1,100 of which had already been received.

FEDERAL CAVALRYMAN WITH FRENCH PINFIRE REVOLVER

LEFAUCHEUX REVOLVER

The only nonpercussion revolver issued in quantity and one of the few foreign handguns ordered by the North, the .41-caliber Lefaucheux required a self-exploding "pinfire" cartridge. Pulling the trigger drove a pin on the cartridge's side into an explosive cap, firing the bullet. Most of the nearly 12,000 Lefaucheux purchased went to arm Yankees in the Western theater.

12-MM PINFIRE CARTRIDGE

FEDERAL CAVALRYMAN WITH STARR REVOLVER

STARR ARMY REVOLVER

At the urging of the U.S. Ordnance Department, the Starr Arms Company of New York scrapped its expensive self-cocking, or double-action, Army revolver for this conventional hand-cocked, single-action design. Gratified, the Union bought 25,000 of the .44-caliber six-shooters at $12 each.

SAVAGE NAVY REVOLVER

The .36-caliber Savage revolver, easily identified by its heart-shaped trigger guard, was an inaccurate arm. Its peculiar dual-trigger construction—a ring trigger for rotating the six-shot cylinder and cocking the hammer, and a forward trigger for firing—unbalanced the gun and made it difficult to aim. Even so, the Union purchased some 12,000 of them.

Privately Purchased Sidearms

During the Civil War, the number of handguns privately purchased by Yankee soldiers easily exceeded the quantity issued by the Federal government. Although few foot soldiers ever found a use for such arms, fewer still went to battle—initially, at least—without a sidearm in reserve. Likewise, the properly equipped officer never ventured forth without a revolver strapped to his side, although in his case, too, it was little used.

Infantrymen and officers paid an average of $20 for such handguns, creating a whole class of so-called secondary martial arms that were extremely popular—with volunteers who had yet to campaign. Although thousands were sold each month, many were lost, sent home, or given away later by owners grown tired of the extra burden.

ALLEN & WHEELOCK ARMY REVOLVER

In 1861, the U.S. government bought 536 of these Allen & Wheelock Army revolvers. The predecessor of this .44-caliber percussion arm, the Allen & Wheelock lipfire revolver (a self-priming arm), saw more use as a personal sidearm but was discontinued because of a patent-infringement suit.

MASSACHUSETTS ADAMS REVOLVER

The Massachusetts Adams, the American-made version of the respected English Adams revolver, was a .36-caliber five-shooter with a self-cocking, double-action trigger. Between 1857 and 1861, the government purchased 500 of the percussion arms from the Massachusetts Arms Company of Chicopee Falls.

COLT MODEL 1862 POLICE REVOLVER

Weighing only one pound 10 ounces, the small, five-shot .36-caliber Colt Model 1862 police revolver was a favorite personal sidearm of Union officers, although it was never purchased under government contract. About 28,000 of the Model 1862s were manufactured.

A FEDERAL CAVALRYMAN POSES WITH HIS MODEL 1862 COLT POLICE REVOLVER

SMITH & WESSON NO. 2 ARMY REVOLVER

This .32-caliber rimfire revolver, its blued finish rubbed away by extensive use, probably belonged to a trooper in the 7th Kentucky Cavalry. During the War, the state of Kentucky purchased 700 of the No. 2s from the arms dealer B. Kittridge & Company of Cincinnati, Ohio, and issued them to the 7th Kentucky Cavalry. Thousands more were privately obtained by Union enlisted men and officers, who found the gun a serviceable, well-crafted sidearm.

EDGED WEAPONS

Major General Romeyn B. Ayres, whose sword appears below, led a V Corps division during the Battle of Five Forks in Virginia on April 1, 1865—a Union victory that presaged the War's end. Ayres fought with the Army of the Potomac from the First Battle of Bull Run to Appomattox, distinguishing himself at Antietam and Fredericksburg.

MAJ. GEN. ROMEYN B. AYRES

This regulation 1850 staff and field officer's sword worn by Ayres bears the letters *US* amid the pierced floral designs on the brass guard. Field officers with the rank of major and above, and all general staff officers, carried this sword or variations on it.

Swords and Sabers for Service and Show

Among the enlisted men in the Union army, only cavalrymen, sergeants, some artillerymen, and musicians were issued swords, and the weapons they received were generally utilitarian—designed for fighting, although rarely used for such. Officers' swords, by contrast, were usually more decorative than useful and served mainly as a symbol of rank. Only the sabers carried by cavalry and light artillery officers were truly serviceable weapons. How often a cavalryman actually drew his saber, however, depended on whether his commander favored blades or firearms.

Nearly all regulation swords carried by Union soldiers were patterned on weapons of the French army. Enlisted men's swords were made by private American firms—primarily the Ames Manufacturing Company of Chicopee, Massachusetts—or purchased abroad. European manufacturers provided the majority of officers' blades, which were based on an 1850 pattern.

Throughout the Civil War, grateful groups of citizens and loyal military subordinates gave specially made presentation swords to officers as tokens of recognition for exceptional service or as symbols of general esteem. For the most part, however, these highly ornate, costly, and usually impractical swords were worn for formal occasions only.

Staff and Field Officers' Swords

A graceful, decorative sword with a light, frail blade, the 1860 model above failed to gain wide approval. Most Civil War officers preferred the sturdy 1850 pattern.

At the sides of several of the Union surgeons pictured at left are medical staff swords similar to the one above, which was carried by Surgeon G. C. Bennett of the 1st New York Mounted Rifles. The pineapple-shaped pommel secures the blade to the grip. Most medical officers wore the swords for dress occasions only.

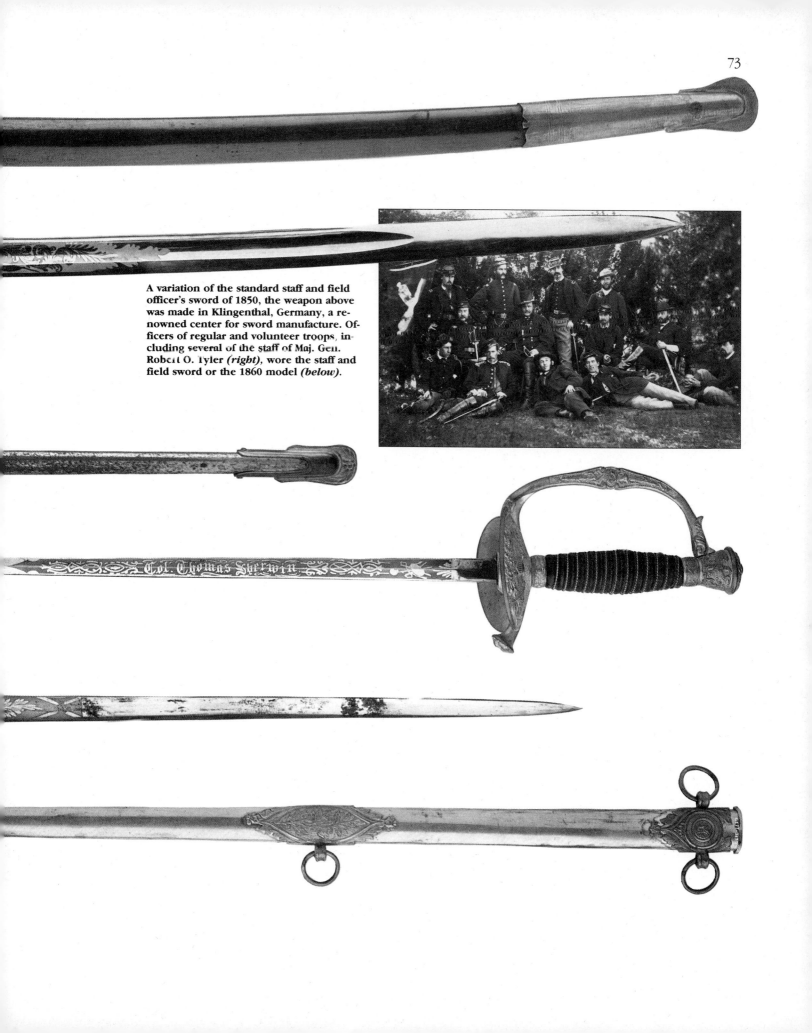

A variation of the standard staff and field officer's sword of 1850, the weapon above was made in Klingenthal, Germany, a renowned center for sword manufacture. Officers of regular and volunteer troops, including several of the staff of Maj. Gen. Robert O. Tyler *(right)*, wore the staff and field sword or the 1860 model *(below)*.

Col. Thomas Sherwin

Foot Officers' Swords

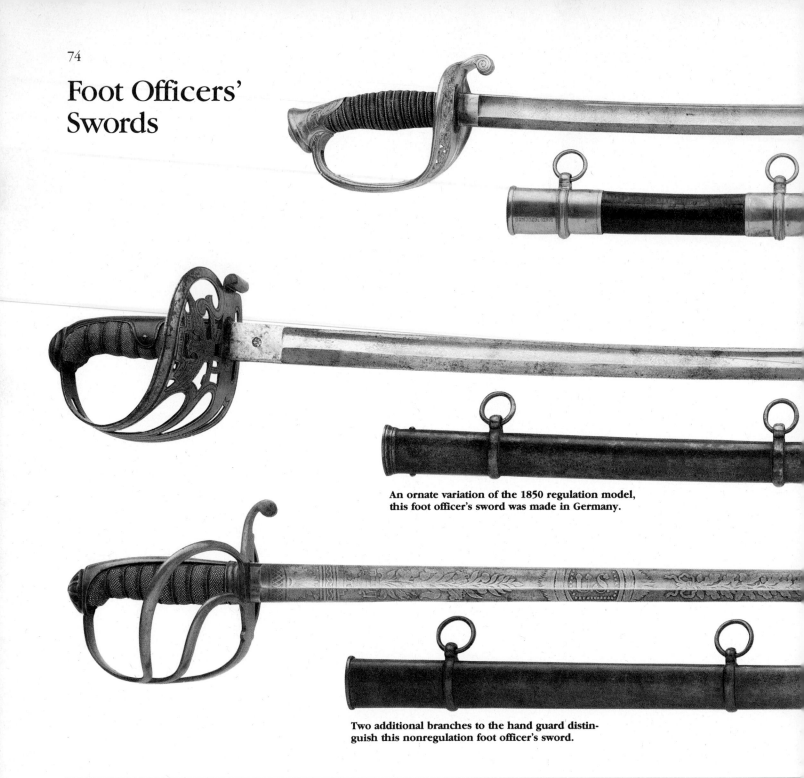

An ornate variation of the 1850 regulation model, this foot officer's sword was made in Germany.

Two additional branches to the hand guard distinguish this nonregulation foot officer's sword.

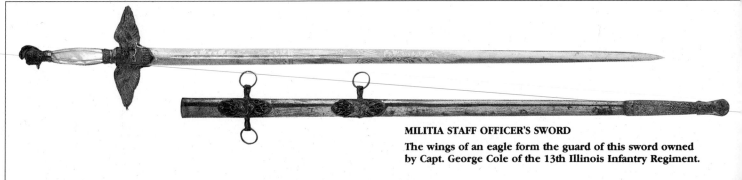

MILITIA STAFF OFFICER'S SWORD

The wings of an eagle form the guard of this sword owned by Capt. George Cole of the 13th Illinois Infantry Regiment.

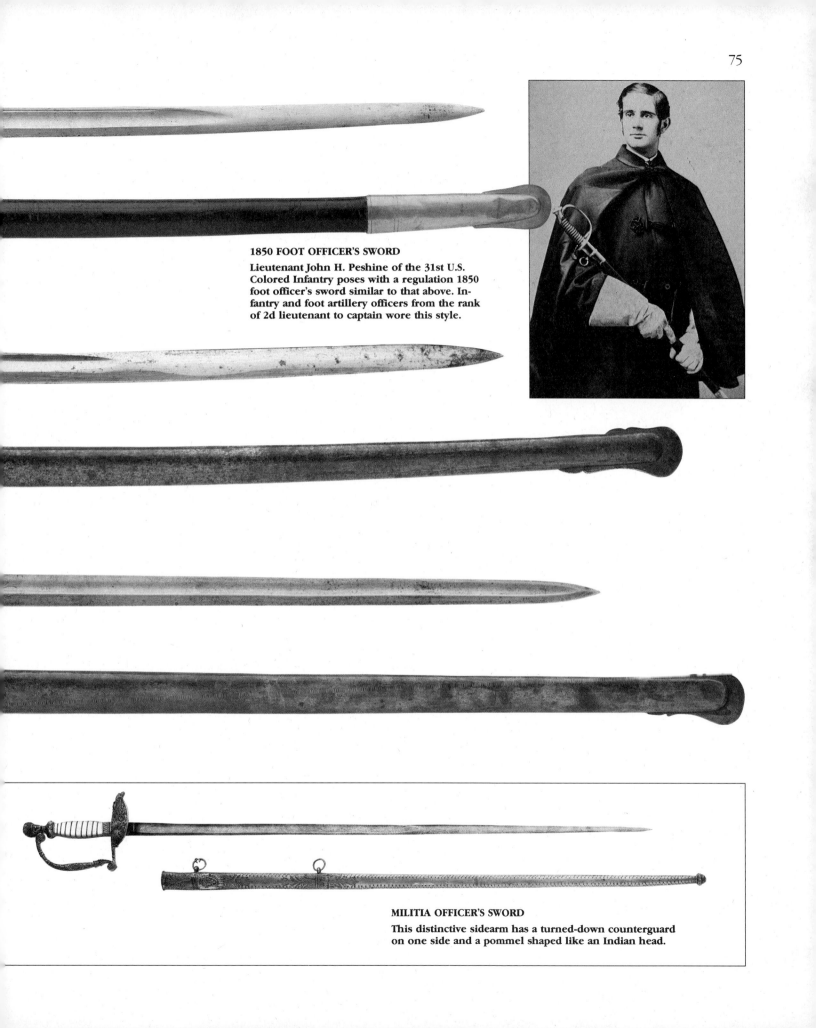

1850 FOOT OFFICER'S SWORD

Lieutenant John H. Peshine of the 31st U.S. Colored Infantry poses with a regulation 1850 foot officer's sword similar to that above. Infantry and foot artillery officers from the rank of 2d lieutenant to captain wore this style.

MILITIA OFFICER'S SWORD

This distinctive sidearm has a turned-down counterguard on one side and a pommel shaped like an Indian head.

Mounted Officers' Swords

1840 CAVALRY OFFICER'S SABER
Wrapped around the iron scabbard of this heavy, wide-bladed saber—of a type used mainly in the early days of the War—is a regulation officer's sash. A raised oak-leaf pattern adorns the sword's pommel.

Gripping an 1840 cavalry saber, an unidentified captain in gleaming boots and spotless gloves strikes a solemn pose for the camera.

With his 1860 cavalry saber at his side, Capt. Henry Page stood beside his mount for this photograph taken in August of 1863 at the Army of the Potomac's headquarters near Bealeton, Virginia. Page served as assistant quartermaster.

1860 OFFICER'S LIGHT CAVALRY SABER

This regulation saber was carried by Lt. T. D. Leslie of the 2d Ohio Cavalry.

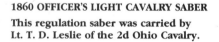

1840 LIGHT ARTILLERY OFFICER'S SABER

Styled after a French pattern, this saber was worn by many field artillery officers, although some preferred to carry the regulation cavalry officer's saber.

Mounted Soldiers' Swords

1840 DRAGOON SABER
Called Old Wristbreaker by the men who used it, this heavy saber was carried early in the War, although the lighter 1860 model was more popular.

1860 LIGHT CAVALRY SABER WITH ACCOUTERMENTS

Sergeant Charles Darling of the 4th Massachusetts Cavalry owned this saber, scabbard, and belt. The sword knot attached to the hand guard served as a wrist strap.

1860 LIGHT CAVALRY SABER

This 1860 cavalry saber had a curved 34-inch blade and a ridged grip for sure handling. The swept-back hand guard protected the trooper's fingers.

Cradling an 1840 light artillery saber, a young Union sergeant sits for the camera. Based on a French pattern, the handsome weapon remained the regulation sword for light artillery until about 1890.

Sergeant Henry DeGroff of the 8th Michigan Cavalry poses with saber in one hand and hat and gloves in the other. His sword belt has a special "Sam Browne" shoulder strap—named after the one-armed British general who devised it—to help support the heavy saber.

With sabers held at rest, the 7th New York Cavalry stands for review before Brig. Gen. Innis N. Palmer and his staff. Also called the Black Horse Cavalry, the regiment was formed in November of 1861 and discharged the following March without once engaging in combat.

Foot Soldiers' Swords

1840 MUSICIAN'S SWORD

The sword worn by a musician—such as the drummer at right—was not purely for decoration but was instead a serviceable weapon. Although musicians were not normally expected to fight, they did accompany troops into battle and at times found it necessary to defend themselves. The musician's regulation sword was similar to that carried by non-commissioned officers *(below)* but was four inches shorter.

1840 NONCOMMISSIONED OFFICER'S SWORD

The sergeant's sword was elegant in design but heavy and poorly balanced. Worn throughout the Civil War, it remained in service until around 1910.

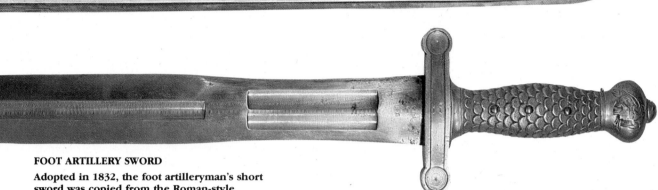

FOOT ARTILLERY SWORD

Adopted in 1832, the foot artilleryman's short sword was copied from the Roman-style weapon of Napoleon's gunners. A federal eagle was added to the pommel. An unwieldy weapon, the sword had little practical value but remained regulation until about 1870.

Federal infantrymen stand at rest with their rifles, while the group's sergeants pose with 1840 noncommissioned officers' swords.

Presentation Swords

MAJ. GEN. GEORGE G. MEADE
Made by Bailey & Company, Philadelphia silversmiths, this silver sword and scabbard were presented to General Meade in 1864 by the Pennsylvania Reserve Corps. Renowned for his intolerance of bungling subordinates, Meade was nicknamed Old Snapping Turtle by his aides.

MAJ. GEN. GOUVERNEUR K. WARREN
A gift from the citizens of his native Cold Spring, New York, this ornate sword in a rosewood case was presented to General Warren in Culpeper, Virginia, on September 30, 1863. According to Col. Theodore Lyman, who witnessed the ceremony, Warren "was extremely nervous at the idea of the sword presentation. This valiant warrior, who don't care a button for missiles, looked much as if about to be married."

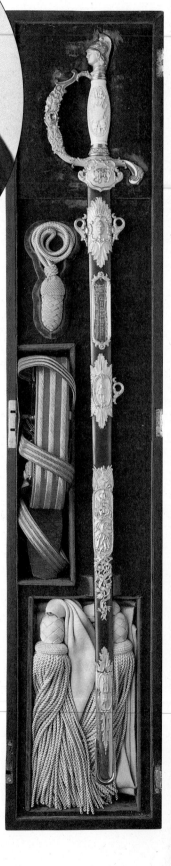

COL. GEORGE C. BURLING

An eagle adorns the gilded guard
of the sword at right given to
Colonel Burling by the officers of
his old regiment, the 6th New
Jersey Volunteers. The blade is
ornamented with the U.S. shield
and emblazoned with the motto
We Never Surrender. On the scabbard are engraved portraits of
Gen. Joseph Hooker, Gen. Daniel
Sickles, and Burling himself.

COL. PETER C. ELLMAKER

A costly variation of the 1850 staff
and field officer's sword, the
weapon at right was presented to
Colonel Ellmaker on January 1,
1862, by the men of his command: the 1st Regiment, Gray Reserves, Pennsylvania National
Guard. An engraved eagle encir-
cled by a sunburst and the U.S.
shield decorate the blade of the
sword, which was produced by
Horstmann & Sons, Philadelphia.

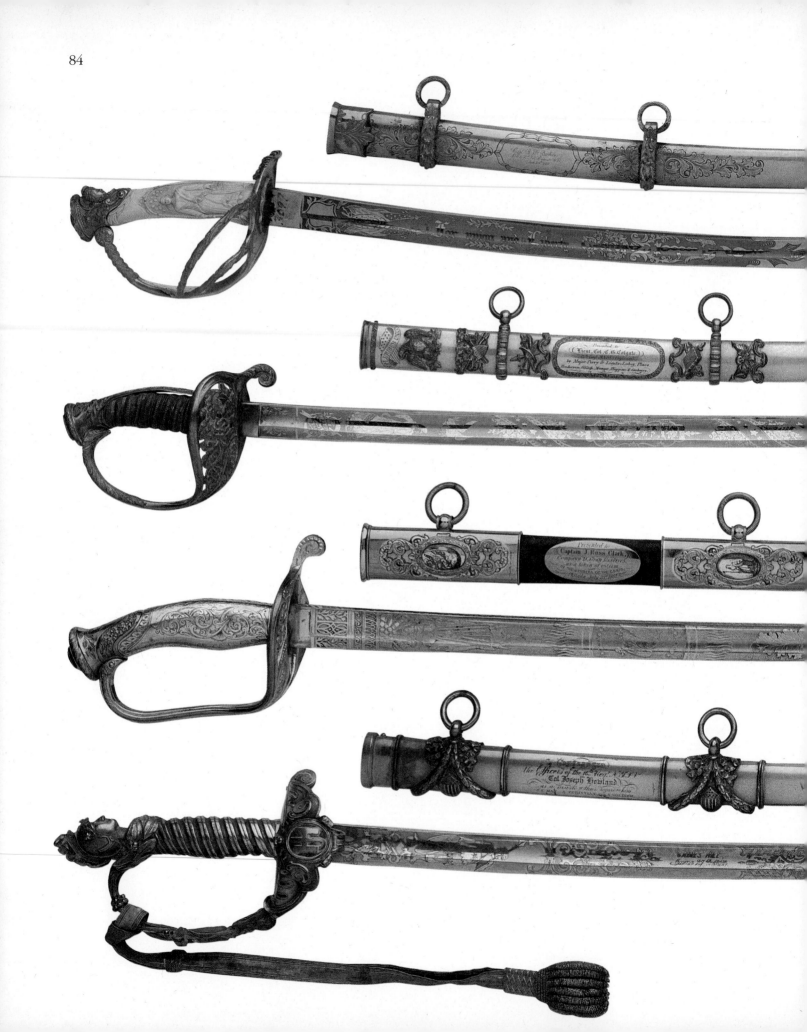

CAPT. G. W. BAKER

Presented to Baker on January 29, 1864, by the 2d New York Veteran Volunteer Cavalry, this sword has a stylized helmet pommel and an ivory grip carved with the figure of Liberty. On the blade are the words *For Union and Liberty*.

LT. COL. C. G. COLGATE

Inscribed on the scabbard of Colgate's blade—an ornate version of the 1850 staff and field officer's sword—are the names of the eight officers of the 15th New York Engineers who gave him the set.

CAPT. J. ROSS CLARK

Captain Clark was given this presentation version of the 1850 foot officer's sword by the members of Company D of the 1st Regiment, Gray Reserves, Pennsylvania National Guard. An eagle and the U.S. shield adorn the blade.

COL. JOSEPH HOWLAND

This sword was presented to Colonel Howland by the officers of his regiment, the 16th New York. An oval plaque on the guard bears his initials. On the blade, the name *Gaines' Mill*—where Howland received a brigadier general's brevet for gallantry—is inscribed, along with the date of the battle.

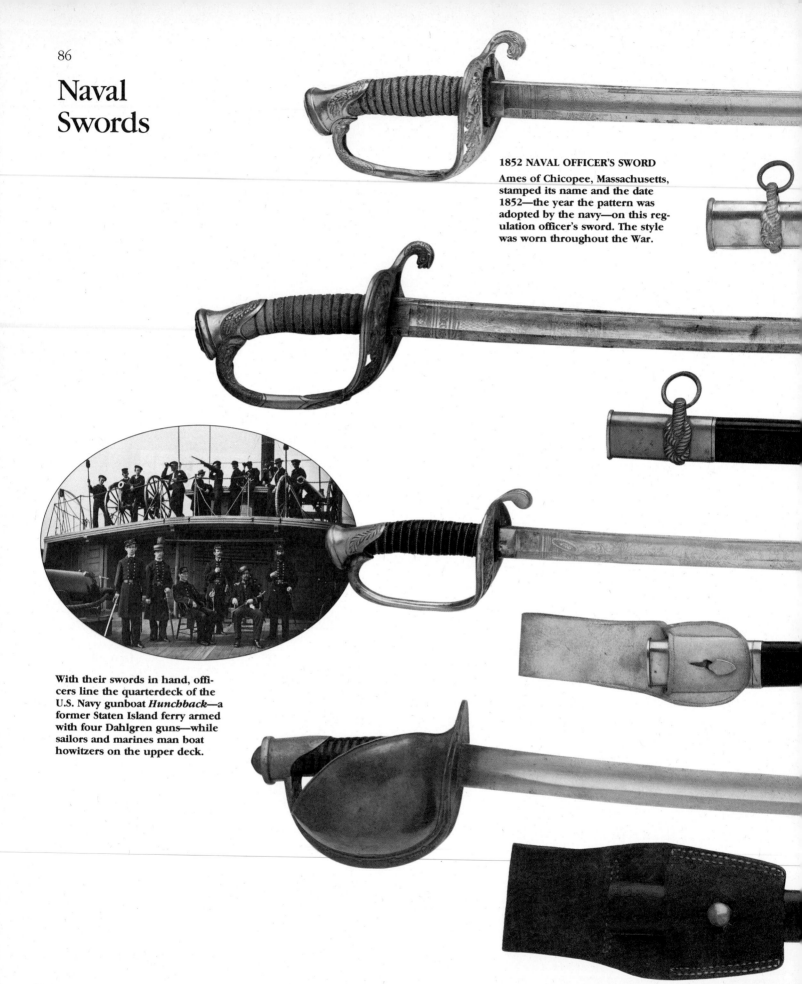

Naval Swords

1852 NAVAL OFFICER'S SWORD
Ames of Chicopee, Massachusetts, stamped its name and the date 1852—the year the pattern was adopted by the navy—on this regulation officer's sword. The style was worn throughout the War.

With their swords in hand, officers line the quarterdeck of the U.S. Navy gunboat *Hunchback*—a former Staten Island ferry armed with four Dahlgren guns—while sailors and marines man boat howitzers on the upper deck.

1852 NAVAL OFFICER'S SWORD

The letters *USN* adorn the counterguard of this regulation sword. The ends of the knuckle guard and the drag on the scabbard are in the form of a dolphin's head.

MARINE CORPS NONCOMMISSIONED OFFICER'S SWORD

The sword worn by marine noncommissioned officers was almost identical to the 1850 army foot officer's sword.

1860 NAVAL CUTLASS

Worn by enlisted sailors, the cutlass adopted around 1860 had a slightly curved blade. The large guard was designed to protect the hand and fingers during close shipboard combat.

UNIFORMS

When Abraham Lincoln issued his call for 75,000 volunteers in April 1861 to suppress the Confederate rebellion, a pattern of dress for the U.S. Army had long been established. Most of the recruits who answered the call, however, had their own notions of proper military attire. They were members of local militia units whose uniforms were bewilderingly diverse. A reporter who visited Camp Dennison in Ohio, where such units were molded into regiments, likened the training ground to "an Eastern bazaar, in which every variety of costume under heaven is to be found." He noticed a soldier who looked something like a member of the Regular Army, in cloth "blue as a jay bird," but nearby another recruit stood watch "in flannel as red as a flamingo."

The units reporting to Confederate camps at this time were no less motley. Indeed, the Southerners, with their resistance to centralized authority and their small industrial base, moved only slowly and tentatively toward uniformity in military dress. By contrast, Federal officials imposed considerable regularity within a year or so. The transition was not a smooth one. The rush to procure factory-made uniforms fostered a good deal of inferior workmanship, even corruption, before the government took firm control of the contractors. And even when the Federal dress pattern was well established, various units continued to assert their sartorial independence, embracing exotic alternatives such as Zouave outfits replete with baggy scarlet pants.

Providing uniforms for the U.S. Army was the official responsibility of the U.S. Quartermaster's Department, which had been supervising the design and manufacture of clothing for enlisted men at the Schuylkill Arsenal in Philadelphia since the War of 1812. Periodically, the regulations had been revised to reflect changes in military fashion and the practical needs of the troops.

The last revision before the Civil War occurred in 1858. For foot troops, the code prescribed the uniform coat—a single-breasted woolen frock coat with a relatively tight fitting body and skirt, cut from a separate piece of material, that extended halfway between the hip and the knee. The coat was inconvenient for men on horseback, so mounted troops were allotted the uniform jacket. Both the uniform coat and the uniform jacket were of dark blue, which the Army had long regarded as the national color. The regulations stipulated that soldiers wear the coat or jacket—along with blue trousers and a tall, stiff black felt hat—on all occasions except fatigue or work duties. For such informal times, the regulars were issued a soft woolen forage cap and a flannel sack coat—a loose-fitting garment with a single row of four buttons.

With minor modifications, these items, along with other trademarks of the prewar Regular Army, eventually became standard issue for most Union troops. But in the hectic months after the fall of Fort Sumter, the Federal government lacked the means of imposing such a pattern on the tens of thousands of Federal volunteers. Unable to conjure up so many uniforms at short notice, the War Department asked the states to outfit their own regiments and apply to Washington for reimbursement. But the states too needed time to organize their efforts. As a result, many early regiments were uniformed primarily at local expense with such help as the state was able to provide.

Volunteer militia units generally furnished the nucleus for these early regiments, but it was not always possible to dress those who filled out the complement in the distinctive manner of the veteran militiamen. The Irish-American militia company that became the 69th New York Regiment, for example, was unable to supply its new recruits with the blue-and-red artillery frocks worn by its original members, so the state supplied coarse gray overshirts as a stopgap until simple blue frocks could be tailored and delivered to the Irishmen in Washington.

In the North as in the South at this time, communities pitched in to produce uniforms for their volunteers. In Greenfield, Ohio, a local tailor cut out uniforms from whole cloth and passed the pieces to local women to be sewn together. The town council dipped into its treasury to buy buttons. Those who did the work were not all as handy as they were patriotic. One soldier recalled that half of his regiment's homemade coats were "two feet too large around the chest."

A few raw regiments actually departed for the nation's capital with none of their members in uniform. The 1st and 2d Ohio were summoned to Washington so soon after they were organized that their leaders elected to pick up uniforms along the way. Finding the market in Pennsylvania monopolized by the state's purchasers, their agent settled for raw materials—"coarse black pilot cloth for overcoats, and cadet gray cloth for pants"—and had the garments sewn by Pennsylvania vendors. The regiments' hastily fabricated sack coats were casual in the extreme—some had no buttons. In the end, the deficits were remedied, and the Ohio agent proudly reported that he had uniformed the men of the two regiments at a price of $12.76 per man, less than half the cost of outfitting a Regular Army soldier when war broke out. Some of the fancier Eastern outfits looked down on such makeshift units, however, branding them "pauper regiments."

Local initiative might have been enough to clothe the Union army if the War had been the short, triumphant affair many Northerners anticipated. But by late July 1861, the Battle of Bull Run had shattered that vision,

and in the meantime the three-month terms of the original recruits were expiring. Congress authorized a volunteer army of half a million men serving three-year terms, and the states geared up in earnest to clothe the new regiments. Some states had already acted. New York, for instance, had decided in late April to issue all its new regiments a standard outfit, including a dark blue woolen jacket, closing in front with eight state-seal buttons; light blue trousers and overcoat; and a dark blue fatigue cap. By the end of July, the state had agreed to purchase more than 32,000 jackets from nine different contractors. But there was not enough dark blue cloth to go around, so the firm of Brooks Brothers was allowed to substitute 7,300 gray jackets. Not only was the color irregular but the fabric was inferior. A soldier who wore the jacket described the cloth as a "coarse, fluffy, flimsy material." At the slightest provocation, it began to fall apart, "irritating the skin, and covering the floor with refuse."

Such cheap work inspired a new derogatory term—*shoddy*—and in the rush to obtain ready-made uniforms in bulk, many states were saddled with it. One observer characterized shoddy as "a villainous compound, the refuse stuff and sweepings of the shop, pounded, rolled, glued, and smoothed to the external form and gloss of the cloth, but no more like the genuine article than the shadow is to the substance." Stories of new uniforms disintegrating after a few days' use scandalized the Union and led to inquiries.

By the autumn of 1861, some order was emerging from the chaos. The purchase of foreign-made cloth and uniforms had the effect of stimulating American manufacturers to improve standards and increase production. And on September 23, 1861, the War Department, in an effort to end deadly confusion on the battlefield, asked the governors and other officials of Northern states to stop furnishing gray uniforms to their soldiers; the color had been popular with Northern militia before the War, and many states, including Maine, Vermont, and Wisconsin, had elected to stick with it. Troops who had already been issued gray uniforms continued to wear them for a while. But by mid-1862 gray had been banished, and Quartermaster General Montgomery C. Meigs had usurped from the states the role of contracting for and distributing uniforms.

Although the states would regain some responsibility in those matters later, the increased authority of the quartermaster general enabled him to make the blue uniform of the Regular Army the standard for most units while allowing for certain regimental exceptions. To supplement the output of Philadelphia's Schuylkill Arsenal, new Union depots for the manufacture or purchase of clothing were established at New York, Boston, Cincinnati, Louisville, Indianapolis, St. Louis, and Springfield, Illinois. Federal inspectors examined the clothing there before it was disbursed, and the uniforms were stamped with labels identifying the inspector and the maker to ensure that shoddy work was no longer foisted on the troops.

Improvements in quality and consistency did not necessarily make the new uniforms any more comfortable than their predecessors. When the regulation clothing arrived at training camp, one recruit recalled, "Coats, trousers, and the other clothes were piled up in separate heaps, and each man was just thrown the first garment on the top of the heap; he took it and walked away. If it was an outrageous fit, he would swap with someone if possible, otherwise he got along as best he could." The short and the tall seldom found a good fit, and men of all sizes complained of the stiffness and scratchiness of the clothing—following the orders of the War Department, Northern mills used wool much of the time, even for underwear. "The shirts are rather coarse," an Indiana volunteer wrote, "and the sox—well, I think I shall wear the ones I brought from home and have Mother knit me some more when they are worn out. As to the shoes, they are wide and big enough, goodness knows! No danger of cramped feet with them! They may be very good but surely they are not very stylish."

Under the pressures of campaigning, the troops inevitably lightened their loads by paring down their wardrobe to a few basic necessities. "With the opening of spring camp, away would go all extra clothing," one veteran recalled. "A choice was made between the dress coat and blouse, for one of these must go. In brief, when a campaign was fairly under way the average infantryman's wardrobe was what he had on." The troops could afford to be somewhat wasteful, because the Federal distribution system generally ensured that they would be resupplied in the fall. Taste rather than necessity dictated other choices. The tall black felt hat was unpopular with many of the troops who received it, and it was often traded away or discarded in favor of the soft forage cap.

Sometimes entire units departed from the Federal norm as a matter of ethnic pride, expressed typically by a distinctive headdress. The men of the 79th New York, known as the Cameron Highlanders, wore glengarry caps for the length of their enlistment, while their fellow Scotsmen of the 12th Illinois wore tam-o'-shanters. The Poles of the 31st New York Volunteer Infantry donned traditional square-topped Polish caps. And the Italians of the 39th New York wore the feathered hats of their homeland's *bersaglieri* and called themselves the Garibaldi Guard.

The strongest foreign influence on Union army apparel was exerted by France—not because it had furnished the North with droves of immigrants, but because the imperial army of Napoleon III had earned a reputation for military excellence and high style. The French-influenced uniforms were of two broad categories: Zouave and chasseur. Zouave garb originated in the French colonies of North Africa, and the Zouave regiments of the French army were generally admired for their dashing performance in Italy and the Crimea. In America, Colonel Elmer Ellsworth's United States Zouave Cadets, a smart militia unit that toured the country on the eve of the Civil War, sparked a rage for Zouave attire and acrobatic drill. Among the Federal units that embraced the style was the 5th New York Regiment, also known as Duryée's Zouaves, which was organized in New York City in the spring of 1861 and served for two years with the Army of the Potomac. Its uniform was a close copy of the French, including a red fez with tassel, a dark blue jacket trimmed in red, and baggy red trousers tucked into leggings or gaiters. Many other regiments adopted similar dress. Some abandoned pantaloons in favor of pleated trousers, while several Western units combined a Zouave-style jacket with regulation trousers and forage cap.

The chasseur uniform, which originated with the French light infantry, enjoyed less of a vogue in the Union army than the Zouave outfit, perhaps because it was less exotic. Its salient feature was an abbreviated frock coat with short skirts slitted at the sides and usually piped or trimmed around all edges. Unlike the open Zouave jacket, it closed with a single row of buttons. The style evidently appealed to Quartermaster General Meigs, because in late 1861 he ordered 10,000 chasseur uniforms from France. The colorful dark blue jackets were trimmed with yellow and bedecked with dark green epaulets with a yellow crescent. The trousers, baggy but long-legged, were of blue-gray and trimmed on the legs and pockets with yellow cording.

A dress shako of leather was included as well. Unfortunately, the uniforms were cut too small for the typical American frame, and only a few regiments made use of them.

After this experiment with foreign dress, the quartermaster general adhered to the Regular Army pattern for the most part. But state regiments devoted to Zouave dress or to distinctive trim or colors managed to obtain new uniforms of that style by special order through the central depots. Schuylkill produced such a surplus of regulation clothing that it was able to compete with private contractors to procure nonregulation regimental uniforms for volunteer units. And aside from the Navy and Marine Corps—separate services with their own clothing regulations—certain branches of the Union army were allotted special uniforms. The so-called Invalid Corps, for example, later known as the Veteran Reserve Corps, adopted a version of the chasseur outfit when it was instituted in 1863. And when Colonel Hiram Berdan organized his United States Sharpshooters in 1861, he arranged for them to be clothed in regulation pattern but in a nonregulation color—dark green.

Most Union officers and men, however, cared little for such distinctions and were content simply to have enough clothing—something the Confederates could not always count on. To be sure, long campaigns occasionally strained the Federal supply system and left more than a few Yankees ragged and barefoot. "Our reg is purty naked," an Ohioan reported in his diary during a period of need. He added that his outfit looked "more like a reg of secesh than northern troops." But the very fact that the Yankees at their threadbare worst likened themselves to Confederates indicated that, overall, the Union was winning the war of the supply lines, and that the boys in blue enjoyed a distinct advantage.

A Peacetime Legacy

In the decades before the War, the states gradually abandoned the old compulsory militia system, in which every able-bodied white male citizen was required to muster for drill once or twice a year. Military-minded men continued to band together, however, in volunteer militia units at private expense. The volunteer companies designed their own uniforms, striving to make them as distinct as possible from other militia units.

For full dress, militias favored the swallow-tailed coat popular with civilians in the 1840s. Although by 1860 this garment had fallen out of fashion, militiamen stubbornly kept their tail coats and wore them proudly when their companies volunteered for war.

**UNIDENTIFIED MILITIAMAN
NATIONAL LANCERS
BOSTON, MASSACHUSETTS**

Traditional headgear for soldiers since the Napoleonic Wars, the shako was a favorite with the volunteer militia in 1861. The owner of this shako later joined the 4th Massachusetts Light Artillery.

NEW ENGLAND GUARDS
BOSTON, MASSACHUSETTS

Despite regulations issued in 1852 calling for a state militia uniform, the New England Guards were unwilling to lose their regimental identity by giving up their dark blue tail coat and trousers.

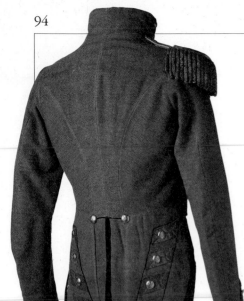

ALEXANDER STERN NEW YORK STATE MILITIA RIFLE REGIMENT

Stern's gold-trimmed, gray militia dress coat *(left and below)* represents the standard style for volunteer militia uniforms of the 1850s. By that decade, New York, the largest and wealthiest Northern state, had organized its several hundred independent militia companies into 51 active, uniformed regiments.

79TH NEW YORK STATE MILITIA

Designated by the number 79 in honor of the Cameron Highlanders, the 79th regiment of the British army, this unit's highland garb included a blue doublet *(below)* and glengarry cap with feathers.

UNIDENTIFIED CORPORAL 79TH NEW YORK STATE MILITIA

SHAKO, NEW YORK RIFLEMEN

7TH NEW YORK STATE MILITIA

The full-dress uniform of the 7th New York, including the swallow-tailed coat *(far right)* and shako *(below),* typifies the garb of militia companies in the first half of the 19th century. In response to Lincoln's call, 945 men from the 7th New York arrived in Washington in April 1861.

UNIDENTIFIED PRIVATE
7TH NEW YORK
STATE MILITIA

PHILO RUGGLES 51ST NEW YORK STATE MILITIA

Revolutionary War uniforms inspired the costume *(right)* of Ruggles' regiment. This group later formed the nucleus of the 12th New York Infantry, which fought in the First Battle of Bull Run.

Early War Volunteers

**PVT. JOHN CROZIER
1ST DELAWARE INFANTRY**

Crozier's frock coat (*right*) was made of sati-net, a fabric woven with a cotton warp and a woolen weft to produce a shiny surface. The companies that mustered to form the 1st Delaware wore either their militia uniforms or whatever clothing they could obtain locally, since their state did not provide uniforms.

When the first waves of troops marched into Washington, D.C., in 1861, one observer wrote that it seemed as if "all the able-bodied men in the country were moving, on the first of May, with all their property on their backs, to agreeable but dusty lodgings on the Potomac."

These soldiers wore the best uniforms they could scrape together, parading past the White House clad in blue, gray, and the garish colors of the Zouave companies. The spectacle was said to be "more like a grand gala season than the serious work of war."

7TH NEW YORK STATE MILITIA

So strict was the sense of propriety of the "kid-glove militia" that when they set up camp in Washington, D.C., in 1861, they reportedly did not even pull a single flower or disturb a fence rail. Members of the 7th New York State Militia, such as the soldier at right, wore gray jackets (*left*) and kepis (*below*) in 1862.

When the 1st Rhode Island Infantry arrived in the nation's capital in 1861, the "absence of smart trappings" made the unit *(right)* "look ready for business," wrote one observer. The scarlet blankets were distinctive to the regiment.

PVT. EDWARD N. WHITTIER
1ST RHODE ISLAND INFANTRY

The 1st Rhode Island was organized and commanded by Col. Ambrose E. Burnside, a former tailor who personally supervised the manufacture of its uniforms. Private Whittier wore the regiment's characteristic homemade pants *(above, left)*, kepi *(below)*, and "Rhode Island blouse" *(left)*.

COMMAND/STAFF

**GEN. GEORGE G. MEADE
ARMY OF THE POTOMAC**

For fatigue and field service, General Meade *(far left)* replaced his frock coat *(left)* with a sack coat. When officers did wear frock coats in the field, they substituted gilt-edged shoulder straps for their dress epaulets. Meade commanded the Army of the Potomac from April 1863 until the end of the War. His failure to pursue the Confederates after the Battle of Gettysburg proved him to be, in the eyes of his critics, "an ordinary general."

**KEPI AND HAT
GEN. GEORGE G. MEADE**

Uniforms for the Brass

The dress regulations issued by the Federal government in 1851 dictated the style of the general officer's uniform during the War. These regulations called for a double-breasted dark blue frock coat and plain dark blue trousers. The only major changes came in 1858, when a black felt hat became the official headgear and the new-pattern forage cap was introduced.

The army's dress regulations stipulated a system of button arrangements to designate the rank of general officers. The buttons on a major general's frock coat, like Meade's *(above),* were grouped in three sets of three; those on a brigadier general's coat *(right)* were arranged in four sets of two.

GENERAL OFFICER'S SHOULDER BOARDS

GEN. GEORGE CUSTER ARMY OF THE POTOMAC

Renowned for his showy dress, Custer *(left, in his signature scarlet necktie)* designed his own distinctly nonregulation uniform jacket *(above)* made of dark blue velvet with gold lace galloons on the sleeves. Custer's appearance in this garment prompted one officer to exclaim, "He looks like a circus rider gone mad!"

GENERAL OFFICER'S SASH

GEN. SAMUEL CRAWFORD PENNSYLVANIA

A note in the pocket of this officer's sack coat *(left)* identified it as belonging to General Crawford. Portrayed above in his full-dress major's uniform, Crawford holds the traditional chapeau bras, or cocked hat, authorized for optional wear with full dress by the army regulations of 1858.

Staff Officers' Uniforms

Relegated to unsung and often obscure service, staff officers nonetheless performed invaluable functions. These men served as the eyes and ears of their commanders. They relayed orders and reported on battlefield situations; they were advisers, correspondents, confidants, and at times even replaced their field commanders in battle.

Although 1851 Federal regulations prescribed the standard dark blue frock coat for staff officers, once the War broke out these men displayed unlimited variation in their dress. Each general set the tone for his own staff. Some expected uniformity; others cared little how their aides dressed.

**COL. WILLIAM GODDARD
1ST RHODE ISLAND INFANTRY**

Cited for his gallantry at First Bull Run, Goddard *(right)* preserved his frock coat, trousers, and kepi *(below)*. He served as aide-de-camp to General Burnside at Fredericksburg; after the War he was appointed chancellor of Brown University.

STAFF OFFICERS' BUTTONS

GENERAL STAFF

TOPOGRAPHICAL
ENGINEERS

ENGINEERS

ORDNANCE
DEPARTMENT

SIGNAL CORPS

These buttons are of the type worn by the general staff and by the specialized branches of the staff corps. Most military buttons from this period were mass-produced and given a gilt finish.

**CAPT. CHARLES PIERCE
GEN. HENRY JUDAH'S STAFF**

Formerly a sergeant with the 10th Massachusetts Infantry Regiment, Pierce married General Judah's daughter and soon thereafter, it is said, was promoted to captain on the general's staff. His captain's uniform, shown here, adhered to regulations with the exception of the white vest.

General John Sedgwick's staff relaxes outside their log cabin quarters near Brandy Station, Virginia, in early 1864, where Sedgwick's VI Corps had its winter headquarters. The officer seated astride his chair *(center)* is Arthur McClellan, younger brother of Gen. George McClellan.

MEDICAL OFFICER'S SASH

ASST. SURG. DAVID R. BEAVER 191ST PENNSYLVANIA VOLUNTEER INFANTRY

Privately purchased officers' sack coats often boasted five buttons, like Beaver's coat *(right)*; government-issue sack coats had only four buttons.

LT. GEORGE YOUNG
143D NEW YORK INFANTRY

Attached to the staff of Col. James Robinson, Lieutenant Young *(above)* was riding as a courier in the heat of the Battle of Peach Tree Creek in July 1864 when a Minié ball passed through his horse's body and lodged in his right leg. The ball splintered two of Young's bones just below the knee. His regimental surgeon salvaged the limb, but the injury rendered him unfit for duty and plagued him the rest of his life. After enduring the pain of chronic infection for nearly 45 years, Young died of his wound in March 1909. Among his effects, he left the uniform shown here, including the trousers *(above, right)* that bear the mark of the bullet that ended his service.

2D MASSACHUSETTS CAVALRY
Officers and men of this regiment were assigned the futile task of pursuing the "Gray Ghost," John Singleton Mosby, the celebrated Confederate guerrilla leader.

**LT. COL. AUGUSTUS W. CORLISS
2D RHODE ISLAND CAVALRY**
Corliss (above) modified his uniform by creasing the crown of his hat and adding gold tape to the collar and sleeves of his regulation frock coat.

"Feathered Cap and Flashing Saber"

As the War began, America's imagination was captured by the vision of the dashing cavalryman, "all leather and jingling harness, feathered cap and flashing saber." From this romantic tradition emerged officers who delighted in asserting personal styles in their uniforms. Forsaking the regulation frock coat, many cavalry officers adopted the short uniform jacket, which they had tailored to their taste. Originally intended to be worn by mounted troops, the jacket proved to be more comfortable for riding.

1ST LIEUTENANT'S CAVALRY JACKET

Nonregulation trefoils of gold braid adorn the sleeves of this jacket, which belonged to an officer of the First Troop of the Philadelphia City Cavalry. Raised from one of the wealthiest volunteer militia companies in the country, the unit saw action between 1861 and 1863. Their field uniform was a far cry from their showy militia garb, which included a bearskin-crested helmet.

Black ostrich feathers decorated the left sides of cavalry officers' hats: three for field officers, two for company officers, and one for enlisted men.

1ST LT. CHARLES E. MORTON 2D U.S. CAVALRY

Morton, pictured at left in his cavalry officer's dress, served for only six months before he became ill and died at Outpost Station, Louisiana, in August 1863.

CAPT. JAMES H. WORKMAN 6TH PENNSYLVANIA

A member of Rush's Lancers—the only Union cavalry regiment officially issued lances—Workman served throughout the War despite being captured in 1863 and wounded the following year. His cavalry jacket and trousers are another variation on cavalry officers' dress.

Standard Garb for Cavalrymen

The two enlisted cavalrymen at right wear uniform jackets made in the regulation Federal pattern. Forage caps like theirs officially replaced the black felt cavalry hat in 1859.

**D. E. TAFT
U.S. CAVALRY**

Taft's cavalry jacket and trousers are probably products of the St. Louis Arsenal; he purchased the vest and hat himself. Single rows of yellow braid on his jacket collar are a modification of the standard U.S. Army pattern embellishing the collars of the two jackets at the bottom of the facing page.

**U.S. ARMY HAT
4TH U.S. CAVALRY**

Authorized by the U.S. Army as its official cavalry dress headgear in 1858, the black felt hat *(right)* was often modified for field use.

SGT. FRANKLIN SMITH 4TH MASSACHUSETTS CAVALRY

Smith *(right)* wore this flannel fatigue sack coat, kepi, and trousers. The trousers are equipped with instep straps that he slipped over his riding boots. After a 10-month stint in the cavalry, Smith was captured in Magnolia, Florida, in 1864; he was confined for six months in the prison camp at Andersonville, Georgia.

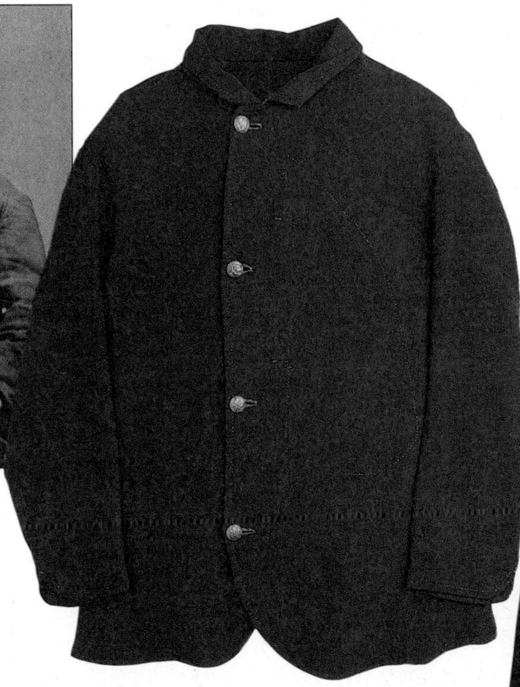

PRIVATE'S JACKET U.S. MOUNTED RIFLES

Early in the War, mounted troops included not only cavalry but also the more heavily armed dragoons and mounted riflemen. Dragoons, such as the horseman pictured above, wore jackets piped in orange. Dragoon musicians' jackets *(right)* bore a more elaborate pattern of orange trim. Jackets owned by members of the mounted rifles *(left)* were piped in green.

DRAGOON MUSICIAN

Uniforms of Volunteer Troopers

In the first frantic months of the War, Northern states attempted to uniform and equip their regiments as best they could with what stores were available. This system resulted in volunteers arriving in Washington, D.C., in 1861 wearing a grab-bag medley of different uniforms.

Even though the Federal quartermaster general had procured sufficient uniforms to clothe the 550,000 members of the Union army by early 1862, a number of states elected to provide clothing for their own troops, including the volunteer cavalry. State-manufactured cavalry jackets, like the ones shown here, varied in piping design, cut, number of buttons, and collar height.

The fully equipped cavalryman, such as the sergeant at right, has been described as "a moving arsenal and military depot, who must have struck surprise, if not terror, into the minds of his enemies."

SGT. CHARLES DARLING 4TH MASSACHUSETTS CAVALRY

Sergeant Darling's uniform *(right)* was probably custom-tailored. While on furlough in November 1864, Darling encountered three Rebels at a house in Virginia, and a skirmish ensued. Darling was wounded in the fight but managed to escape on his horse. After hearing of the incident, his commanding officer decided to burn down the house and gave Darling the "satisfaction of applying the torch."

The Fighting Butterflies

Among the rough-and-ready horsemen of Gen. Philip Sheridan's Cavalry Corps, the 3d New Jersey was decidedly out of the ordinary, at least in its resplendent appearance. To attract recruits, New Jersey authorities outfitted the unit in a distinctive uniform—visorless forage cap, elaborately braided jacket, and a hooded cloak, or talma—that resembled the brilliant garb worn by hussar regiments of European armies.

When the 3d New Jersey Cavalry reached the front at the Wilderness in 1864, the gaudily clad recruits were derisively dubbed butterflies by the army's veterans. But the regiment proved itself as tough as any, fighting bravely under Sheridan in the Shenandoah Valley at the battles of Winchester and Tom's Brook.

TROOPER OF THE 3D NEW JERSEY CAVALRY

HUSSAR-STYLE JACKET AND TALMA

This assortment of Pennsylvania cavalry jackets *(left, far left, and below)* illustrates the diversity found in volunteer cavalry soldiers' clothing.

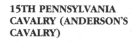

PVT. WALTER GREGORY 2D MISSOURI CAVALRY

Noted for the variety and peculiarity of its militia dress, the state of Missouri did not issue clothing during the War. The trim on Private Gregory's jacket *(above)* appeared on jackets of other Western-states cavalrymen.

15TH PENNSYLVANIA CAVALRY (ANDERSON'S CAVALRY)

6TH PENNSYLVANIA CAVALRY (RUSH'S LANCERS)

ARTILLERY

Called the "forgotten branch of the service," the artillery was always the smallest arm of the Union forces. Its officers, like those at right wearing regulation frock coats, drilled their men as many as three times a day. This repetition was crucial, since the din of battle often drowned out verbal commands.

Although ordered to wear the full-brimmed "Hardee hat" in 1858, light artillery commanders, such as the officer above, insisted on keeping the dragoon-style "Ringgold cap" with its red horsehair plume and cords, named for the hat worn by the men of Bvt. Maj. Samuel Ringgold's artillery company before the Mexican War.

LIGHT ARTILLERY DRESS CAP

Artillery Officers' Uniforms

Prior to 1861, two of the 12 companies of U.S. Army artillery were equipped and trained as light, or field, artillery. The remaining 10 companies garrisoned coastal forts, manning the heavy artillery, big defensive cannon. When the War broke out, new companies were added; 14 of the regular artillery companies converted to horse artillery for greater mobility, and the other five remained foot artillery.

Although they found jackets more practical for mounted service, artillery officers retained the regulation frock coat for dress occasions. Enlisted men of the heavy artillery were uniformed the same as foot troops. The color of their trim—scarlet instead of light blue—distinguished them from infantry.

1ST LT. FLORANCE W. GRUGAN
2D PENNSYLVANIA HEAVY ARTILLERY

Grugan, whose jacket and trousers are shown here, served for most of the War as the regiment's acting assistant adjutant general. This post required good horsemanship, good penmanship, and the ability to "know the right flank from the left."

In 1860, the government authorized a special jacket for light artillery officers. These new undress jackets incorporated "Russian shoulder knots" made of gilt cord to replace the fringed epaulets found on earlier models. The officers above have modified their jackets by adding breast pockets.

1ST LT.
EDWARD WHITTIER
5TH MAINE LIGHT
ARTILLERY

The guns of Whittier's regiment were positioned along the front lines at Fisher's Hill, Virginia, in September 1864. There, Whittier later reported, they were "most hotly engaged for the day, playing mostly upon the enemy's infantry." Awarded a Medal of Honor for his conduct in this battle, Whittier *(right)* owned this 12-button jacket and kepi.

Enlisted Artillerymen

**SGT. GEORGE M. TURNER
3D RHODE ISLAND HEAVY ARTILLERY**

As was typical of men in the foot artillery, Sergeant Turner wore a light artillery jacket *(right)*. His forage cap *(below)* is probably a private purchase; his trousers appear to be regulation for heavy artillery.

Members of Battery D of the 1st New York Light Artillery man their gun at Stafford Heights, Virginia, across the river from Fredericksburg, in April 1863. Assigned to the Army of the Potomac, Battery D lost 13 men in battle and 14 men to disease throughout its four-year service.

SGT. AUGUSTUS BRADBURY 7TH BATTERY MAINE LIGHT ARTILLERY

A lumberman before the War, Sergeant Bradbury *(right)* received a $300 bonus from the government for his 18-month service. The 7th Battery, which was mustered in December 1863, participated in the siege of Petersburg between June 1864 and April 1865. Nonstandard belt loops on Bradbury's jacket *(far right)* were added to support a heavy saber belt.

1ST MAINE HEAVY ARTILLERY

As members of a heavy artillery regiment, the men of the 1st Maine were armed and equipped as infantry but wore the regulation uniform of the Federal heavy artillery, which consisted of a red-trimmed frock coat *(right)* and a forage cap with crossed-cannon insignia *(below)*.

UNIDENTIFIED PRIVATE 8TH NEW YORK HEAVY ARTILLERY

The 8th New York did garrison duty at Forts Federal Hill, Marshall, and McHenry in Maryland before joining the Army of the Potomac in the field in May 1864.

Officers of the 82d Illinois relax in camp at Atlanta, Georgia, in the autumn of 1864. Their regiment was among the Federal troops that occupied Atlanta from September to late November of that year.

Uniforms of the Infantry Command

The use of the frock coat for officers of the United States Army dated back to the 1820s. By the time of the Civil War, the regulation uniform for infantry officers differed from other branches only in its addition of eagle "I" buttons and light blue shoulder straps. Although the regulation color for trousers was sky blue after December 1861, infantry officers also wore dark blue trousers with sky blue welts throughout the War.

As the War wore on, however, infantry officers appeared in the field more frequently in short jackets and loose sack coats, finding these garments more comfortable than their regulation frock coats, especially in hot weather.

INFANTRY OFFICER'S SASH

COL. JOHN L. CHATFIELD
6TH CONNECTICUT INFANTRY

On the evening of July 18, 1863, Chatfield, whose forage cap, frock coat, and pants are shown left and below, led his regiment in an assault on Fort Wagner on Morris Island, South Carolina. Chatfield was severely wounded in the attack and died the following month.

MAJ. SAMUEL S. LINTON
39TH ILLINOIS INFANTRY

Since custom dictated that an officer's shirt front should not be revealed, some officers, such as Major Linton, added a vest *(above)* to their uniforms so they could wear their coats open. Linton's hat bears the insignia of the X Army Corps, to which his regiment belonged. These troops were involved in Gen. Benjamin Butler's operations on the south side of the James River in 1864.

Infantry Officers

MAJ. CHARLES G. GOULD
5TH VERMONT INFANTRY

Owner of the frock coat above, Major Gould was hailed by his commander for his daring in the capture of a fort at Petersburg in April 1865. Gould stormed the fort, slashing right and left with his sword, until a Rebel soldier thrust a bayonet through his jaw. He survived the wound.

LT. ISAIAH S. BEAL
16TH OHIO INFANTRY

Officers' clothing followed Federal standards more closely than the dress of enlisted men. This was true in Ohio, where even though the state's soldiers dressed in non-Federal-pattern uniforms, its officers, such as Lieutenant Beal, wore the regulation single-breasted frock coat, trousers, and black felt hat (left and below).

**LT. JOHN C. WHITE
1ST NEW YORK INFANTRY**

Regulations dictated a single-breasted frock coat *(right)* for captains and lieutenants. White served as the assistant adjutant general of his regiment during the Chancellorsville campaign in 1863. A vest and pale blue striped trousers completed his uniform.

Officers of the 2d Rhode Island Infantry gather behind their colonel, Elisha Hunt Rhodes *(seated at far left).* Just before the fighting started at Sayler's Creek, Virginia, on April 6, 1865, Capt. Charles Gleason, the tall officer at center, said to Rhodes, "This will be the last battle—if we win—and then you and I can go home." Within moments, Gleason was shot in the head and killed.

Officers' Fatigue Uniforms

Known as the Green Mountain photographer, G. H. Houghton took this portrait of Vermont infantry officers at their camp near Manassas, Virginia, in 1862. The officer in the middle wears a frock coat; the other two sport loose-cut sack coats.

LT. COL. EDWARD L. GAUL 159TH NEW YORK INFANTRY

Lieutenant Colonel Gaul's fatigue uniform, shown here, consisted of a blue jacket, pants, and kepi. Stationed in Louisiana with his regiment, Gaul contracted typhoid fever in early 1863. After several recurrences of the disease, he requested a discharge in 1864, saying, "I am unable to endure the effects of this climate."

**COL. CHARLES P. HERRING
118TH PENNSYLVANIA INFANTRY**

Colonel Herring designed his jacket *(right)* to mimic the button pattern on a colonel's frock coat. Both his kepi *(below)* and his jacket bear the Maltese cross that signified the V Army Corps.

OFFICER'S SACK COAT

The extra length, black velvet collar, and five eagle "I" buttons of the officer's sack coat below, manufactured by Niehaus & Hock, were common features of infantry officers' field garb.

CAPT. EDWIN DILLINGHAM, 10TH VERMONT INFANTRY
Captain Dillingham omitted the prescribed shoulder straps on his sack coat in an attempt to remain inconspicuous on the battlefield.

**MAJ. SAMUEL S. LINTON
39TH ILLINOIS INFANTRY**

Linton's sack coat *(left)* bears the mark of the bullet that pierced the lower part of his left lung during the Battle of Proctor's Creek in Winchester, Virginia, in May 1864. He rejoined his regiment in August after a three-month stay in the hospital.

**MODEL 1858
ENLISTED MAN'S
FORAGE CAP**

**MODEL 1858
U.S. ARMY
HAT**

The 8th U.S. Infantry, dressed in regulation sack coats and forage caps, stands in formation at Fairfax Courthouse, Virginia, in June 1863.

U.S. INFANTRY TROUSERS

ENLISTED MAN'S VEST

The Foot Soldier's Dress

The North's first flood of eager volunteers rushed to join the infantry, envisioning themselves marching off to war, their guns gleaming in the sun. As enlisted men, they were required by 1858 regulations to wear a single-breasted dark blue frock coat with dark blue trousers. In December 1861, light blue trousers were authorized to reduce expenses for dye.

But while the soldiers may have thought themselves handsomely dressed, not everyone found their garb appealing. "The Federal uniform," observed Sir Richard Burton during his travels in the United States in 1860, "consists of a blue broadcloth tunic, too dark and dingy to please the eye. Its principal merit is a severe republican plainness."

**MODEL 1858 CORPORAL'S
UNIFORM COAT**

**BUCKTAIL BADGE
150TH PENN-
SYLVANIA**

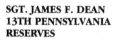

PVT. FRED CORTES *(LEFT)*, **PENNSYLVANIA BUCKTAILS,
AND PVT. HENRY CORTES, 18TH U.S. INFANTRY**

**SGT. JAMES F. DEAN
13TH PENNSYLVANIA
RESERVES**

Named for the strips of
deerskin they wore in
their caps, the "Buck-
tails" were a regiment
of Pennsylvania back-
woodsmen. Dean's frock
coat *(right),* of officer's
quality, was probably
tailor-made.

**FIFE MAJOR JOHN CURRIER
6TH NEW HAMPSHIRE INFANTRY**

The devices on the shoulders of Currier's
distinctively plain frock coat *(right)* are
fittings for brass scale ornaments.

SGT. CHARLES A. HUNTER 34TH MASSACHUSETTS INFANTRY

Hunter, whose kepi, frock coat, and trousers are pictured here, won the Medal of Honor for his valor during the Federal assault on Fort Gregg outside Petersburg in March 1865.

Maj. Gen. John Gibbon *(in front of tree)* stands with his staff and an escort of Medal of Honor recipients including Sgt. Charles Hunter *(seventh from right, holding flag)*. Later that day, May 1, 1865, General Gibbon presented 71 surrendered Confederate flags to the War Department in Washington.

Enlisted Men's Fatigue Dress

Clad in a variety of Federal
fatigue clothing, members of
Company F of the 7th Illinois
Infantry Regiment gather on
Lookout Mountain near Chatta-
nooga, Tennessee, in June 1864.

SCHUYLKILL ARSENAL

CINCINNATI ARSENAL

UNLINED SACK COAT

These sack coats illustrate three variants of Federal patterns. The coat on the right, of unknown provenance, is unusual in that it was manufactured without a lining.

PVT. HENRY H. ADSIT 44TH NEW YORK INFANTRY

Private Adsit's regiment was known as Ellsworth's Avengers in honor of a fellow New Yorker, Col. Elmer Ellsworth, the first Union officer to be killed in the Civil War. Adsit's fatigue jacket *(right)* typifies the 1861 New York State pattern. The jacket was worn with shoulder straps and belt loops.

SGT. JOHN C. SUNDERLIN 5TH VERMONT INFANTRY

Sunderlin's sack coat *(below)* was a commercially made pattern from the last year of the War.

SGT. HENRY H. STONE 11TH MASSACHUSETTS INFANTRY

After Gettysburg, Sergeant Stone's family asked him to send home his jacket *(above)* as a souvenir. But Stone *(right)* refused to part with the garment in which he had survived action in five battles, including a gunshot wound at Gettysburg. In May 1864, during fierce fighting at Spotsylvania Courthouse, Stone was captured and interned at Andersonville, Georgia.

PVT. SILAS BLAIR 63D OHIO INFANTRY

Shirts and Trousers

U.S. ARMY NECK STOCK

ENLISTED MEN'S SHIRTS

Generally distributed at the rate of three a year, Federal-issue shirts were often made of heavy, coarsely knit wool that soldiers found uncomfortable next to their skin. The two white wool flannel examples *(above)* demonstrate the variety of Federal-issue pullover shirts; the blue one with the placket front was issued by the state of Massachusetts.

**PVT. EDGAR YERGASON
22D CONNECTICUT INFANTRY**

Yergason's mother made this plaid shirt *(right)* for her son. The unidentified Federal soldier above sports a similar style.

FEDERAL-ISSUE UNDERWEAR

Drawstrings around the ankles of these flannel long johns, which belonged to a soldier from a Connecticut regiment, prevented the legs from riding up under the wearer's trousers. They also helped keep out the damp cold of winters in Virginia.

SGT. ABRAHAM RYERSON 5TH NEW YORK LIGHT ARTILLERY

Noncommissioned officers' trousers were striped in their branch-of-service color, red for artillery here. The width of the stripe indicated rank: 1½ inches for a sergeant and ½ inch for a corporal.

U.S. ENLISTED MEN'S TROUSERS

Federal-issue trousers *(below)* varied according to branch of service. Infantry trousers *(far left)* bear the dark blue branch-of-service stripe. The seat of trousers for mounted troops *(center)* was saddled, or reinforced, for durability. Issued by the Schuylkill Arsenal, dark blue trousers were worn by Regular Army soldiers.

Overcoats

INFANTRY OFFICER'S OVERCOAT

Four frogs and loops of black silk cord fasten this regulation dark blue officer's overcoat. Called a cloak coat, the garment was a copy of the official greatcoat worn by French officers.

FOUL-WEATHER GEAR

Officers—such as Lt. Col. Edward Whitaker *(inset)*—and enlisted men alike wore such commercial rubber-coated linen raincoats as the one above, owned by Pvt. George Stinchfield of the 12th Maine.

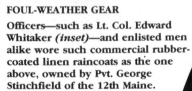

COL. EZRA A. CARMAN 13TH NEW JERSEY INFANTRY

Faded black trim and a bright blue lining accent this greatcoat owned by Colonel Carman. On March 13, 1865, he was made a brevet brigadier general for gallant and meritorious service.

BRIG. GEN. THOMAS G. STEVENSON

General Stevenson *(inset)* led the 1st Division, IX Corps, of the Army of the Potomac from April 19 to May 10, 1864. The five lines of black silk braid on the sleeves of the coat cloak he wore *(above inset)* denote his rank.

Lt. Francis E. Brownell *(left)* wears a regulation officer's overcoat with cape. In Alexandria, Virginia, on May 24, 1861, Brownell, then a corporal with the New York Fire Zouaves, killed the Confederate sympathizer who had just slain his regimental commander, the popular Col. Elmer Ellsworth. Brownell was promoted to second lieutenant in the Regular Army.

MOUNTED ENLISTED MAN'S OVERCOAT

A double-breasted front, a stand-and-fall collar, and a longer cape distinguished the mounted man's greatcoat *(above and left)* from the foot soldier's variety. Regulations stipulated that capes for mounted men extend down to the cuffs of the sleeves.

SGT. WILLIAM WELLS, 16TH MAINE INFANTRY

Made of sky blue wool kersey, Sergeant Wells' regulation overcoat has a short cape and a stand-up collar. Wells was wearing it in December of 1862 at the Battle of Fredericksburg—his first and only taste of combat—where he suffered a wound that resulted in the amputation of a leg. Late in 1861, officers, too, were authorized to wear sky blue overcoats on the battlefield to make them less conspicuous targets.

PVT. EDMUND STARRETT 24TH MAINE INFANTRY

Made of jean cloth, Private Starrett's state-contract overcoat is typical of the garments produced by private contractors in the first years of the War. A shortage of the regulation sky-blue kersey in 1861 and 1862 resulted in thousands of dark blue, black, and even brown coats.

The Dashing Zouaves

Colonel Abram Duryée, standing at far right, recruited the 5th New York Infantry, known as Duryée's Zouaves. During a charge on a Confederate battery at Big Bethel, Virginia, in June 1861, the regiment lost six men. Viewing the slain Zouaves, a Rebel remarked that the garish uniforms "contrasted greatly with the pale, fixed faces of their dead owners."

COL. GOUVERNEUR K. WARREN 5TH NEW YORK INFANTRY

LT. COL. WILLIAM FOWLER 146TH NEW YORK INFANTRY

In spring 1863, as the two-year enlistment of Duryée's 5th New York Infantry drew to a close, the V Army Corps was threatened with the disappearance of its only Zouave color. To forestall this, the 146th Infantry adopted Zouave garb. Its officers wore a gold-trimmed jacket (left) and kepi (below).

LT. WILLIAM H. MALLORY 5TH NEW YORK INFANTRY

Lieutenant Mallory (above) cut quite a dashing—and conspicuous—figure on the battlefield in his bright red trousers (right). A blue frock coat and red kepi would have completed his officer's uniform.

COL. ELMER ELLSWORTH
11TH NEW YORK INFANTRY

At daybreak on May 24, 1861, Colonel Ellsworth and his regiment of Fire Zouaves put ashore at Alexandria, Virginia, where they soon spotted a large Confederate flag flying from the roof of the Marshall House inn. Ellsworth dashed upstairs, cut down the flag, and was on his way down when the innkeeper, James Jackson, blasted him at point-blank range with a shotgun. Ellsworth fell forward "with the heavy, horrible headlong weight which always comes with sudden death." The frock coat worn by the Union's first casualty *(left)* bears the mark of Jackson's shotgun slug.

MAJ. JOHN GLENN
23D PENNSYLVANIA VOLUNTEERS

Glenn's blue kepi followed the French chasseur pattern of dark blue as opposed to the scarlet cap worn by many Zouave officers.

2D LT. CHARLES R. CARVILLE
165TH NEW YORK INFANTRY

The uniforms of the 165th New York Infantry Regiment, including Lieutenant Carville's frock coat and baggy red trousers *(left)*, closely copied the North African costume adopted by French regiments in the 1840s. Carville *(above)* was killed in action during the Federal siege of Port Hudson, Louisiana, in May 1863. He was 19 years old at the time.

Early Enlisted Zouave Garb

Frank E. Brownell
11
U.S.A

**PVT. FRANCIS E. BROWNELL
11TH NEW YORK INFANTRY**

Like other members of Col. Elmer Ellsworth's Fire Zouaves, Brownell *(left)* substituted a red fireman's shirt for the traditional Zouave vest under his uniform jacket. In this portrait, Brownell also wears his fireman's belt. Based on Ellsworth's own design, the 11th Infantry's gray jackets were made of a flimsy material that literally fell apart in service.

11TH NEW YORK INFANTRY FEZ FOUND NEAR RICKETTS' BATTERY, MANASSAS

Soldiers of the 11th New York Zouaves, captured at Bull Run in July 1861, pose inside their prison, Castle Pinckney, in Charleston Harbor. These former members of the New York City Fire Department hand-lettered the signs in the background to make light of their unhappy situation.

UNIDENTIFIED PRIVATE 11TH NEW YORK INFANTRY

When the first Zouave uniforms of the 11th New York wore out, they were replaced with dark blue Zouave jackets and trousers. But the regiment, including the soldier at left, retained their red firemen's shirts. "I want the New York Firemen," Ellsworth said when he recruited this regiment, "for there are no more effective men in the country."

ZOUAVE VEST AND PANTS 10TH NEW YORK INFANTRY

In the spring and summer of 1861, the 10th New York received two quasi-Zouave uniforms, neither of which stood up to service conditions. Their later outfits, which included a striking yellow-trimmed vest *(left)* and full-cut blue trousers striped with red *(below),* arrived in September.

SGT. JAMES E. TAYLOR 10TH NEW YORK INFANTRY

Taylor *(right)* wears the uniform of the 10th New York, also known as the National Zouaves. After serving two years with his regiment, Taylor became an artist-correspondent for *Leslie's Illustrated Newspaper*. Among his sketches were those depicting the fighting in the Shenandoah Valley.

Duryée's Zouaves

ZOUAVE SASH

**CPL. WILLIAM C. RYER
5TH NEW YORK INFANTRY**

Red trim on the front of Corporal Ryer's collarless Zouave jacket *(above)* forms a loop-and-trefoil design called a tombeau.

ZOUAVE PANTALOONS

**PVT. JOHN L. SLOANE
5TH NEW YORK
VETERANS**

A member of the 5th New York *(center)* carries freshly baked bread to the troops of the III Corps at their winter camp at Stafford Heights, Virginia, in April 1863. Scheduled to end their term of service in May, the men of the 5th New York asked to be excused from the coming campaign. Their request was denied and they fought at Chancellorsville, but quit promptly on May 14, the day their term expired.

**SGT. HENRY VREDENBURG
5TH NEW YORK VET-
ERAN VOLUNTEERS**

ZOUAVE FEZ WITH WHITE TURBAN

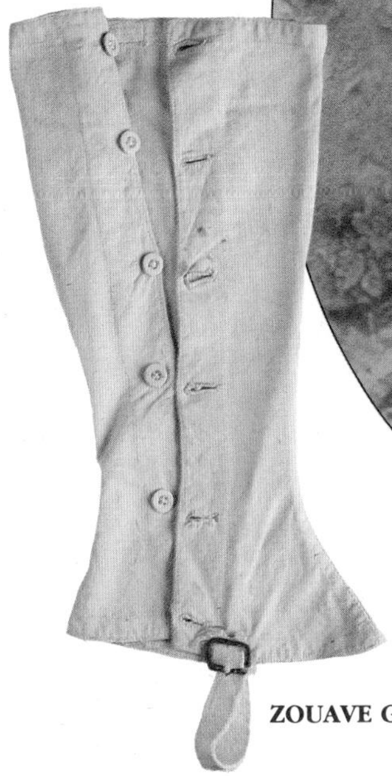

ZOUAVE GAITER

**SGT. HENRY VREDENBURG
5TH NEW YORK VETERAN VOLUNTEERS**

Organized in October 1863, this regiment
adopted a Zouave jacket *(above)* and Arab
pantaloons *(left)* similar to those worn by
Duryée's Zouaves. By allowing volunteers
to reenlist as veterans, many regiments
were able to stay in existence after their
original mustering-out date had expired.

Empire State Zouaves

CPL. THEODORE D'ESCHAMBAULT 165TH NEW YORK

Color guard Corporal D'Eschambault *(left)* was killed during the first Federal assault on Port Hudson, Louisiana, on May 27, 1863. Of the 165th New York's eight-member color guard, only one emerged from the battle unscathed.

ZOUAVE JACKET 165TH NEW YORK

Originally recruited as the second battalion of Duryée's 5th New York Zouaves, the 165th was formed in November of 1862. The 2d Duryée's Zouaves, as they became known, adopted the uniforms of their parent group, including a dark blue jacket with red tombeaux *(above)* and a blue-tasseled red fez *(left)*.

U.S. ZOUAVE FEZ, 165TH NEW YORK

137

146TH NEW YORK FEZ

ZOUAVE UNIFORM
146TH NEW YORK INFANTRY

Among the first Federal units engaged in the Wilderness was Brig. Gen. Romeyn Ayres' hard-fighting Zouave brigade, which included the 146th New York. The regiment's uniform *(left)*, which copied the attire worn by elite French North African troops, boosted the men's morale. "We had the vanity to think there was no organization in the army superior to us," one officer recalled.

146TH NEW YORK LEGGINGS

**UNIDENTIFIED SERGEANT
9TH NEW YORK INFANTRY**

**SGT. LATHAM A. FISH
9TH NEW YORK INFANTRY**

Federal arsenals copied the uniform of the 9th New York—Hawkins' Zouaves—*(above and right)* to such an extent that it became the standard-issue Zouave dress. Their trousers, unlike the French uniform they mostly mimicked, were dark blue and only slightly baggy. Organized by Rush C. Hawkins as a pre-War military club in New York City in 1860, the 9th New York was the first New York Zouave regiment to be mustered into Federal service.

ZOUAVE JACKET AND VEST
164TH NEW YORK INFANTRY

The jacket *(left)* worn by the 164th New York closely resembled that of Hawkins' Zouaves. The regiment's side-buttoned vest *(above)* was typical of the original French Zouave attire.

Green tassels on their blue fezzes signified the Irish lineage of members of the 164th New York, shown here in Alexandria, Virginia, in fall 1863.

Collis' Zouaves

**PVT. THADDEUS PAXSON
114TH PENNSYLVANIA INFANTRY**

Fabric for Private Paxson's jacket, trousers, and fez *(below)* was imported from France. According to one of the regiment's musicians, their uniforms "pricked up the pride of the new recruits, and gave us an imposing and warlike appearance."

Members of Company G of the 114th Pennsylvania assemble in full dress at their camp near Petersburg, Virginia, in August 1864.

French Mary's Wartime Odyssey

Among the Union wounded at Fredericksburg was "French Mary" Tepe *(left),* a *vivandière*—a woman who carried provisions to sell to the soldiers—attached to Col. Charles Collis' Zouaves. She washed and mended the men's clothes and often carried her small keg of whiskey to the front lines to comfort the wounded and encourage the faint of heart. Her bravery at Fredericksburg earned her a decoration from her corps.

Mary was a French immigrant who married the Philadelphia tailor Bernardo Tepe. When he enlisted in 1861, according to legend, Mary followed him to Virginia and braved 13 battles. The wound she suffered in her heel in Fredericksburg continued to cause such pain that it may have contributed to her suicide in 1900.

VIVANDIÈRE'S JACKET AND SKIRT

In most cases, vivandières were wives of soldiers in the regiment to which they were attached. This lace-trimmed jacket *(above)* and knee-length skirt *(left)* followed the traditional French pattern. Vivandières wore pantaloons under the short skirt.

Variant Zouave Uniforms

Sergeant Solomon Miller *(far left)* and Pvt. Henry Baker of the 76th Pennsylvania, a regiment known as the Keystone Zouaves, took part in the unsuccessful Federal charge on Lee's defenses at Deep Bottom, Virginia, in August 1864. Private Baker was killed in the action.

ZOUAVE JACKET 155TH PENNSYLVANIA

Yellow tombeaux distinguishes this jacket. The regiment switched from regulation blue uniforms to Zouave dress in 1863.

76TH PENNSYLVANIA FEZ

CPL. WALTER H. MALLORIE 76TH PENNSYLVANIA

General McClellan described the French Zouave, "with his graceful dress," as the "beau ideal of a soldier." The collarless jacket and Arab-style trousers *(above)* allowed free movement.

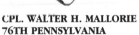

76TH PENNSYLVANIA JAMBIÈRES

76TH PENNSYLVANIA GAITERS

ZOUAVE JACKET
140TH NEW YORK INFANTRY

Americanized versions of Zouave attire appeared in various regiments. The jacket worn by the 140th New York *(left)* incorporated flaps that closed the garment, creating the illusion that the soldier was wearing a buttoned vest under his jacket.

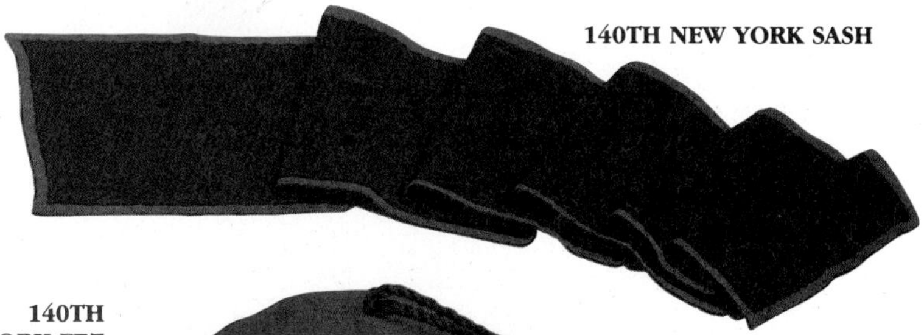

140TH NEW YORK SASH

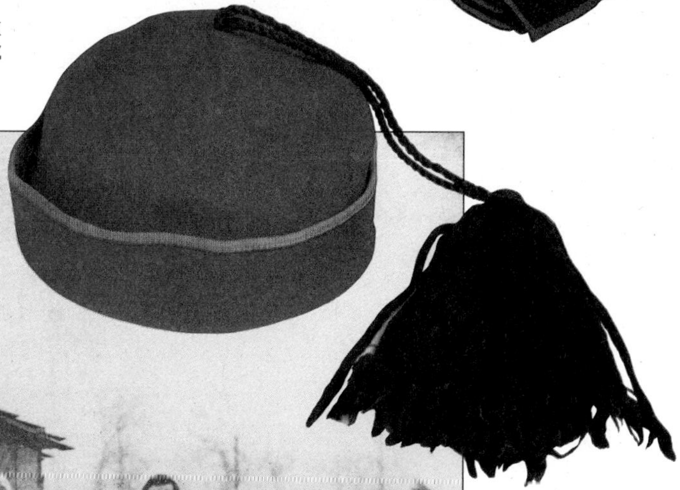

**140TH
NEW YORK FEZ**

With a shout that its adjutant said "drowned all other sounds," the 140th New York, some of whom are pictured here at Warrenton Junction, Virginia, led the charge at the Battle of the Wilderness in May 1864. Despite its tenacity, the regiment lost nearly a third of its men at the Wilderness.

Birney's Zouaves

**PVT. ROBERT ELLIOT
23D PENNSYLVANIA INFANTRY**

When he fought at Gettysburg with the 23d Pennsylvania—Birney's Zouaves—Private Elliot wore the kepi and I.D. badge that appear in his portrait *(above)*. Many soldiers purchased I.D. badges so their bodies could be easily identified if they were killed in battle.

**SERGEANT'S JACKET
23D PENNSYLVANIA INFANTRY**

The red trim on the jacket above poorly approximates the tombeaux on French Zouave uniforms. In the wake of the Federal defeat at First Bull Run, four new Zouave regiments—including the 23d Pennsylvania—were raised.

LEFT TO RIGHT: CAPTAIN'S COOK, CAPT. LOUIS HILDE-BRAND, SGT. WILLIAM PED-DLE, 23D PENNSYLVANIA

KEPI, 23D PENNSYLVANIA

LEATHER ZOUAVE LEGGINGS

**TROUSERS
23D PENNSYLVANIA**

**UNIDENTIFIED PRIVATE
11TH INDIANA INFANTRY**

**PVT. A. G. GARRETT
34TH INDIANA VETERAN
VOLUNTEER INFANTRY**

**PVT. LEE MATTHEWS
76TH OHIO INFANTRY**

Men of the 11th Indiana—Wallace's Zou-aves—seem to have initiated the style of the integral vest, which was widely copied by other midwestern regiments. First clothed in a gray quasi-Zouave uniform as a three-month regiment, Wallace's Zouaves later traded their gray garb for blue to distinguish it from the color generally worn by the Confederates. Their permanent uniforms consisted of black Zouave jackets with light blue trim and a dark blue front; trousers were army regulation.

Pennsylvania Zouaves

**HOSPITAL STEWARD R. B. HEINTZELMAN
95TH PENNSYLVANIA INFANTRY**

**ZOUAVE JACKET
95TH PENNSYLVANIA INFANTRY**

Organized in Philadelphia in August of 1861, Gosline's Zouaves wore a jacket *(left)* with ball buttons that resembled the one designed by Col. Elmer Ellsworth for his Chicago zouave cadets in 1860. The Pennsylvania regiment added a low-standing collar.

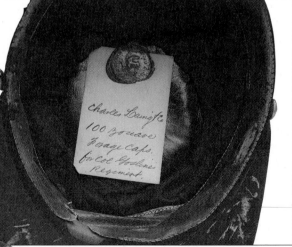

This kepi *(left)* served as the pattern piece for the 95th Pennsylvania's uniform hat. The wax seal *(above)* marked it as the official model at the Schuylkill Arsenal.

PVT. EDWARD A. FULTON
72D PENNSYLVANIA INFANTRY

Fulton, who was killed in action at Antietam in September 1862, wore a jacket *(below)* nearly identical to that worn by Gosline's Zouaves. Unlike Gosline's regiment, however, the 72d Pennsylvania's uniform included a red-trimmed vest *(right)* and light blue trousers.

UNIDENTIFIED MUSICIAN 72D PENNSYLVANIA INFANTRY REGIMENT

The heroic 72d Pennsylvania helped defend the Angle in the Union lines against the Confederates in Maj. Gen. George Pickett's charge at Gettysburg in July 1863.

A member of the 14th New York State Militia—commonly known as the 14th Brooklyn—wears his regiment's unique chasseur uniform. The style was adopted by the regiment in 1860 and worn until its men were mustered out in 1864.

Chasseur Uniforms

On the eve of the Civil War, several state militia units were sporting uniforms patterned after the distinctive garb worn by the French light infantry, or *chasseurs à pied*. Chasseur jackets were generally single-breasted, with a five- or six-inch skirt extending below the waist. The trousers were full and pleated at the waist.

The chasseur trend spread with the outbreak of war: In August 1861 the Federal quartermaster general ordered 10,000 complete chasseur uniforms from a Paris military outfitter. They arrived in November and were distributed throughout the army, although most soldiers found them uncomfortably small. The chasseur style remained popular all through the War and for some time after.

14TH NEW YORK STATE MILITIA

Worn by an unknown sergeant, the dark blue jacket and red trousers are typical of the regiment's unusual chasseur garb. The buttons down the jacket front are for show only: A mock vest sewed within the garment actually fastened it. Although this uniform is that of an enlisted man, the red kepi *(below)* is an officer's cap.

FRENCH CHASSEUR CLOAK, JACKET, AND HAT

Among the regiments issued French-made chasseur uniforms were the 62d and 83d Pennsylvania, the 18th Massachusetts, and the 49th and 72d New York. Included were a hooded cloak *(left)*, a dress coat *(above)*, a leather shako *(below)*, and more. The shako plate was designed for this uniform.

CLOAK, OR TALMA

FRENCH-PATTERN SHAKO

109TH PENNSYLVANIA (CURTIN LIGHT GUARDS)

The 109th Pennsylvania chose a chasseur-style jacket with regulation trousers, ornamented with a distinctive red-white-and-blue piping. This jacket, made at the Schuylkill Arsenal late in the War, features piped shoulder straps and belt loops.

Q.M. SGT. EDWARD WELCH 65TH NEW YORK INFANTRY

90TH PENNSYLVANIA (NATIONAL GUARDS)

A wax seal inside the chasseur jacket at right identifies it as an official pattern model for the Schuylkill Arsenal in Philadelphia. The jacket's nine gilt buttons, bearing the initials *N.G.* for National Guards and the motto *Nonsibi Sed Patriae* ("Not for oneself but for the country"), were provided through the arsenal. These were the only regimental buttons authorized during the War.

12TH NEW YORK STATE MILITIA

At the outbreak of war, the 12th New York adopted the traditional chasseur uniform worn by the soldier at right. A low kepi *(below)* completed the outfit. In March of 1862, an official board of officers recommended—without success—that chasseur dress be issued to all Union troops.

VETERAN RESERVE CORPS

Dark blue trim accents this sky-blue chasseur jacket worn by a sergeant in the Veteran Reserve Corps—officers and men unfit for full combat duty but able to serve as guards, clerks, cooks, or hospital nurses.

Soldiers of the Veteran Reserve Corps stationed in Alexandria, Virginia, gather for a group picture. Some men hold weapons, while others amuse themselves with playing cards *(bottom, right),* and a few play musical instruments *(bottom, left).* On the far right, a barber gives a soldier a shave.

Confined to guarding their home state for most of the War, the Pennsylvania Gray Reserves, pictured here at Camp Logan near Philadelphia in 1861, were called up in September 1862 for 15 days to help resist Lee's invasion of Maryland. "The assembling of so large a body of men arrayed for war, put into the field in so brief a period," wrote a regiment historian with considerable exaggeration, "has scarcely a historic parallel."

1ST REGIMENT, PHILADELPHIA RESERVE BRIGADE

The gray frock coat and Hardee hat at right were worn during the War by members of the 1st Regiment Infantry who formed part of the Philadelphia Reserve Brigade. Probably a self-purchased item, the dark blue sack coat *(below)* belonged to Sergeant Sutton of the same regiment.

Wartime Militia and National Guard

In 1861, militia companies scrambled to reorganize themselves into uniformed regiments in response to President Lincoln's call for 75,000 men. By this time some states, notably New York and Pennsylvania, were requiring regimental uniforms for their members.

Most states organized militia regiments specifically for guard duty at home. Few of the home guard units—designated National Guard in some states—actually saw action during the War. The uniforms on these pages were designed for units who stayed at home, ever ready to perform emergency service.

1ST REGIMENT PHILADELPHIA RESERVE BRIGADE

Shoulder straps indicate that a lieutenant or a captain wore this frock coat *(left)*. Before he joined the 119th Pennsylvania in 1862, Col. Peter Ellmaker donned the Hardee hat below as a member of the Reserve Brigade.

PENNSYLVANIA-ISSUE SHELL JACKET

Pennsylvania issued a gray shell jacket, like this one, to its Reserve Corps. These men may have taken their gray jackets with them but probably never wore them in battle lest they be mistaken for Confederate soldiers.

18TH NEW YORK MILITIA

Members of the 18th, like the drum major who owned this colorful uniform, never saw action in the War.

9TH NEW YORK MILITIA

Originally called the City Guard, the 9th New York State Militia volunteered for three years' service in 1861, becoming the 83d New York Infantry. Men of this regiment marched off to war wearing militia uniform jackets like the one below.

UNIDENTIFIED SOLDIER FROM THE 9TH NEW YORK STATE MILITIA

SGT. HARLAN COBB
COMPANY B, U.S. CORPS OF
ENGINEERS

A brass turreted castle, the official insignia of the Corps of Engineers, ornaments the front of Sergeant Cobb's felt hat. The same emblem is pinned to the chest of his regulation frock coat. The coat and yellow-striped trousers were probably worn for formal occasions only. Engineers in the field, such as the group at right photographed near Petersburg in September of 1864, generally dressed in infantry fatigues. Sergeant Cobb sits in the front row of soldiers, third from the left.

On May 1, 1863, members of the 15th New York Engineers and the U.S. Corps of Engineers pose in front of the pontoon bridges they constructed over the Rappahannock River at Franklin's Crossing during a lull in the Second Battle of Fredericksburg. Three days later, after the Federal defeat at Salem Church, the engineers moved the pontoons upriver to evacuate the Union VI Corps.

**SERGEANT'S FROCK COAT
U.S. CORPS OF ENGINEERS**

Special Support Corps

In addition to its three combat arms—the infantry, cavalry, and artillery—the Union army had a host of support organizations throughout the War. Among these were the U.S. Corps of Engineers, whose members cut roads through the wilderness, dug earthworks and canals, and built pontoon bridges; the Ordnance Department, which claimed responsibility for the distribution and maintenance of weapons and ammunition; and the Signal Corps, whose signalmen established observation posts and oversaw field communications, operating primarily with visual signals such as flags and torches.

Ordnance Department

SERGEANT'S TROUSERS

A now-faded stripe of crimson—
the official branch color for ordnance—runs the length of these
regulation trousers.

1858 U.S. ARMY HAT

The Ordnance Depart-
ment brass shell and
flame insignia adorns
this enlisted man's hat.

PRIVATELY PURCHASED UNIFORM

Of finer quality than regular-
issue uniforms, the frock coat,
trousers, and slouch hat above
probably belonged to a senior
ordnance N.C.O. Ordnance men
carried the same arms and equipment as infantrymen.

Signal Corps

MOUNTED SIGNALMAN'S TROUSERS
Shown front and rear, these trousers are similar to cavalry pants. Indeed, a man who joined the Signal Corps in December of 1862 remarked that for uniforms he and his comrades had "cavalry jackets and cavalry trousers, with reinforced seats."

Wearing a jacket much like the one above, Signalman Hamilton Clark stands for a portrait taken soon after the end of the War. The jacket bears red-and-white crossed flags on the sleeve, the emblem of the Signal Corps authorized in 1864.

PRIVATE D. B. BYAM

Private Byam's 11-button fatigue jacket was the model worn by enlisted men of the Signal Corps, which was created on March 3, 1863, although signalmen and officers had operated since the beginning of the War.

Medical Department

ASST. SURG. WILLIAM F. TIBBALS, 5TH OHIO VOLUNTEER INFANTRY

Tibbals *(below)*, who interrupted his medical studies to enlist, was promoted to assistant surgeon in May 1862. During the War, each Federal regiment included one surgeon and one assistant surgeon whose appointments were confirmed—not always judiciously—by their state's medical examining board. As the editor of a leading medical journal complained in 1861: "Indeed, these examinations have in some cases been so conducted to prove the merest farce."

HOSPITAL STEWARD'S UNIFORM

The yellow-piped, green half-chevrons on the sleeves of the regulation jacket above bear the caduceus, the distinctive symbol of the medical profession that was first authorized for army use in 1851. The sky-blue trousers and dark blue vest are regulation issue. Hospital stewards were warrant officers, ranking above the first sergeant of a company. Besides the surgeons, they were the only men permanently attached to the Medical Department.

An ambulance convoy pauses in its journey to the large Federal hospital at City Point, Virginia, during the siege of Petersburg in 1864. Four-wheeled ambulances like these had folding bunks for wounded men. At times the vehicles were so grossly overcrowded that the wounded were in danger of being smothered en route. The Army of the Potomac established its Ambulance Corps in August of 1862. Regulations called for its personnel—which consisted of drivers, attendants, blacksmiths, and saddlers—to wear a broad green band around their caps *(below)* so that they might be easily distinguished in the field.

HOSPITAL STEWARD'S FROCK COAT

Hospital stewards of the IX Corps enjoy a rare moment of relaxation outside a field hospital near Petersburg in November of 1864. Like the regulation frock coat at left, their coat sleeves all bear a green chevron with caduceus.

**RUBBER BUTTON
U.S. SHARPSHOOTERS**

Outfitted like "Robin Hood's merry outlaws," in the words of a *New York Post* reporter, members of Berdan's Sharpshooters, including Pvt. C. Maltby *(left)*, carried a Prussian-pattern knapsack of fur-covered calfskin *(below)*.

**FROCK COAT AND FORAGE CAP
1ST U.S. SHARPSHOOTERS**

Resembling a regulation infantry frock coat in all aspects but color, the coat worn by this regiment was piped in light green. Members of Berdan's Sharpshooters, who "rarely missed a man at a mile," according to a Rebel soldier, decorated their green forage caps with a black plume.

Deadeyes in Green

In June 1861, Hiram Berdan, a New York inventor and the nation's foremost marksman, won approval from President Lincoln for his idea of forming his own regiment of sharpshooters. Handpicked by Berdan, men from companies in eight different states were recruited directly into Federal service as United States Volunteers. A number of additional regiments were created this way during the War; all received the standard uniform of the U.S. Army.

The first and second regiments of U.S. Sharpshooters, which resulted from Berdan's request, were issued instead dark green uniforms of Berdan's own design that set them apart from the regular infantry regiments and earned them the nickname Green Coats.

Black Troops for the Union

"Let the colored men accept the offer of the President, take arms, join the army, and then we will whip the rebels," said one black private in response to Lincoln's authorization of full-scale recruitment of black soldiers in late 1862. Although the first black regiments were formed by state governments, in early 1863 the Federal government began organizing regiments of United States Colored Troops who were mustered directly into the army. By August 1863, 14 black regiments were serving all branches of the Union army, and 24 more were in the process of formation.

Largely restricted to menial military tasks such as building fortifications and roads, black troops never realized their full potential in battle because of the Union commanders' hesitation to let them fight. Even so, during the last three years of the War, black Federal regiments saw action in more than 33 major battles.

One company of the 4th U.S. Colored Troops, pictured above serving guard duty near Washington after the War, lost 178 men in the Federal attacks on Fort Harrison at Petersburg, Virginia. "When we were ordered to do our duty," one of the soldiers wrote, "we went like men."

Slated for promotion, Pvt. Louis Troutman (above) served with the 108th U.S. Colored Troops. The only action his regiment saw was at Owensboro, Kentucky, in October 1864. Mustered directly into Federal service, black soldiers received U.S. regulation uniforms, such as the frock coat at right.

162

FROCK COAT AND VEST LT. CHARLES E. CLARK

Some officers added a vest *(below)* to their uniform so they could comfortably wear their frock coats open or with the lapels turned back. The rank insignia displayed on the shoulders and cuffs of Lieutenant Clark's coat *(left)* dates from late in the War.

Officers of the U.S. Navy

Historically, uniforms were not necessary to distinguish rank aboard a ship since crew members knew virtually everyone on board. Naval uniforms developed out of the desire of British Royal Navy officers in the 18th century to differentiate themselves from army officers in public.

Once called "the working coat of the navy," the frock coat served U.S. Navy officers for both undress and service dress. As prescribed by regulations in 1852, the navy frock coat was dark blue and double-breasted with two rows of nine buttons and a roll collar. Unlike the army, the navy did not use different-colored trim to indicate branch of service or function of its officers. Instead, it employed a complicated—and ever-changing—system of insignia to differentiate the ranks.

Officers and crew of the U.S.S. *Mendota (right)* appear fresh despite the oppressive, swamplike climate they endured while escorting Federal supply schooners and troop carriers up the James River from the Chesapeake Bay. A double-bowed side-wheeler laden with guns, the *Mendota* could reverse direction without turning around because of its arrangement of twin rudders and wheelhouses.

OFFICER'S SACK COAT ASST. SURG. JACOB SOLIS-COHEN

This assistant surgeon's white linen sack coat bears no sign of its owner's rank. Not officially authorized until 1865, the officer's sack coat appeared in many styles, single- and double-breasted, before then.

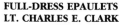

FULL-DRESS EPAULETS LT. CHARLES E. CLARK

Clark probably did not find much use for his epaulets (above) since the full-dress uniform was reserved, in the words of a U.S. admiral, "for exceptional occasions, to show we had it; but otherwise it was generally done up in camphor."

OFFICER'S FROCK COAT ASST. ENG. WILLIAM A. DRIPPS

Although regulations originally prescribed a single-breasted frock coat for staff officers, engineers were authorized to wear double-breasted coats (right). By the end of the War, U.S. Navy staff officers could be distinguished from line officers only by their insignia.

OFFICER'S FROCK COAT ENS. L. H. POLLOCK

As a midshipman who had passed his exams for promotion to lieutenant, Pollock (inset) was awarded the title of ensign. The cuff insignia on his frock coat (right) bears the single star that all U.S. Navy line officers wore after May 1963.

Navy Enlisted Blues

For service at sea, Seaman, First Class George Washington Brown wore this regulation blue seaman's frock and wide-bottomed trousers, which adhered to navy regulations. The visorless blue cloth cap *(below)* belonged to Petty Officer John Cook, who used the homemade plaid liner to help the cap hold its shape. First designated to be worn only at sea, the blue cap became the sailor's dress headgear at the beginning of the War, when seamen began ornamenting their caps with black silk ribbon.

U.S. NAVY STRAW HAT

Aboard ship, enlisted navy men had the option of wearing a white straw hat intended for warm weather, like the one modeled by the sailor in the portrait at left. The hat above was lined with cloth to deflect the sun's glare.

A black sailor aboard the U.S.S. *Hunchback* entertains shipmates with a tune from his banjo *(foreground).* Originally built as a wooden steam ferryboat, the *Hunchback* was purchased by the U.S. Navy in 1861. Assigned to the North Atlantic Blockading Squadron, the ship's crew participated in the capture of Roanoke Island in early 1862.

PETTY OFFICER JOHN COOK

Cook wore this double-breasted regulation shell jacket *(right)* over his blue frock *(above)* for dress occasions. The prescribed eagle-anchor-star device on the left sleeve of his jacket indicates his rank. A similar, but hand-embroidered, version of this insignia appears on his frock sleeve.

U.S. NAVY SEA BAG

The navy issued canvas sea bags in which sailors carried personal possessions. Handy with a needle and thread, the owner of this bag embroidered it with naval motifs, including a representation of the pre-War sloop *Albany*. Decorative embroidery was a traditional pastime among sailors.

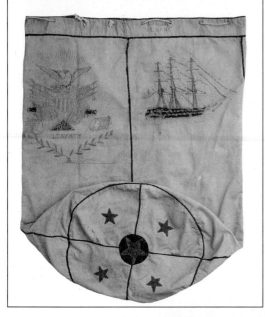

SEAMAN'S UNIFORM
GEORGE WASHINGTON BROWN

In hot weather, the traditional seaman's blue uniform was replaced by summer whites, typified by Brown's frock, trousers, and cap cover shown here. Brown embellished the edges of his frock's blue dungaree collar and cuffs with embroidery. His white dress trousers *(left)* differ from his work pants mainly in the addition of decorative blue lining inside the front flaps.

Blue frocks worn by crew members of the U.S.S. *Unadilla* exhibit several of the various yoke styles that were made during the War. The *Unadilla,* one of the screw gunboats that was hastily constructed in less than three months after the outbreak of the War, was struck six times during the bombardment and capture of Forts Walker and Beauregard in Port Royal Sound, South Carolina, in November 1861. The boat sustained only minor damage.

U.S. NAVY SEAMEN'S UNDERSHIRTS

Although naval regulations never mentioned undershirts, these garments were widely worn by sailors throughout the War. The owners of these two shirts proudly adorned them with elaborately stitched designs. Some sailors turned their skill with a needle and thread into a profitable venture, offering to embroider their shipmates' garments for a price.

HEADGEAR

Seaman, First Class George Washington Brown sewed an insignia onto the top of his fatigue cap *(left),* as did many sailors to prevent snipers aloft from shooting their own men. Sou'westers were worn by crew who manned the deck in foul weather.

U.S. Marine Corps

On July 20, 1837, James Buckner (shown above as a marine sergeant while serving aboard the U.S.S. *Mahaska* during the War) strode at the age of seven into the U.S. Marine Corps headquarters in Washington, D.C., and enlisted. Young Buckner was assigned to drum major Robert Tray for instruction in Marine music. After mastering the fife, Buckner went to sea as a Marine Guard aboard the war sloop *St. Louis*.

**U.S. MARINE CORPS DRESS UNIFORM
PVT. JOHN HAMMOND**

The 1859 model Marine Corps enlisted man's uniform, exemplified by Private Hammond's dress trousers, frock coat, and shako, remained essentially unchanged until 1875. Although a seven-button double-breasted frock coat replaced the tail coat worn before 1859, the corps retained the system of gold lace collar and cuff loops piped with scarlet that was characteristic of the earlier coat. The red worsted pompon on Hammond's shako indicated his enlisted status; gold net pompons adorned officers' shakos.

LT. P. C. POPE

For undress, Marine Corps officers such as Lieutenant Pope *(left)* wore frock coats with two rows of eight buttons. A four-lobed gold cord knot called a quatrefoil decorated each shoulder. The dark blue cloth fatigue cap was made with a straight visor in the chasseur pattern.

In 1859, the Marine Corps numbered about 2,000 officers and men, its ranks swelling to 3,900 during the War. Sent to sea in small detachments, marines performed guard duty, repelled boarders, and spearheaded landing operations. The marine below wears regulation sky blue trousers with narrow legs resembling those worn by the army.

ENLISTED FATIGUE UNIFORM U.S. MARINE CORPS

Enlisted men wore a single-breasted frock coat for undress, but noncommissioned officers kept the chevrons *(left)* as in full dress. A blue flannel fatigue sack *(above)*, worn by enlisted men aboard seagoing vessels, was introduced in 1859. In that year, the Marine Corps adopted the light infantry bugle insignia for all its fatigue caps.

DECORATIONS / INSIGNIA

Medals for Valor

The first American military medal was awarded by the Continental Congress to Gen. George Washington for his role in driving the British forces from Boston in 1776. Prior to that time, the Founding Fathers had been reluctant to bestow honors on their own, sharing as they did a distaste for what they considered the trappings of European royalty.

At the outbreak of the Civil War, no American medal existed to honor gallantry or distinguished conduct. In July of 1862, Congress authorized the five-pointed bronze Medal of Honor for enlisted men of the army. It was awarded to some 2,100 Union soldiers. As the War continued, a number of other decorations were adopted by various army commands, state governments, and civil bodies.

SUMTER MEDAL

Issued to the officers and men who defended Fort Sumter in April 1861, the bronze Sumter Medal bears the profile of the fort's commander, Gen. Robert Anderson, on the obverse.

CONGRESSIONAL MEDAL ISSUED TO ULYSSES S. GRANT

In March 1865, Congress honored General Grant with the unique gold medal at right. As one officer described it, the award "was three pounds in weight, on one side a bad likeness of Grant; on the reverse a goddess in an impossible position."

CAPT. ABNER W. TURNER 4TH MAINE INFANTRY

Captain Turner (above) was one of the 317 men who earned the Kearny Medal for his bravery during the War.

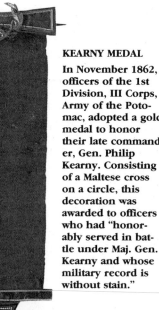

KEARNY MEDAL

In November 1862, officers of the 1st Division, III Corps, Army of the Potomac, adopted a gold medal to honor their late commander, Gen. Philip Kearny. Consisting of a Maltese cross on a circle, this decoration was awarded to officers who had "honorably served in battle under Maj. Gen. Kearny and whose military record is without stain."

KEARNY CROSS

Brigadier General D. B. Birney, who succeeded Kearny, authorized a bronze "cross of valor" for enlisted men in his command who distinguished themselves in battle.

GILLMORE MEDAL PVT. WALCOTT WETHERELL

One of 400 bronze medals awarded after the Federal attack on Fort Sumter in August 1863, this was given to Pvt. Walcott Wetherell of the 6th Connecticut Volunteers *(below)*.

Sergeant Major Christian Fleetwood *(back row, fourth from right)*, standing with officers of the 4th U.S. Colored Troops, displays the Medal of Honor he won after the Battle of New Market Heights in September 1864.

Medal of Honor

Presented to

Private Walcott Wetherell
6th. Regiment Conn Vols Co. A

Q. A. Gillmore

Major General
Commanding Department
of the South

MEDAL OF HONOR SGT. CHARLES HUNTER

Sergeant Hunter earned this Medal of Honor in March 1865 after planting the Union flag in Fort Gregg, outside Petersburg, Virginia.

1ST MASS. INFANTRY

U.S. ENGINEERS BATTALION

3D NEW JERSEY CAVALRY

2D NEW JERSEY CAVALRY

118TH PENNSYLVANIA INFANTRY, V CORPS

118TH PENNSYLVANIA V CORPS

1ST DIVISION VI CORPS

IX CORPS

Emblems of Unit Pride

Officially prescribed by Brig. Gen. Joseph Hooker in 1863 to boost his army's flagging spirits, corps and division insignia provided a means by which commanders could identify their units in the field.

The first corps badges were distinctive shapes cut from colored cloth. In time, more elaborate badges appeared, especially among officers who purchased them from sutlers, or commissioned jewelers, to fashion them to individual specifications. Materials for the badges ranged from solid gold to coin metal and bone.

PVT. MARINER FICKETT U.S. ENGINEERS BATTALION

1ST NEW JERSEY CAVALRY

U.S. ARMY CORPS BADGES

The popular corps badges reflected soldiers' pride in their outfits. The shape of the badge denoted the corps, while its color designated the division: red for first, white for second, and blue for third.

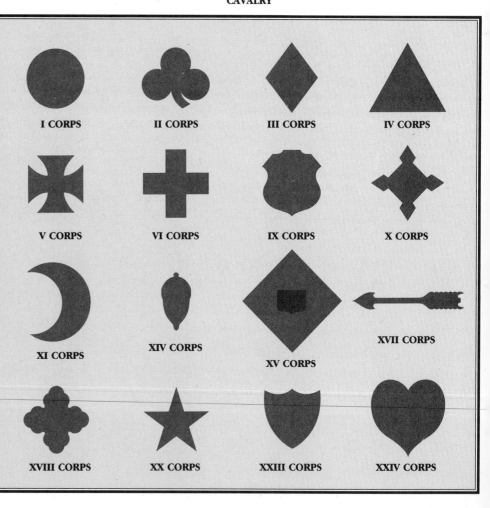

I CORPS
II CORPS
III CORPS
IV CORPS
V CORPS
VI CORPS
IX CORPS
X CORPS
XI CORPS
XIV CORPS
XV CORPS
XVII CORPS
XVIII CORPS
XX CORPS
XXIII CORPS
XXIV CORPS

IX CORPS

5TH OHIO
INFANTRY
XII CORPS

1ST VERMONT
ARTILLERY
VI CORPS

132D
PENNSYLVANIA
INFANTRY, II CORPS

19TH
PENNSYLVANIA
CAVALRY

6TH OHIO
CAVALRY

5TH NEW YORK
INFANTRY, V CORPS

CHRISTIAN COMMISSION

III CORPS

PROVOST GUARD

XII CORPS

U.S. SIGNAL CORPS

CAPT.
GEORGE G. MEADE
V CORPS HEADQUARTERS

2D KENTUCKY INFANTRY
IV CORPS

1ST DIVISION
VI CORPS

ISAAC CHESTER, 173D
PENNSYLVANIA INFANTRY

A member of the Provost
Guard, Chester *(right)*
proudly exhibits his XX
Corps badge *(above)*.

As war casualties mounted, men purchased name-tags *(right)*, which they wore so that their bodies could be easily identified if they were killed in battle. Distributed by the civilian Christian Commission, which provided aid to soldiers, parchment tags *(bottom, right)* were water-resistant.

PVT. BENJAMIN F. HANNIFORD
20TH MASSACHUSETTS INFANTRY

PVT. SIDNEY BREWSTER
18TH CONNECTICUT INFANTRY

PVT. AZRA MILLS
9TH MAINE INFANTRY

Rank and Service Branch Insignia

STAFF OFFICER'S HAT BADGE

INFANTRY OFFICER'S HAT BADGE

**OFFICER'S GENERAL
SERVICE HAT BADGE**

CAVALRY OFFICER'S HAT BADGE

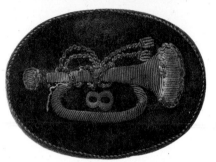

U.S. RIFLEMAN'S HAT BADGE

U.S. ARMY BUTTONS

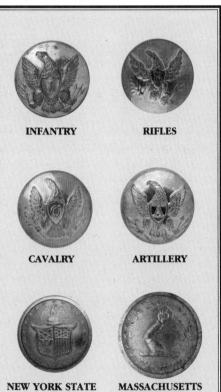

INFANTRY   **RIFLES**

CAVALRY   **ARTILLERY**

**NEW YORK STATE
BUTTON**   **MASSACHUSETTS
STATE BUTTON**

ARTILLERY OFFICER'S HAT BADGE

U.S. SANITARY COMMISSION HAT INSIGNIA

Buttons issued by the Federal
government bore branch-of-
service initials, with the exception of the general service eagle
button. Only two states, New York
and Massachusetts, issued large
numbers of buttons to their own
soldiers throughout the War.

**SHOULDER SCALES
U.S. SERGEANT MAJOR**

**FULL-DRESS
EPAULETS,
MAJ. GEN.
AMOS B. EATON**

**SHOULDER BOARD
MAJ. GEN. AMOS B. EATON**

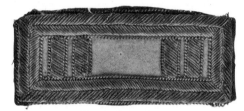

**SHOULDER BOARD
GEN. PHILIP KEARNY**

In Chantilly, Virginia, on September 1, 1862, Gen. Philip Kearny, inadvertently riding behind enemy lines, was killed by a Rebel's bullet. Federal surgeons returned the bullet *(left)* and one of Kearny's shoulder straps *(above, left)* to the general's family.

**SHOULDER BOARD
COLONEL, ARTILLERY**

**SHOULDER BOARD
CAPTAIN, CAVALRY**

**SHOULDER BOARD, LT. COLONEL
MEDICAL CORPS OR RIFLES**

**SHOULDER BOARD
1ST LIEUTENANT, STAFF**

**SHOULDER BOARD
MAJOR, INFANTRY**

**SHOULDER BOARD
2D LIEUTENANT, ARTILLERY**

HEADGEAR

CHAPEAU BRAS

Two examples of the cocked hat, or chapeau bras, one belonging to a member of the New York State Militia *(left)* and one to Gen. John Knapp *(above)*, illustrate the traditional, formal headdress of general officers and their staffs. The chapeau bras was eliminated in the 1851 dress regulations but reauthorized in 1859.

FORAGE CAP
15TH NEW HAMPSHIRE
VOLUNTEER INFANTRY

New Hampshire contracted with local tailors for forage caps to issue to the state's volunteers in 1861. The caps, including this one and the one held by the infantryman *(far right)*, displayed the silver-plated brass letters *NHV*—for New Hampshire Volunteers.

EARLY-WAR FORAGE CAPS

Variations on the 1858 regulation forage cap included a rounded brim (*far left*) worn by an officer with the 7th Connecticut Infantry. Officers' caps typically had an embroidered branch-of-service insignia, like the one on the cap at left; enlisted men decorated the tops of their forage caps with polished brass insignia.

FEDERAL OFFICER'S KEPI

Resembling an enlisted man's kepi with its low-cut sides and straight, square brim, the example at left was worn by a New York officer. The glazed leather chin strap attaches to the crown with two New York State brass eagle buttons.

2D LT. GEORGE W. TAYLOR 4TH MASSACHUSETTS LIGHT ARTILLERY

This cross between a havelock and a forage cap, modeled by a New Hampshire infantryman (*far right*), was patented in July 1861 by John F. Whipple, an agent with the Seamless Clothing Company in New York. The hat featured a brim that could be adjusted up or down.

Kepis for Union Officers

CAPT. ELLIOT C. PIERCE
13TH MASSACHUSETTS INFANTRY

Because Pierce was a staff officer in the Ambulance Corps, the I Corps badge on his kepi *(left)* combined the red, white, and blue colors representing all three divisions of the Federal army corps.

LT. WATERS W. BRAMAN
93D NEW YORK INFANTRY

Privately purchased from local tailors, officers' kepis exhibited subtle variations. McClellan-style kepis, such as Lieutenant Braman's *(left),* had a square, duckbill brim, influenced by the French chasseur.

LT. AUGUSTUS W. CORLISS
15TH U.S. INFANTRY

Manufactured by Shute & Sons in Boston, Corliss' hat *(above)* exemplifies a nonregulation, McClellan-style kepi. Lieutenant Corliss, formerly commander of the 2d Rhode Island Cavalry, enlisted in the Western army's Regular Brigade in early 1865 after his Rhode Island regiment was disbanded.

Tailors cut kepis in differing heights. This high-cut example *(right)* was worn by a member of the 161st New York Infantry. The low-cut model *(above)* bears the circle badge of the I Army Corps.

**OFFICER'S KEPI
114TH PENNSYLVANIA INFANTRY**

The officer in Col. Charles H. T. Collis' Zouave regiment who owned this bright red kepi *(left)* commissioned a tailor-made insignia for the front. Most officers personalized their hats by purchasing metal numbers to indicate their regiments.

**LT. MATTHIAS JOHNSON
165TH NEW YORK INFANTRY**

Chasseur-pattern kepis, such as the one at right worn by Lieutenant Johnson, cost more to make than the plainer McClellan-style kepi. Rows of gold braid along the sides and atop the hat's crown denoted the officer's rank.

**COL. GEORGE BURLING
6TH NEW JERSEY INFANTRY**

Officers usually wore their corps badges—if they wore them at all—on the left breast of their frock coats. Burling's kepi is unusual in that his III Corps badge covers the officer's braid on the crown of his hat.

**CAPT. SELLECK L. WHITE
10TH CONNECTICUT VOLUNTEERS**

On August 15, 1864, Captain White, who owned this chasseur-style kepi *(right)*, deployed his company to support the 2d brigade troops at Deep Bottom, Virginia. In the ensuing skirmishes, White was mortally wounded. His commander lamented losing one of his "most brave and valued officers, whom the regiment can ill spare."

Officers' Forage Caps

**UNIDENTIFIED OFFICER'S CAP
63D NEW YORK INFANTRY**

The chin strap on this cap once fastened to its sides by two now-missing buttons. The 63d New York, predominantly Irishmen, was attached to the Army of the Potomac's II Corps.

**SGT. W. O. LINCOLN
1ST MASSACHUSETTS CAVALRY**

Narrow, crescent-shaped brims and high crowns characterize the McDowell-style forage cap *(above)*. Unlike the square-brimmed private-contractor models, the McDowell type was usually made without binding on its brim.

McDOWELL-STYLE FORAGE CAP

Described by an officer as "light, comfortable, military, and cheap," the forage cap was first issued to the U.S. Army in 1858. Officers' caps, like the one here, were lined with silk.

These officers were members of the 45th Illinois Infantry—known as the Washburn Lead Mine Regiment—which boasted a long and successful battle record in the Army of the Tennessee. The officer in the foreground displays his McDowell-style forage cap on a table.

**CAPT. LINDLEY COLEMAN
19TH MAINE INFANTRY**

Captain Coleman added a brass ventilator to his forage cap *(above)*. The ventilators sold by sutlers were supposed to keep air circulating through the dark cloth crowns in hot weather.

**CAPT. J. HENRY SLEEPER
10TH MASSACHUSETTS LIGHT
ARTILLERY**

While commanding his regiment at Reams' Station, Virginia, in late August 1864, Sleeper was painfully wounded but fought on until the firing ceased nearly a half-hour later. For his courage, Sleeper, whose forage cap *(above)* features an embroidered crossed-cannons insignia, was awarded the rank of brevet major.

CAPT. WATERS WHIPPLE BRAMAN, 93D NEW YORK VOLUNTEERS

Captain Braman, who owned this McDowell-style forage cap, commanded Company C of the 93d New York. Eight months of hard campaigning reduced his regiment's ranks from 998 officers and men to some 250.

Enlisted Men's Headgear

ENLISTED FORAGE CAP

General Kearny instituted corps badges to identify his men after he mistakenly reprimanded officers not of his command. His own red blanket furnished material for the first squares that were sewn, like the one above, to the tops of his men's caps.

PVT. JOSEPH BAKER
1ST PENNSYLVANIA RESERVES

Private Joseph Baker wore this forage cap, which bears the Maltese cross signifying the V Army Corps.

105TH OHIO INFANTRY

This forage cap belonged to a sergeant of the 105th Ohio, which came under siege at Chattanooga in fall 1863. The regiment was in Brig. Gen. Absalom Baird's division, whose great losses at Chickamauga "attest[ed] to the determination with which my men fought," Baird wrote.

PVT. FRANK ELLIOT
KEYSTONE BATTERY

A member of Matthew Hastings' Keystone Battery of the Pennsylvania Independent Artillery, Private Elliot poked ventilation holes into the top of his forage cap *(above)*. His III Corps badge is sewn to the cap's right side.

UNIDENTIFIED UNION INFANTRYMAN

High-crowned forage caps, like the one worn below, proved popular. "There is room for a wet sponge, green leaves, a handkerchief, or other protection against the sun," one soldier declared.

PVT. JOHN FLORY 107TH OHIO INFANTRY

The cap insignia for the X Corps (above) represented a fort with four bastions. The round hunting horn of the French light infantry was adopted as the official device of the U.S. Infantry in 1836.

PRIVATE WIEDERSHIEM 119TH PENNSYLVANIA INFANTRY

The Greek cross on this cap (below) identified its owner as a member of the VI Corps. In battle, cap badges enabled officers to pinpoint stragglers and deserters and send them back to the proper commands.

PVT. JACOB MUSCHBACH 128TH PENNSYLVANIA VOLUNTEERS

This forage cap bears Private Muschbach's company letter atop its red star-shaped XII Corps badge, as well as his regimental numbers denoting the 128th Pennsylvania.

FORAGE CAP 31ST MAINE INFANTRY

U.S. Army depots manufactured more than 41,000 forage caps and purchased some four million more for issue to Federal troops during the War. Jean cloth was used for the caps throughout the War; the jean-cloth cap at left was worn by a member of the 31st Maine, a regiment organized in the spring of 1864.

Slouch Hats

DRESS HAT

In 1858, officials authorized a black felt dress hat for officers *(right)* and enlisted men *(photo)*. This headgear was dubbed the Hardee hat for Maj. William J. Hardee, a future Confederate general who served on the board that chose the style. Most soldiers disliked the official Hardee hat for its stiffness, and modified their own or bought other types from private contractors. The recessed crown of the example shown here classifies it as nonregulation.

U.S. ARMY HAT

A twisted black silk and gold bullion cord ending in two acorns surrounds the crown of this hat belonging to an unidentified Federal infantry officer. Federal regulations directed infantrymen to loop up the right side of their hats, cavalrymen the left, fastening the brim of the hat to the crown with a stamped brass national eagle. Officers used an embroidered eagle.

Federal officers dressed in headgear ranging from kepis to a regulation Hardee hat *(officer, center)* enjoy the view from Lookout Mountain, Tennessee, in 1863.

GEN. THOMAS G. STEVENSON
ARMY OF THE POTOMAC

Silk grosgrain tape binds the brim of General Stevenson's black slouch hat *(below)*. Stevenson, who recruited the 24th Massachusetts Infantry, was killed in action at Spotsylvania in May 1864.

MAJ. GEN. JOHN SEDGWICK

When his aides cautioned him against unnecessary exposure to enemy fire on the battlefield at Spotsylvania, General Sedgwick, who owned the well-worn slouch hat above, disparaged the Confederates' marksmanship. Moments later, a sharpshooter's bullet struck him below the left eye, killing him instantly.

CAPT. DAVID C. TAYLOR
118TH NEW YORK INFANTRY

The practical soldier preferred a wide-brimmed slouch hat like the one worn by Captain Taylor *(left)*. This style was popularized by Louis Kossuth, a renowned Hungarian patriot who visited the United States in 1851.

CAPT. CHARLES NASH
19TH MAINE INFANTRY

This slouch hat, pierced by a bullet at the left rear of the crown, bears the cloverleaf emblem of the Federal II Corps. Its owner, Captain Nash, was leading a company against Gen. James Longstreet's Confederates in the Wilderness on May 6, 1864, when a bullet sent the hat flying; Captain Nash was not harmed.

**LT. HENRY BREWSTER
57TH NEW YORK INFANTRY**

Brewster purchased this expensive French hat *(left)* from an outfitter in New York City. He was wearing it when a bullet shattered his right arm during the Battle of Fredericksburg in December 1862.

**INFANTRY OFFICER'S
SLOUCH HAT**

Faded machine-woven bullion cord adorns this hat from the 9th regiment of an unknown state's infantry. In the field, nonregulation headgear was the rule rather than the exception.

**LT. BARTLETT
13TH NEW HAMPSHIRE INFANTRY**

The gray felt slouch hat above reflected popular civilian fashion of the time. Distinguished by a low, rounded crown, the hat could be worn bowler style, with the brim upturned.

**CAPT. ROBERT S. JOHNSTON
4TH NEW JERSEY INFANTRY**

Rebel bullets riddled Johnston's slouch hat *(right)* during the Federal assault on the Confederate line near Spotsylvania Courthouse in May 1864. Fortunately, the spent ball that hit Johnston knocked him unconscious but did not kill him.

PVT. JOHN M. MITCHELL 79TH ILLINOIS VOLUNTEER INFANTRY

Soldiers often modified their issue hats by poking them in or creasing them to achieve the effect they desired. Private Mitchell folded in the crown of his Federal-issue Hardee hat *(left)* in order to lower the crown. The hat was pierced by a bullet at Liberty Gap, Tennessee, in June 1863, but Mitchell was not seriously harmed. The enlisted cavalryman above wears similar headgear.

UNIDENTIFIED ENLISTED MEN 102D NEW YORK INFANTRY

Although more popular with Western troops, broad-brimmed slouch hats similar to the one bearing the five-pointed star of the XII Corps *(far right)* were occasionally found in Eastern regiments. Enlisted men shunned regulation dress hats that, according to one Pennsylvania private, "were high, stiff affairs, with enough brass fixings about them to make a copper kettle."

Foul-Weather and Fatigue Headgear

FEDERAL HAVELOCKS

Popularized by Sir Henry Havelock of the British Army during the Sepoy Rebellion in India in 1857, the havelock was a linen or cotton drape made to cover a soldier's cap and shield him from the sun. In the beginning of the War, soldiers who wore havelocks, typified by the three models above, soon found that these covers cut off air circulation around their heads and actually made them hotter. After his regiment received a full complement of havelocks from ladies in their home county, "We sent home thanks," said one Pennsylvanian, "and threw the head bags away."

FEDERAL SOLDIERS' CAMP HATS

Colonel William Hatch, who commanded the 4th New Jersey Volunteer Infantry before he was killed in action at Fredericksburg, Virginia, in December 1862, wore this unique fur-trimmed folding camp hat *(above)*. The colorful hand-embroidered hat at left resembled the smoking hats that were popular in the civilian fashion of the time; it was worn when its owner lounged around camp.

RAIN HEADGEAR

Foul weather inspired several different types of headgear for Federal soldiers. Issued to Philadelphia's State Fencibles militia company, the oilcloth kepi below was intended as a rain hat. Men who could afford them purchased vulcanized rubber rain covers *(portrait and far left),* which were more durable than the state-issue oilcloth versions.

Stationed early in the War at Hilton Head Island, South Carolina, men of the 3d New Hampshire Volunteer Infantry *(left)* "battled sand fleas so thick they could streak a man's trousers black," according to one colonel. The tricolor knitted tam *(below)* belonged to one of the New Hampshire men; the brown-and-red camp hat *(lower left)* was worn by a soldier in the 1st Rhode Island.

FOOTWEAR

LEATHER GAITERS U.S. ARMY OF THE POTOMAC

LEATHER-REINFORCED CANVAS GAITERS, U.S. ARMY OF THE POTOMAC

Leather leggings, known as gaiters, buckled over soldiers' shoes and pant legs as protection from sand and dust. Some gaiters, such as those worn by a member of Berdan's Sharpshooters *(above),* reached up to the knee. Made both in thick cotton canvas and in leather, the leggings were copied from French infantrymen.

Shoes for the Soldiers

For soldiers who marched 10 miles a day while on campaign, good shoes made the difference between simple exhaustion and misery. "If you find a foot soldier lying beat out by the roadside," said one veteran campaigner, "five to one his heels are too high, or his soles too narrow, or too thin, or his shoe is not made straight on the inside, so that the great toe can spread into its place as he treads."

This knowledge was not always implemented by the contractors who manufactured shoes for the Federal government. The average life of a pair of contractor's shoes, such as the low-cut regulation Jefferson boots issued to foot soldiers, was estimated to be between 20 and 30 days.

PRIVATE-PURCHASE CAMP SHOES 22D CONNECTICUT INFANTRY

FEDERAL-ISSUE SHOES

Variously called mudscows and gunboats by Federal soldiers, squaretoed brogans were issued for $1.96 a pair in 1861. Soles with exposed stitching *(right)* wore out quickly and were often replaced by more durable pegged soles *(below)*.

**FEDERAL-ISSUE SHOES
5TH MASSACHUSETTS INFANTRY**

For comfort, soldiers occasionally cut down their brogans with the help of a local shoemaker. This low-cut version *(right)* boasts a brass reinforcement at the instep, a mid-War improvement that made the shoes more durable.

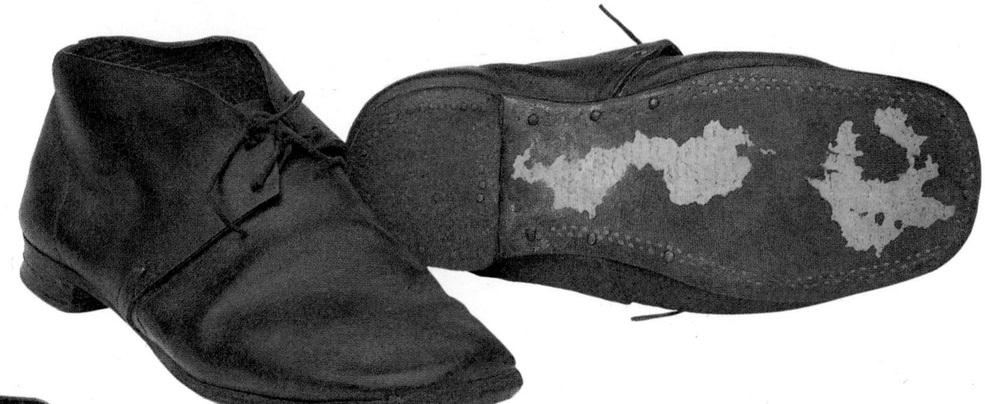

**U.S. ARMY SHOES
SGT. GILBERT BENTLEY
37TH MASSACHUSETTS
VOLUNTEER MILITIA**

FEDERAL-ISSUE VARIANT-STYLE JEFFERSON BOOTS

192

Despite regulations to the contrary, caval-rymen, including the soldier above, often tucked their pant legs inside their boots.

U.S. CAVALRY BOOTS

Made of heavy bridle leather, these privately purchased cavalry boots feature a high flap to shield the wearer's vulnerable knees from abrasion.

**PVT. EDGAR S. YERGASON
22D CONNECTICUT INFANTRY**

Although worn by many infantry-men early in the War, boots, like the Napoleon-style pair above, soon proved to be "heavy and irk-some on long marches," accord-ing to one foot soldier.

FEDERAL-ISSUE SOLDIER'S BOOTS

Both mounted and foot soldiers favored heavy, rigid Wellington boots *(above)* that rose to just below the knee in front. Leather pulls are sewn to the top of each boot.

A sergeant in the 45th Massachusetts purchased these deerskin mocca-sins *(left)* to protect his legs from being cut while foraging in the woods. Strapped to the heel like spurs, metal-studded ice creepers *(below)* were popular with officers who used them on icy ground in winter quarters.

U.S. ARMY SPURS

The medieval-looking spiked spurs *(top)* bought by Capt. J. H. Sleeper, commander of the 10th Massachusetts Artillery, contrast with a regulation pair *(left)* and a screw-attached type *(above)*.

OFFICER'S BOOTS

Traditionally, the army issued boots to men in the mounted service. Officers preferred an expensive, soft leather style *(above)* that emulated those worn by 17th-century cavaliers.

FEDERAL OFFICER'S BOOTS

Tapered toes on this pair of regulation officer's boots *(right)* typify boot construction prior to 1865.

GEN. GEORGE MEADE ARMY OF THE POTOMAC

Recounting Meade's infamous bad temper, one of his officers wrote, "I don't know any thin old man, who, when he is wrathy, exercises less Christian charity than my well-beloved chief." Meade's high-cut boots appear above.

EQUIPMENT

The Union's superior industrial power generated an endless supply of high-quality equipment for use by the Northern armies. So much gear was amassed by the U.S. Ordnance and Quartermaster's departments, in fact, that the result was the first true military surplus in American history.

The accouterments of the Union soldier at the beginning of the War were essentially those that had been adopted in 1839, with minor modifications introduced in the mid-1850s. These items were little more than updated versions of the basics that had been carried by all the world's soldiers for the previous 100 years.

From the outset, Yankee soldiers had plenty of complaints about their equipment, most of which were justified. Entrepreneurs began to pay attention to the complaints. The surplus provided an interval for experimentation, and as the War wore on, efforts were made to devise more efficient and comfortable accouterments. The results were sound, battle-tested alternatives to many roundly despised items.

The Civil War infantryman wore a waist belt and a shoulder belt, from which hung a cartridge box. The standard, old-pattern cartridge box was a wooden block enclosed in a leather case. Holes were drilled in the blocks for the paper-wrapped cartridges, and a tin tray underneath held extra ammunition and tools. The new 1839-model box featured two separate but identical tin compartments that sat side by side in the leather case and slid upward for removal. Each compartment was divided into two sections. One section, open at the top, was intended for ready ammunition; the lower section, open at the front, held reserve cartridges, carried still wrapped in packets of 10 rounds. With a capacity of 40 rounds, the cartridge box was made in three different sizes, for .58- and .69-caliber Minié balls and for .69-caliber round balls. On the flap of the cartridge box was an oval, lead-filled plate with *US* in relief, intended both as insignia and as a weight to hold down the flap.

The shoulder belt, which had been white buff leather in the Mexican War, was blackened with dye by the mid-1850s, and during the Civil War it was often made of black bridle leather. It carried the same eagle insignia that had been in use since 1828.

The waist belt, also black at the time of the War, had a "US" oval buckle. The leather bayonet scabbard was attached to the belt by a leather loop known as a frog. One newer item, introduced in the 1840s, was a pouch for carrying the percussion caps that ignited the musket cartridges. It was made of pressed leather and was carried on the waist belt to the right of the belt plate.

Officers and noncommissioned officers wore their swords suspended from waist belts. Many officers' versions had a narrow shoulder strap attached to help support the sword. The belts were fastened by a rectangular brass plate emblazoned with a standard motif: the American eagle surrounded by an applied German-silver wreath. Cavalrymen carried their revolvers in holsters fastened to the waist belt, an innovation resulting from then-Captain George B. McClellan's assignment as an observer in the Crimean War in 1856. Before then, cavalry officers and troopers carried pistols or revolvers in saddle holsters, and many officers' saddles still sported holsters during the Civil War.

The carbine sling, a cavalry fixture since before the Revolution, was still in use. The sling, a wide leather strap attached to the carbine with a snap hook, rode over the left shoulder, the carbine hanging at the trooper's right side, muzzle down. Carbine cartridge boxes, smaller versions of the infantryman's box, were worn either on the carbine sling or on the waist belt.

The standard canteen was an oblate-spheroid model, made of two tinned-iron halves soldered together, with a pewter or tin spout, three loops for a leather or cotton sling, and a woolen cover. It was made either with smooth sides or with a pressed concentric "bulls-eye" pattern for reinforcement.

The haversack, or "bread bag," designed to carry rations and eating utensils, was made of cotton drill painted black, with an inner bag of unpainted cotton, which was removable for washing. Sutlers and manufacturers offered several types of specially designed haversacks. Many were of patent leather or oilcloth, with several compartments to divide the soldier's rations.

The infantryman's knapsack, designed to carry extra clothing and personal effects, was based on the current French pattern but may have been influenced by the Russian version. Foot artillerymen also carried these knapsacks; cavalrymen and horse artillery carried their personal belongings in saddlebags. Like the haversack, the standard-issue knapsack was made of cotton cloth coated with black paint. Other models, mostly state issue or private purchases, were fashioned from cloth covered with India rubber or gutta-percha. Many early militia versions featured heavy wooden inserts to maintain a neat, boxlike appearance.

Civil War soldiers cursed their knapsacks, which weighed 50 pounds or more when fully loaded. They complained that the straps that crossed their chests rubbed the skin raw and constricted breathing. In addition, the pack tended to sag and ride uncomfortably on the back. And in the heat of Southern summers, the black paint that coated the pack tended to melt and become sticky.

One short march usually sufficed to educate a foot soldier about the torment that had been designed into his equipment. Private Warren Lee Goss of the U.S. Regular Engineers described such a march when his regiment passed through Boston en route to the front: "We were marched through the streets—the first march of any consequence we had taken with our knapsacks and equipment on. Our dress consisted of a belt about the body, which held a cartridge box and bayonet, a crossbelt, also a haversack and tin drinking cup, a canteen, and, last but not least, the knapsack strapped to the back. The straps ran over, around, and about one, in confusion most perplexing to our unsophisticated shoulders, the knapsack giving one constantly the feeling that he was being pulled over backward. We marched along, my canteen banging against my bayonet, my cartridge box and haversack flopping up and down—the whole jangling like loose harness and chains on a runaway horse."

Numerous patent-knapsack manufacturers attempted to solve these problems with improved products. The firms of Baxter and Wood devised a frame-and-strap system intended to relieve some of the pressure on the chest and back. Short's knapsack, used extensively by Massachusetts troops, had a strapping system that allowed the knapsack to fall away from the shoulders and spine, thus permitting ventilation across the back and shoulders. Other models, such as Rider's Tent Knapsack, Joubert's, Rush's, and Southward's, were designed to be converted into tents, litters, hammocks, or cots.

Such innovations failed to reach the mass of soldiers, however. Thousands of them came up with their own quick and easy solution to the problem of the knapsack—they threw them away. Private Leander Stillwell of the 61st Illinois Infantry recalled a pivotal, 35-mile march from Bethel to Jackson in Tennessee: "On this march, I did not carry my knapsack. It was about this time that most of the boys adopted the 'blanket-roll' system. Our knapsacks were awkward, cumbersome things, with a combination of straps and buckles that chafed the shoulders and back, and greatly augmented heat and general discomfort. So we would fold in our blankets an extra shirt, with a few other light articles, roll the blanket tight, double it over and tie the two ends together, then throw the blanket over one shoulder, with the tied ends under the opposite arm—and the arrangement was complete. We had learned by this time the necessity of reducing our personal baggage to the lightest possible limit. We had left Camp Carrollton with great bulging knapsacks, stuffed with all sorts of plunder, much of which was utterly useless to soldiers in the field. But we soon got rid of all that. And my recollection is that after the Bethel march the great majority of the men would, in some way, when on a march, temporarily lay aside their knapsacks, and use the blanket roll."

Perhaps the newest pieces of equipment in the soldier's inventory were the rubber blanket and poncho. Theoretically, infantrymen carried the blankets while mounted troops received the poncho, but the two were often issued indiscriminately. Products of the new process for vulcanizing rubber, these waterproof items were to prove invaluable during the War.

The shelter half also made its appearance during the Civil War. It was copied from the French *tente d'abri* and was first distributed in the summer of 1862. These diminutive "dog" or "pup" tents, made of sturdy drill or duck, soon became standard issue to all troops. Each soldier carried half of a tent. Two soldiers would button their halves together, stretch them between poles—or even between rifles stuck bayonet-first in the ground—and stake them to the earth. The tents afforded shelter when the wagons carrying the standard camp wall tents were far to the rear. They also proved useful for roofing winter huts, and were used as blankets and sunshades in the summer. Initially disliked, the shelter half soon proved its worth as a basic part of the soldier's gear.

As with the knapsack, other pieces of Civil War gear were revised, improved, or otherwise altered by private manufacturers who peddled their wares to the states or the Federal government for use by the regiments in the field. Among many items, a number of new canteens were devised, including some with water filters. Factories also turned out special water-filter tubes intended for use in the standard-issue canteen. The filters only succeeded in cleansing the water of visible sediment, however, leaving behind the disease-causing microbes.

In fact, the subject of sanitation did not draw the attention of the providers of Civil War equipment. Mess kits and knife, fork, and spoon sets were patented and produced, but no thought was given to cleaning such gear. Massachusetts veteran John D. Billings recalled what a soldier did—or did not do—after he had eaten: "When he had finished his meal, he did not in many cases stand on ceremony, and his dishes were tossed under the bunk to await the next meal. Or, if he condescended to do a little dish-cleaning, it was not of an aesthetic kind. Sometimes he was satisfied to scrape his plate out with his knife, and let it go at that. Another time he would take a wisp of straw or a handful of leaves from his bunk, and wipe it out. Now and then a man would pour a little of his hot coffee into his plate to cleanse it. As to the knife and fork, when they got too black to be tolerated—and they had to be of a very sable hue, it should be said—there was no cleansing process so inexpensive, simple, available, and efficient as running them vigorously into the earth a few times."

New ways of carrying gear emerged during the War, prompted by widespread complaints of hernia and shoulder damage

197

caused by heavy, off-balance loads. An inventor named William D. Mann developed an innovative system of shoulder straps intended to relieve the stresses and strains imposed by the heavy cartridge box. His system was fielded on an experimental basis in 1864. But despite Mann's aggressive marketing tactics, only small numbers of his invention were used in combat.

New cartridge boxes were developed for the cavalry's various breechloading or repeating carbines. Most of them, however, were throwbacks to the earlier system—drilled, varnished wooden blocks encased in leather. Even the Blakeslee box, intended to hold the magazine tubes of the highy advanced Spencer carbine, was essentially a wooden block with holes for the tubes. Still, it proved effective and useful.

The methods developed to manufacture accouterments for the Yankee soldiers were the result of years of experience on the part of the Ordnance and Quartermaster's departments. Standard patterns were issued to armories and civilian contractors to ensure uniformity. Early in the War, however, when the masses of volunteers created a crisis of supply, many contractors indulged in unscrupulous practices, cutting corners to increase their profits. The extent of the fraud spurred Congressional action. After January 1862, every item of army equipment had to be marked by the contractor with his name and the date of the contract. Army inspectors also marked the items they scrutinized. Such rigid quality control soon eliminated the production of shoddy goods.

Excluded from this rigorous inspection process were the manufacturers who sold their products to individuals or to state governments. These companies had to compete vigorously for contracts, and the competition generally kept the quality of their products high. Among those suppliers were the manufacturers of personal items that the soldiers carried to camp and on campaign. Non-army-issue, personal gear varied with a man's inclinations. Most soldiers took along some extra clothing, sometimes of civilian pattern, as well as amenities such as pipes or cigars, match safes, pocket Bibles, pencils and paper (or more sophisticated writing kits), sewing kits, or "housewives," smoking caps, candles and spiked candleholders, jackknives, and photographs of loved ones. Some men even packed a Jew's harp or a volume of Shakespeare.

Soldiers cherished such items, particularly mementos of home, but they displayed a decidedly casual attitude toward articles of government issue. They tended to accumulate gear when encamped during the winter and then abandon their belongings when they marched off on campaign in the spring. Like their Rebel counterparts, the more experienced Union soldiers found it beneficial to carry the minimum.

Union commanders bemoaned the loss of equipment. General Ulysses S. Grant, observing his troops in the Army of the Potomac in the spring of 1864, wrote: "I saw scattered along the road from Culpeper to Germanna Ford wagonloads of new blankets and overcoats, thrown away by the troops to lighten their knapsacks." Another Federal general declared that an "army half the size of ours could be supplied with what we waste." That the Union soldiers could so casually discard their equipment was, in fact, a testimony to the success of the Union supply effort. Unlike the soldiers of the South, Federal troops could expect their lost gear to be replaced in due time. Particularly in the latter part of the War, there was always extra equipment ready to be distributed when it was needed. As John Billings of Massachusetts put it, waste was simply a "way the Army of the Potomac had of getting into light marching order."

ACCOUTERMENTS

This Federal cartridge-box plate was struck by a bullet during the Battle of Chickamauga. Box plates as well as the identical belt plates were made of thin brass stampings filled with lead to add weight.

FEDERAL INFANTRYMAN IN FULL MARCHING ORDER

MODEL 1858 CANTEEN COMPANY B 21ST MASSACHUSETTS

This smooth, tinned-iron oblate spheroid canteen has a pewter spout closed with a cork stopper.

The leather belt, 1855 cartridge box, and bayonet scabbard shown here were captured by the Rebels from a member of Gen. Truman Seymour's division, X Corps, at the Battle of Olustee, Florida, in February 1864.

PVT. EDGAR S. YERGASON 22D CONNECTICUT INFANTRY REGIMENT

The haversack at right belonged to Private Yergason during his service with the 22d Connecticut, a nine-month regiment serving in the defenses of Washington, D.C., and at the siege of Suffolk, Virginia.

Federal Officers' Equipment

**SWORD BELT
MAJ. GEN. GEORGE G. MEADE**

**MODEL 1851 FIELD- AND
COMPANY-GRADE OFFICER'S
SWORD BELT**

**FIELD GLASSES, LT. COL. CHARLES
PIERSON, 39TH MASSACHUSETTS**

These binoculars were smashed by
the shell fragment that wounded
Pierson at Spotsylvania on May 10,
1864. The glasses had belonged to
his friend Col. Paul Revere of the
20th Massachusetts, who was mortally wounded at Gettysburg.

**CAPT. CHARLES S. EIGONBRODT
2D MASSACHUSETTS CAVALRY**

HAVERSACK
CAPT. E. GRANT
3D MASSACHUSETTS
INFANTRY

HOLSTER
LT. CHARLES TOBEY
58TH MASSACHUSETTS

HOLSTER FOR .44-CAL.
COLT ARMY REVOLVER

OFFICER'S HAVERSACK
WITH U.S. SHIELD DEVICE

PRESSED OILCLOTH
OFFICER'S HAVERSACK

Infantry
Accouterments

GEAR FOR .69-CAL. MUSKET

MODEL 1855 EQUIPMENT

MODEL 1856 BELT AND
FROG FOR SWORD BAYONET

MODEL 1852 N.C.O. AND MUSICIAN'S BELT

MODEL 1859 FOOT ARTILLERY BELT

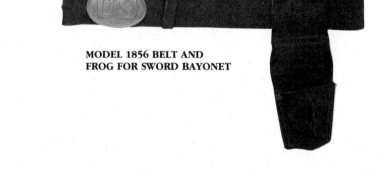

MODEL 1855 RIFLEMAN'S BELT

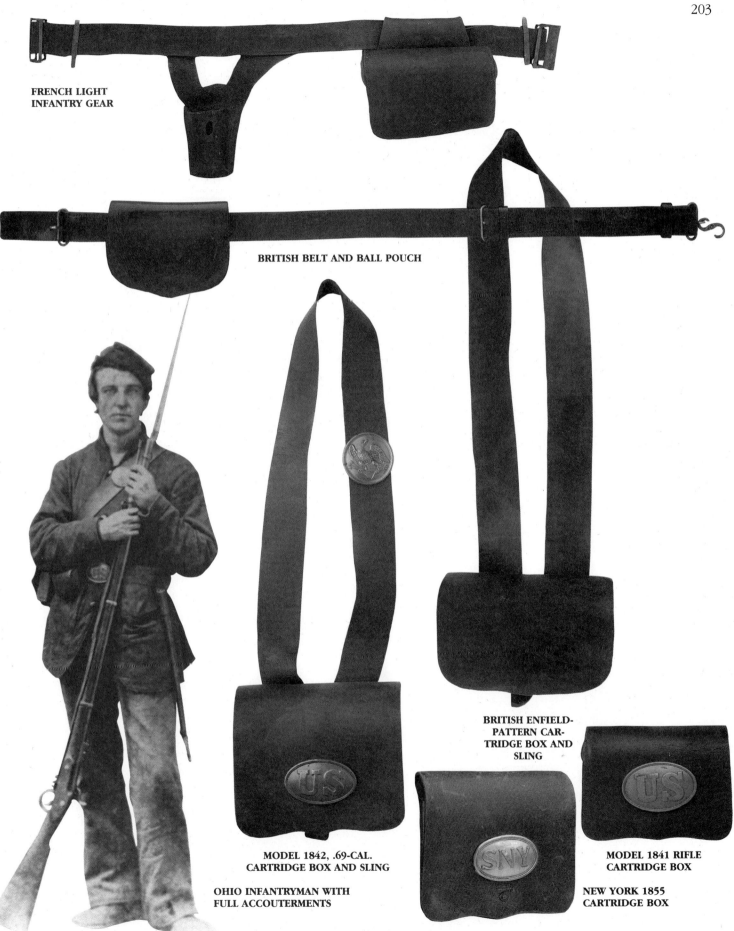

FRENCH LIGHT
INFANTRY GEAR

BRITISH BELT AND BALL POUCH

BRITISH ENFIELD-
PATTERN CAR-
TRIDGE BOX AND
SLING

MODEL 1842, .69-CAL.
CARTRIDGE BOX AND SLING

OHIO INFANTRYMAN WITH
FULL ACCOUTERMENTS

MODEL 1841 RIFLE
CARTRIDGE BOX

NEW YORK 1855
CARTRIDGE BOX

Cavalry Equipment

**CAVALRY PRIVATE WITH
SMITH CARBINE AND GEAR**

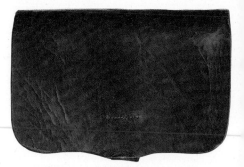

BURNSIDE CARTRIDGE BOX

MULTIPURPOSE CARTRIDGE BOX

SPENCER CARTRIDGE BOX

SHARPS CARTRIDGE BOX

CAVALRY GAUNTLETS

**CAVALRY
ACCOUTERMENTS**

This 1851 dragoon saber
belt, made of black buff
leather, features loops
to add a shoulder strap.
In addition to the saber,
the belt carries a car-
tridge box for .52- to
.56-caliber paper carbine
ammunition, a percus-
sion cap pouch, and a
holster for the Colt
Army revolver.

REVOLVER AMMUNITION BOX

WARTIME 1861 CARBINE SLING

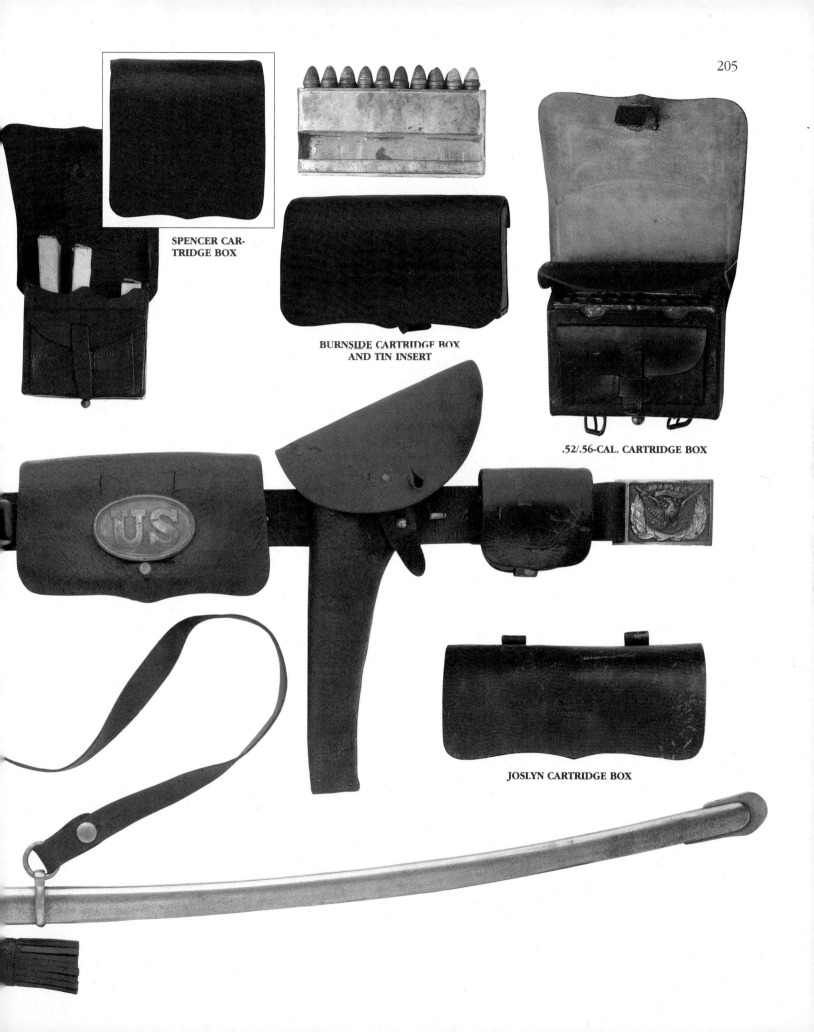

SPENCER CAR-
TRIDGE BOX

BURNSIDE CARTRIDGE BOX
AND TIN INSERT

.52/.56-CAL. CARTRIDGE BOX

JOSLYN CARTRIDGE BOX

The Indispensable Canteen

TIN CANTEEN

In 1859, Philadelphia contractor Albert Dorff made 15,000 canteens with leather slings.

UNIDENTIFIED PRIVATE

The owner of this portrait labeled the photograph "At the Halt."

PVT. WILLIAM PECK 27TH CONNECTICUT

After 1861, certain contractors made canteens with concentric rings for added strength.

9TH MASSACHUSETTS INFANTRY REGIMENT

The owner of this 1858 canteen painted his regimental designation over a I Corps badge.

13TH VETERAN RESERVES

This 1858 canteen features the regulation cotton sling. Covers appeared in blue, brown, or gray cloth.

1858 CANTEEN

The large Roman numeral on this canteen from Pennsylvania may have stood for the V Corps.

MELLIN'S PATENT FILTER

This 1861 patent filter stopper, made to fit the regulation canteen, used felt or sponge as a filtering agent.

CAPT. JONAS COREY 53D MASSACHUSETTS INFANTRY REGIMENT

This popular filter canteen was patented in 1861 by Charles Bartholomae.

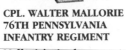

CPL. WALTER MALLORIE 76TH PENNSYLVANIA INFANTRY REGIMENT

Mallorie's tin drum canteen is probably a pre-War militia model.

CANTEL PATENT CANTEEN

Lazare Cantel's 1862 patent specified a leather body lined with tinfoil and joined by copper rivets.

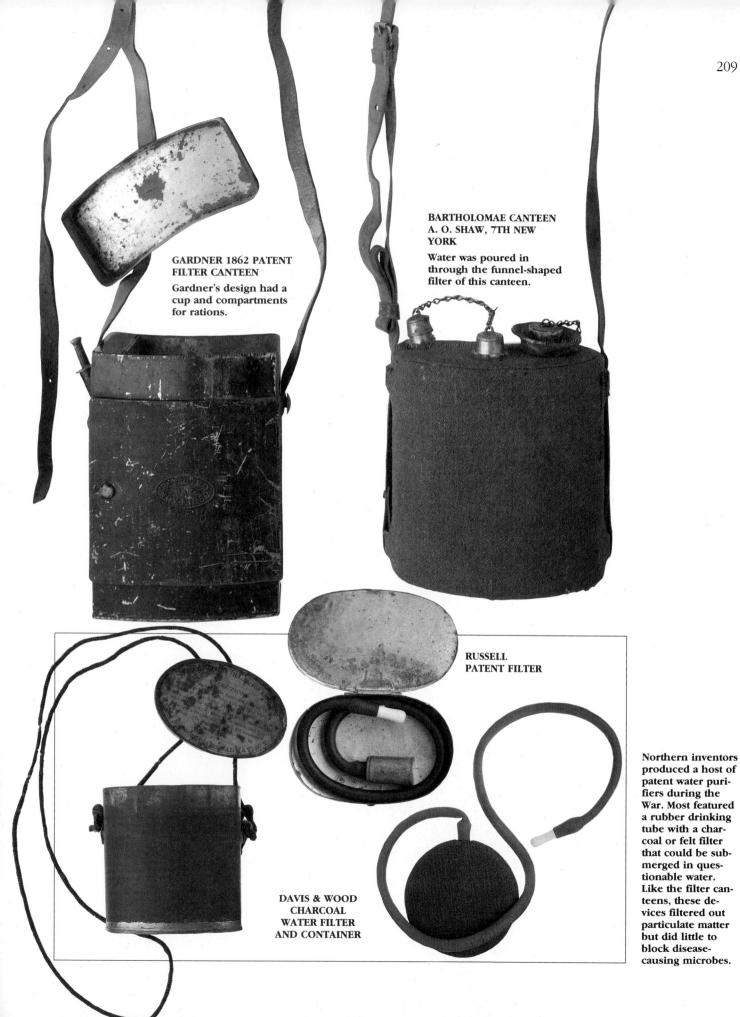

GARDNER 1862 PATENT FILTER CANTEEN

Gardner's design had a cup and compartments for rations.

BARTHOLOMAE CANTEEN A. O. SHAW, 7TH NEW YORK

Water was poured in through the funnel-shaped filter of this canteen.

RUSSELL PATENT FILTER

DAVIS & WOOD CHARCOAL WATER FILTER AND CONTAINER

Northern inventors produced a host of patent water purifiers during the War. Most featured a rubber drinking tube with a charcoal or felt filter that could be submerged in questionable water. Like the filter canteens, these devices filtered out particulate matter but did little to block disease-causing microbes.

Haversacks

**UNIDENTIFIED PRIVATE
1ST PHILADELPHIA MILITIA
"GRAY RESERVES"**

PATTERN 1851 HAVERSACK

This painted linen haversack was carried by a trooper in the 1st New Jersey Cavalry.

MASSACHUSETTS HAVERSACK

Massachusetts issued haversacks in this oilcloth-and-cotton-canvas pattern as well as in smaller, all cotton, versions.

**PVT. LEVI DICKSON
17TH CONNECTICUT
INFANTRY REGIMENT**

Private Dickson carried this haversack when he was wounded at Gettysburg in 1863.

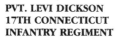

**PATTERN 1851 HAVERSACK
PVT. BROWN, 40TH NEW YORK**

Brown's regulation haversack contains an inner ration bag that could be removed for washing.

**PVT. W. H. COPE
2D OHIO
HEAVY ARTILLERY**

The use of cheap cotton haversacks like this one persisted among western and New England states troops.

Knapsacks

**MILITIA-STYLE BOX KNAPSACK
21ST MASSACHUSETTS INFANTRY
REGIMENT**

Rigid-frame knapsacks *(above, left)*, their sides reinforced with wood, pasteboard, or leather, were commonly acquired by new volunteer regiments early in the War. Experienced soldiers shunned the extra weight and adopted soft knapsacks such as this one.

**MILITIA-STYLE BOX KNAPSACK, REGIMENTAL BAND,
10TH CONNECTICUT INFANTRY REGIMENT**

This knapsack's wood frame gave it a neat appearance on parade.

**PVT. EDGAR S. YERGASON
22D CONNECTICUT INFANTRY REGIMENT**

Knapsack of gutta-percha-lined canvas

MODEL 1853/55 KNAPSACK 71ST NEW YORK INFANTRY REGIMENT

These nonrigid knapsacks of rubberized or painted canvas were the commonest style used during the War. The straps could be hooked to the 1855 rifleman's belt or crossed on the chest.

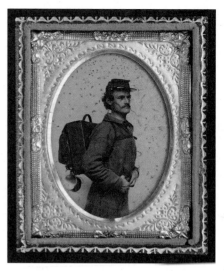

UNIDENTIFIED FEDERAL SOLDIER WITH SHORT'S PATENT KNAPSACK

SHORT'S PATENT KNAPSACK

Joseph Short, of Salem, Massachusetts, designed a knapsack suspension system with a shoulder yoke and belt braces to distribute weight. Short knapsacks of painted and natural canvas were purchased by New York, Massachusetts, and New Hampshire.

MODEL 1853/55 KNAPSACK 29TH CONNECTICUT INFANTRY REGIMENT

The Federal infantryman was expected to carry a double wool blanket, shelter tent, gum blanket, pair of extra shoes, mess equipment, toilet articles, and spare clothing. The knapsack had two compartments and loops for attaching a rolled blanket to the top.

Tents and Blankets

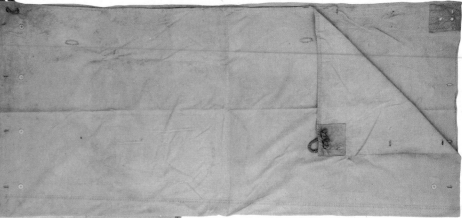

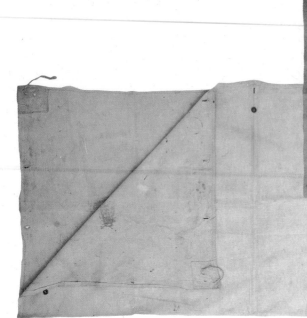

EARLY-ISSUE SHELTER TENT

The shelter tent, patterned after the French *tente d'Abri,* was first issued in 1862. Early tents measured 5'2" x 4'8" and were fastened by bone buttons. Tents in 1864 *(left)* were larger, 5'6" x 5'5", with metal buttons.

LATE-WAR SHELTER TENT

PVT. EDGAR S. YERGASON
22D CONNECTICUT INFANTRY

Yergason carried this gray regulation army blanket during his nine months of service.

LT. J. R. ROYER
156TH PENNSYLVANIA INFANTRY
REGIMENT

In common with most Federal military blankets, Royer's once-gray blanket bears dark stripes at either end and a "U.S." to mark it as Army property.

STATE CONTRACT
BLANKET

Because woolen mills were unable to supply sufficient cloth to fill the army's demands for blankets, the Quartermaster's Department adopted expedients such as this lightweight brown blanket made of a mixture of wool and cotton.

Federal soldiers, bivouacked outside Atlanta, air blankets atop their shelter tents. One soldier, new to the field, remarked that the tents reminded him "forcibly of a hog pen."

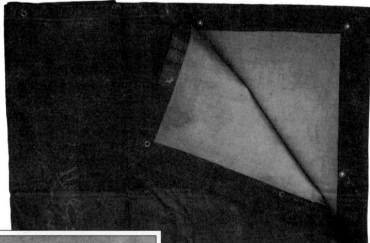

RUBBER BLANKET

The 45″ x 79″ blanket, fitted with brass grommets, was first issued to the infantry in November 1861.

PAINTED BLANKET, PVT. GRAHAM McKENNEDY, 149TH PENNSYLVANIA INFANTRY REGIMENT

McKennedy inscribed a curse against pilferers on his blanket: "May the dogs bite him as a thief." Painted blankets, supplied to make up for a shortage of gum blankets, could be worn as rain cloaks *(left)*.

RUBBERIZED PONCHO

First issued to mounted troops in November 1861, the poncho featured brass grommets and a buttoned slit.

MARINE CORPS EQUIPMENT

At the outset, enlisted Marines wore white buff leather crossbelts *(below)*, supporting the 1839 bayonet and a cartridge box for the 1842 musket. The cap pouch was carried in a white buff waist belt closed with a brass plate. Later most Marines relegated their crossbelts to full dress and wore the bayonet and the cartridge box on their belts *(above)*. Regulations specified fur-covered knapsacks, but most *(below, right)* were of painted canvas.

Navy and Marine Gear

The primary weapons of a warship were its big guns, but on occasion sailors had to repel boarders or fight on shore. Most warships keep small arms and gear tailored to naval requirements. Regulations provided for cutlasses, revolvers, and battle-axes, along with carbines or rifles.

Marines, whose duties included acting as guards, sharpshooters, and landing parties, were equipped and armed as infantrymen. Since the navy and the Marine Corps supplied their own accouterments, the items issued differed considerably from those of the army.

NAVAL MUSKET ACCOUTERMENTS

In 1862 the navy introduced a buff leather belt *(above)* with a japanned iron buckle for "captains of guns and boarders, small-arms men, and the crews of field howitzers." The navy musket cartridge box and cap box were embossed with a "U.S.N." cartouche.

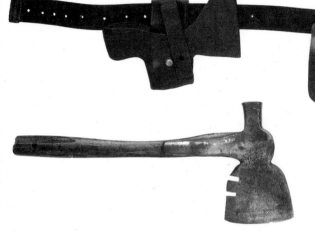

NAVAL REVOLVER ACCOUTERMENTS

The 1841 belt was of buff leather to withstand better salt-water exposure. Also issued were pistol frogs, bottomless scabbards for revolvers, and a battle-ax and carrier.

NAVY DOUBLE BLANKET

This oversize blanket washed ashore from the sunken U.S.S. *Cumberland* near Hampton Roads, Virginia.

Surrounded by companions, a veteran Michigan cavalryman sits astride his McClellan saddle. Military saddles had to be light enough to spare the horse on a long march yet sturdy enough to bear the weight of the rider as well as any clothing and equipment that would be strapped to it.

1859 McCLELLAN SADDLE

George B. McClellan's design featured an open seat covered with rawhide, wooden stirrups, a girth strap of wool yarn, and a thick harness-leather skirt. Basic accessories included saddlebags, a currycomb *(far left)*, a picket pin and lariat *(above)*, a nose bag, and a "thimble" to hold the rider's carbine muzzle. The 1859 dragoon saddle blanket is bordered in orange, the dragoon branch-of-service color.

**MODEL 1863 CAVALRY
BRIDLE AND CURB BIT**

**1847 GRIMSLEY OR
DRAGOON SADDLE**

This saddle was originally
issued to dragoons and
mounted riflemen. De-
spite its gradual replacement by the McClellan
and other saddles, the
Grimsley saw widespread
use during the War. In
service it was equipped
with a valise, carbine
boot, and black leather
saddle holsters, and was
fitted with a crupper
and breast straps, and a
blue woolen girth. The
small pouch contained
spare horseshoes.

OFFICER'S McCLELLAN SADDLE, LT. COL. ISAAC L. CLARKE, 95TH ILLINOIS INFANTRY REGIMENT

Clarke was shot from this saddle "bravely cheering his men" in their defense of Snodgrass Hill during the final stages of the Battle of Chickamauga on September 20, 1863. He died of the wound on September 22. Clarke's saddle was shipped to a friend, Lt. Col. Eugene B. Payne, who had served in Clarke's militia company, the Waukegan Zouaves. Payne commanded the 37th Illinois, part of the Army of the Gulf.

Staff officers L. C. Taylor *(left)* and Marcus Reno display regulation saddle-cloths or shabracks, blue with gold trim.

**1861 ARTILLERY
DRIVER'S SADDLE,
VALISE, AND BRIDLE**

Artillery drivers, who
rode the left, or off, horses
of the team, used well-padded
saddles that did not require a
blanket. Rings on the pommel
and cantle attached to the horses'
harness. The valise *(bottom)* was
carried on the right, or near,
horses, on a reduced version of
the driver's saddle. The artillery
bridle *(above)* features a brass-
faced iron bit issued in 1862.

PERSONAL EFFECTS

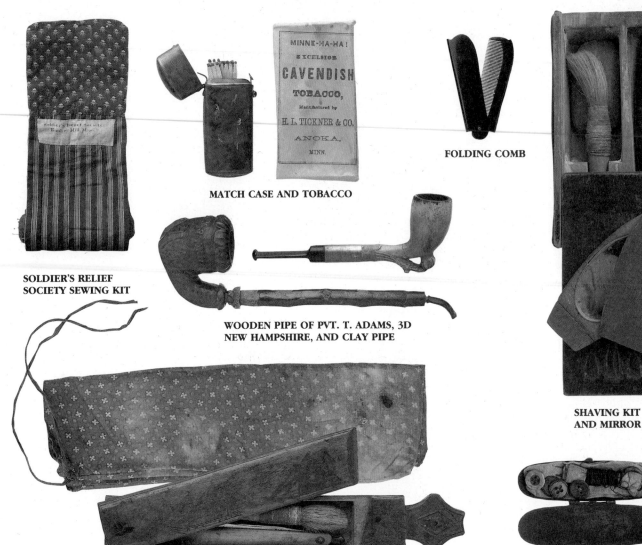

MATCH CASE AND TOBACCO

FOLDING COMB

SOLDIER'S RELIEF
SOCIETY SEWING KIT

WOODEN PIPE OF PVT. T. ADAMS, 3D
NEW HAMPSHIRE, AND CLAY PIPE

SHAVING KIT
AND MIRROR

NAVY SHAVING KIT AND BAG

"HOUSEWIFE," OR SEWING KIT

EARLY-WAR PATRIOTIC PLAY-
ING CARDS

BROOKS' PATENT TOILET AND WRITING KIT
PVT. G. W. GREEN, 1ST MASSACHUSETTS CAVALRY

PROPERTY STENCIL

BAG FOR STENCIL KIT

TOOTHBRUSH

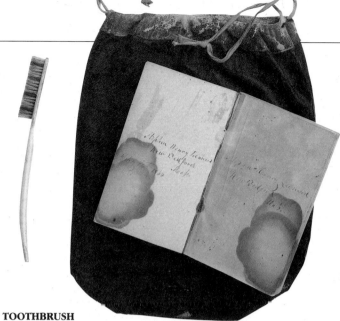

BAG AND DIARY

WALLET AND PERSONAL EFFECTS PVT. STEPHEN HENRY LEONARD 3D MASSACHUSETTS CAVALRY

Leonard died of wounds after the Battle of Winchester in 1864.

HANDKERCHIEF

STENCIL KIT, INK BOTTLE, AND BRUSH

SEWING KIT

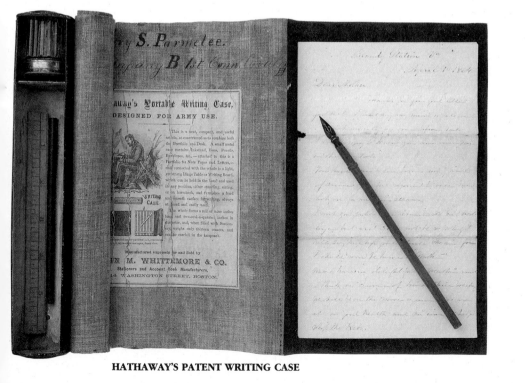

HATHAWAY'S PATENT WRITING CASE

FOLDING LANTERN

LIQUOR FLASK AND SILVER FOLDING CUP

MESS EQUIPMENT

ISSUE AND PRIVATELY PURCHASED TIN ARMY CUPS

Using their knapsacks as a table, two Ohio infantrymen display partially eaten pieces of army bread, or hardtack. Private Wilbur Fisk of the 2d Vermont called it "cast-iron biscuits" and recalled that on the march "hardtack suffered every indignity, and was positively unsuitable fodder for anything that claims to be human."

ARMY HARDTACK CRATE

ARMY-ISSUE MESS UTENSILS

PATENT KNIFE, FORK, AND
SPOON COMBINATIONS

CUP, AUSTIN STEARNS, 13TH MASS.

MESS CHEST, LT.
WILLIAM CAMAC, 1ST
TROOP, PHILADELPHIA
CITY CAVALRY

BARTHOLOMAE MESS SET, A. O. SHAW, 7TH NEW YORK

MEDICAL EQUIPMENT

ARMY DRUG CONTAINERS

These tinned iron containers were provided by government pharmaceutical plants in Philadelphia and New York. Quinine was a vital medication used in the prevention and treatment of malaria.

1863 SURGEON'S FIELD MEDICINE CASE

Dubbed a surgeon's field companion, this supply kit replaced the cumbersome medical knapsack for field use. It contained simple surgical instruments and medicines and was usually carried by a hospital orderly.

Caring for the Wounded

Despite some early confusion and occasional lapses, the U.S. Army Medical Department functioned smoothly and efficiently during four years of war. After 1863, a wounded soldier could expect to be removed from the battlefield to a field dressing station and then evacuated to a field hospital somewhere in the rear in a reasonable amount of time. Basic operations were performed at the dressing station, but less serious injuries were treated at the better-equipped hospital. Unfortunately, the best efforts of even the most skilled surgeon were confounded by a lack of knowledge of the causes of disease and infection. Thousands of soldiers survived wounds and amputation only to die of infections caused by unsterile instruments and unsanitary operating procedures.

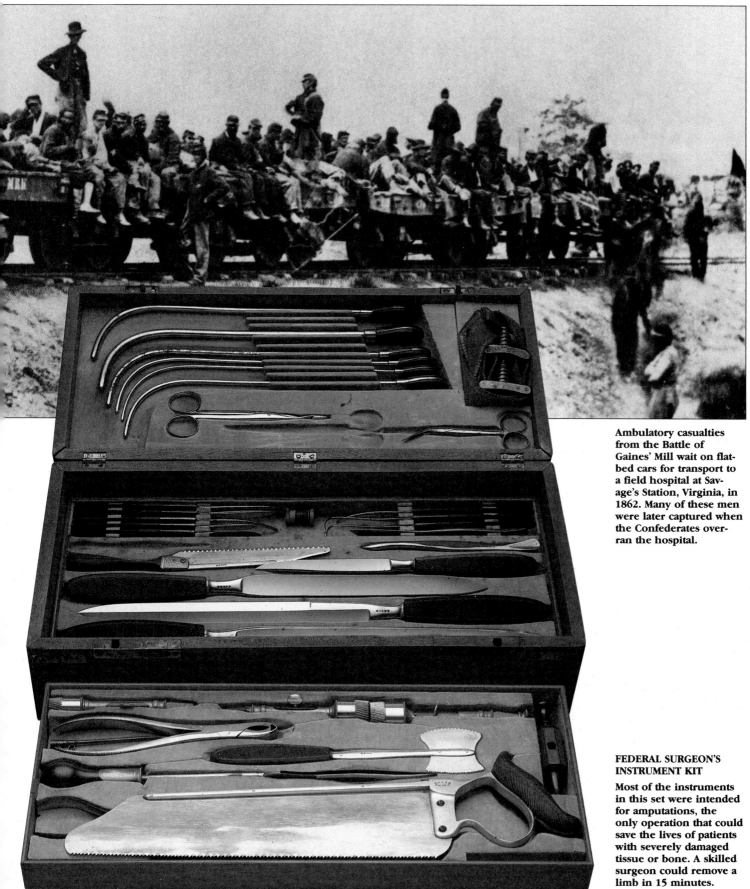

Ambulatory casualties from the Battle of Gaines' Mill wait on flat-bed cars for transport to a field hospital at Savage's Station, Virginia, in 1862. Many of these men were later captured when the Confederates overran the hospital.

FEDERAL SURGEON'S INSTRUMENT KIT

Most of the instruments in this set were intended for amputations, the only operation that could save the lives of patients with severely damaged tissue or bone. A skilled surgeon could remove a limb in 15 minutes.

MUSIC

By late afternoon on August 6, 1862, a throng of 10,000 patriots and passersby had gathered before the steps of the Capitol in Washington, D.C., to hear the U.S. Marine Band. The serenade, a rousing medley of national airs, kicked off an evening of speeches, fireworks, and mass sing-alongs designed to attract fresh recruits to the Union army.

Throughout the North, similar rallies were being held on village greens and town squares. Two days earlier, President Lincoln had issued another call to arms—this time for 300,000 militia to serve nine months. Because of the large number of casualties and the dispiriting string of Union defeats, enlistments were sharply down. To entice young volunteers, recruiters were staging jamborees, replete with refreshments, flag-waving orators, and, importantly, the spine-tingling strains of Yankee Doodle bands. Of one such gathering, U. H. Farr of the 17th Indiana recollected: "The fife was playing, the drums were beating, and the new soldiers fell into line. When I saw among them boys no larger than myself, I suddenly resolved to see if they would take me, and stepped into the ranks with the others."

The power of music to inspire enlistments was not limited to war rallies. Would-be captains and colonels—titles accorded almost anyone who could raise a company or a regiment of men—soon learned that attaching well-known brass musicians to their ranks attracted many volunteers. So keen was the competition among recruiters to sign on accomplished musicians that at least one officer agreed to pay his bandsmen double the standard military stipend, making up the difference himself.

Regimental brass bands were officially sanctioned in May 1861 by a War Department decree that permitted each infantry or artillery regiment one 24-man band; cavalry regiments were allowed 16-man ensembles. An inspection of Union military camps completed by the U.S. Sanitary Commission in October 1861 revealed that nearly 75 percent of all regiments had brass bands.

However, not all regiments had the good fortune or the resources to attract a professional band. Many cobbled together makeshift bands out of musically inclined volunteers—often with cacophonous effect. Infantryman Timothy Pendergast of the 2d Minnesota recalled the formation of his regiment's band: "A wagonload, more or less, of brass instruments, varying in size from a dinner horn to a cartwheel, arrived for our band, and peace fled. For the next two weeks the braying of the horns from one side of the camp would be answered by the braying of the mules from the other side. The poor mules no doubt thought another wagon train was parked over there."

Most brass bands, however, were revered by their regiments. In a letter home written in April 1862, a foot soldier with the 24th Massachusetts noted: "I don't know what we should have done without our band. Every night about sundown, Gilmore gives us a splendid concert, playing selections from the operas and some very pretty marches." In addition to providing nightly concerts when encamped, regimental bands performed at dress parades, guard mount, formal reviews, and funerals. Troops on the march were also serenaded by their bands, which, leading the way, tooted such contemporary favorites as "Hard Crackers, Come Again No More," and "The Girl I Left behind Me."

When not musically engaged, bandsmen served as medical assistants. At Gettysburg's Little Round Top, musicians of the 20th Maine aided surgeons in removing soldiers' shattered limbs. "Frequently the severed arms and legs reached level with the tables, in ghastly heaps," recalled one musician, "when a detail of men would dig long trenches and bury them. All this, too, taking place under the intense heat of a July sun!" Time permitting, musicians played light tunes in the hospital to cheer the wounded.

The few Yankee regiments that failed to muster a band were not entirely without music. Every regimental company was assigned "field musicians"—as a rule, fifers or drummers to infantry units, buglers to cavalry units. The daily cadences of camp life, from roll call to taps, were regulated by these musicians. Their drumrolls and bugle blasts orchestrated tactical movements on the battlefield as well, sounding as many as 67 distinct calls to guide their comrades.

When assembled into a drum corps—usually two field musicians from each of the 10 regimental companies, all under the direction of a drum major—the field musicians achieved a martial splendor seldom approached by brass bands. Wrote the historian of the 17th Maine: "As the first beams of the rising sun begin to tinge the eastern skies, the clear notes of the bugle sounding reveille from headquarters are heard—repeated in turn by the regimental buglers. The drums of one regiment commence their noisy rataplan, which is taken up by another, till every drum corps of the brigade, with accompanying bugles and fifes, joins in the din, and the morning air is resonant with the rattle of drums, the shrill notes of the fife, or the clarion tones of the bugle."

After 1862, many regiments had to rely entirely on their drum corps for daily music. Citing economic cause, the U.S. Adjutant General ordered all volunteer regimental brass ensembles disbanded as of July of 1862. General Order No. 91 was met with dismay by the rank and file. Alonzo Quint, regimental chaplain of the 2d Massachusetts, offered this opinion of the unpopular mandate: "Those who advocate this cannot have an idea of their value among soldiers. I see the effects of a good band continually. It scatters the dismal part of camp life; gives new spirit to the men. Could you see our men when, of an evening, our band comes out and plays its sweet, stirring music, you would say 'Let the men have their music.'"

A few clever colonels did manage to save their regiment's beloved bands by reenlisting the bandsmen as combatants and then detailing them to serve as musicians.

With the demise of regimental bands came the rise of brigade-level bands. General Order No. 91 provided for the formation of brass bands made up of 16 musicians drawn from two or more regiments. These brigade bandsmen were required to trade their horns for muskets when occasion demanded—though often enough, they were drafted to play right through the fray. General Philip Sheridan strongly believed in the effect of music on the fighting capability of his soldiers. Exempt from medical duties during battle, his musicians were led to the front instead. At the battle of Five Forks on March 31, 1865, General Horace Porter observed one of Sheridan's bands under heavy fire, "playing Nellie Bly as cheerily as if it were furnishing music for a country picnic."

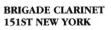

**BRIGADE CLARINET
151ST NEW YORK**

Band member
Enoch Pettit of
Company F, New
York Volunteers,
owned this box-
wood clarinet. The
larger, brigade-
level bands
boasted clarinets
among their in-
strumentation.

**B-FLAT CORNET
MAINE INFANTRY**

Described on his enlistment pa-
pers as blue-eyed and fair-haired,
the musician William Brown
played this cornet for the 7th
and 1st Maine before dying in
1865 of chronic diarrhea.

Saxhorns, cornets, and bass drum at the ready, the 2d Rhode Island Regimental Band spearheads a parade of Northern infantry assembling on a drill field at Camp Brightwood in Virginia.

CIRCULAR CORNET 16TH KENTUCKY

A July thunderstorm claimed the life of Adjutant Joe Dudley, player of this circular cornet for the 16th Kentucky Infantry Band. Dudley died in 1864 when his tent, pitched in a field in Fulton County, Georgia, was struck by a falling tree.

**BAND MEMBERS
11TH PENNSYLVANIA
CAVALRY**

The Zouave Band of the 114th Pennsylvania Infantry, shown here at Brandy Station, Virginia, in 1864, was often called upon to give evening serenades at army headquarters, where—according to the bandmaster—"a few candles in the open air afforded all the light we had in reading difficult manuscript."

E-FLAT ALTO SAXHORN, 28TH NEW YORK

An essential component of the well-balanced brass band, the alto saxhorn commonly numbered among the instruments of Federal bands. This over-the-shoulder alto belonged to 28th New York Volunteer Henry Buckley.

**FEDERAL 12-INCH CYMBALS
WITH LEATHER CARRYING CASE**

Cymbals added brilliance and
vibrancy to many Union bands,
which sounded them in
rhythm with the bass drum.

3D CALIFORNIA REGIMENTAL BAND

Union band members, such as the musicians of the 3d California Infantry ensemble pictured above, played an average of seven and a half hours a day when encamped. They typically earned between $17 and $45 per month, depending on rank.

FEDERAL BASS DRUM

On the march, the bass drum commonly brought up the band's rear, beating time for the footsore troops. The 24-inch-diameter drum was as heavy as it was unwieldy. To play it while under way, the drummer first secured the instrument to his neck with a harness, and then—no longer able to see his feet—pounded away with leather-covered wooden beaters.

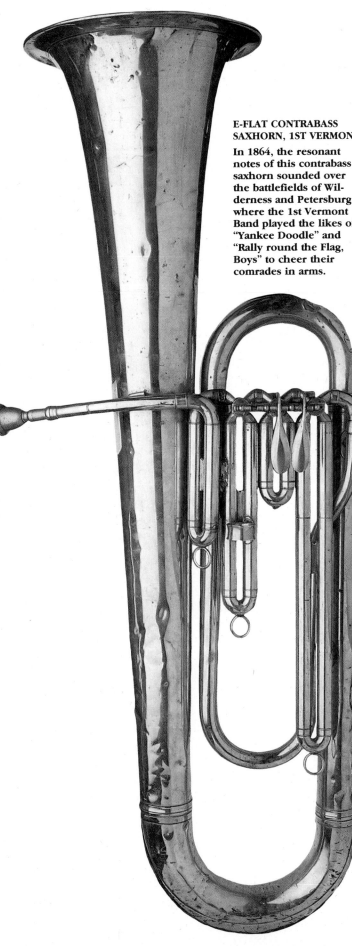

z

235

E-FLAT CONTRABASS SAXHORN, 1ST VERMONT

In 1864, the resonant notes of this contrabass saxhorn sounded over the battlefields of Wilderness and Petersburg, where the 1st Vermont Band played the likes of "Yankee Doodle" and "Rally round the Flag, Boys" to cheer their comrades in arms.

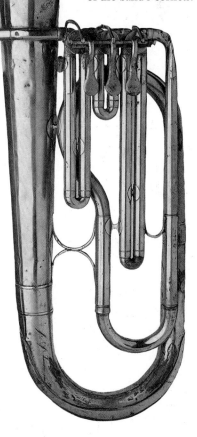

E-FLAT ALTO SAXHORN 1ST DIVISION, 2D CORPS

One of the premier instrument makers of the Civil War period, Isaac Fiske of Worcester, Massachusetts, fashioned this alto saxhorn out of German silver. Used by a musician in the Army of the Potomac, the instrument produced full-bodied tones that balanced the sweet timbre of the band's cornets.

FIELD MUSIC

INFANTRY FIELD MUSICIAN'S COAT

Federal musicians were uniformed identically to the other enlisted men of their corps, except for the addition of worsted lace about the jacket bibs. The color of the lace—here sky blue—was dictated by the color assigned to a particular corps.

FEDERAL DRUM MAJOR'S BATON WITH SILVER HEAD

93D NEW YORK INFANTRY DRUM CORPS

Company fifers and drummers of the 93d New York assume formation behind their drum major in preparation for a formal dress parade at Bealeton, Virginia, in 1863.

Impressively attired drum majors, like the unidentified Federal at left, directed the musical and physical responses of regimental drum corps with baton motions.

Fifers and drummers, such as the young Federals pictured here, were expected to master all 148 calls and tunes described in the Union field-music text, *The Drummers and Fifers Guide,* by the first day of enlistment. Any formal instruction—typically involving rote exercises—was provided by veteran musicians.

FEDERAL WOODEN FIFE WITH LEATHER CASE

**EAGLE DRUM
27TH MASSACHUSETTS**

This side drum once belonged to Union drummer Almon Laird, who was captured by Rebel troops in May 1864 at the Battle of Drewry's Bluff in Virginia. Among the oldest known field musicians, the 48-year-old Laird died in a Confederate prison in Savannah, Georgia.

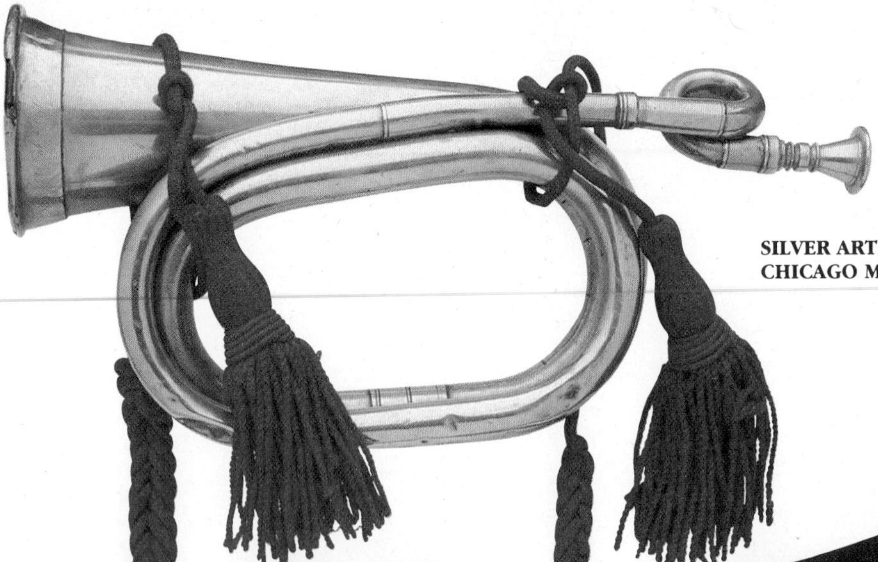

**SILVER ARTILLERY BUGLE
CHICAGO MERCANTILE BATTERY**

**FEDERAL MUSICIAN'S
CAVALRY JACKET**

**BUGLER'S JACKET
UNION HORSE
ARTILLERY**

Phil Kearny's Little Bugler

Gustave Schurmann was barely 11 when he volunteered as a drummer with the 40th New York. Within a year he was selected to be General Philip Kearny's orderly for a day; Kearny presented the boy with a silver bugle *(above)* and a large mare, and challenged him to a gambol over the countryside. When Gus—his legs barely straddling his mount—followed Kearny's charger over a ravine, the general was so impressed he named the young musician his permanent orderly. "From that day until his death, I was always with him," wrote Schurmann. Kearny was killed at Chantilly, Virginia, in 1862.

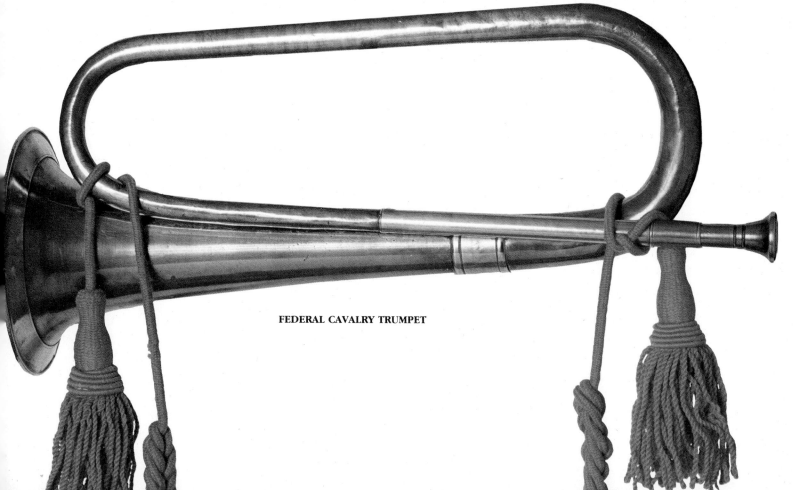

FEDERAL CAVALRY TRUMPET

FLAGS

On the morning of January 29, 1861, Secretary of the Treasury John A. Dix hurried from his temporary quarters in the White House to the Treasury Department. Trouble was brewing down South. Three days earlier, Louisiana had become the sixth state to secede from the Union. And now Dix had learned that the captain of the U.S. cutter *Robert McClelland,* based in New Orleans, was refusing to obey his orders to turn over command of the vessel to the Federal government. In the heat of the moment, Dix, a staunch Unionist, penned a telegraph message to his agent in New Orleans ordering the arrest of the *McClelland*'s commander and closing, "If anyone attempts to haul down the American flag, shoot him on the spot."

Dix's impassioned dispatch never reached his agent. The telegraph operator in New Orleans, true to his Southern blood, refused to deliver the incendiary note. Louisiana state troops seized the *McClelland* and replaced the Stars and Stripes atop its mast with the tricolored Revenue Service flag of the newly formed Confederacy. Despite the loss of ship and flag, Dix's exhortation, published in the Northern press, became a rallying cry for the Union. The American flag, ever a revered symbol of the United States, was henceforth endowed with a near-sacred significance.

About 10 weeks later came the event that would further consecrate the Stars and Stripes in Northern hearts. On April 12, Confederate batteries at Charleston, South Carolina, opened fire on Fort Sumter, whose American flag flew high above the ramparts.

The news of Fort Sumter electrified the North. Robert Stiles, a young Southerner studying law at Columbia University who would soon cast his lot with the Confederacy, later recalled the uproar in New York City: "A wild enthusiasm for 'the flag' seized and swept the entire population, which surged through streets hung with banners and bunting, their own persons bedecked with small United States flags and other patriotic devices." Also in that city, an irate mob of loyalists stormed the offices of the pro-Southern New York *Herald* and, on threat of burning everything in sight, forced publisher James Gordon Bennett to display the Stars and Stripes. In Boston, two weeks after the bombardment of Fort Sumter, the orator and statesman Edward Everett captured the intensity of the flag fever sweeping the Northern states when he observed that the flag, "always honored," was now "worshiped."

Throughout the North, patriotic seamstresses fashioned bunting, silks, cottons—whatever was available—into United States flags. Some of these were strictly for proud public display, but many were made for presentation to the military units hastily forming throughout the Union. In Manitowoc, Wisconsin, on the shore of Lake Michigan, the women of the town prepared a flag for presentation to their local militia, the Manitowoc Guards, later Company A of the 5th Wisconsin. Mrs. G. B. Collins presented the new colors to the company on June 21, 1861, with the request that it serve them nobly: "You go, bearing with you this flag—the gift of willing hearts. In the smoke and din of battle stand by it, because it is the Stars and Stripes—the flag our fathers fought under."

The flag made in Manitowoc followed the general design of the Stars and Stripes, but in its canton was a gold eagle, surrounded by an oval of 34 stars. Like many such flags presented to military units in 1861, indeed throughout the War, it bore the personal stamp of its makers and did not comply with military specifications.

According to the 1861 revision of the U.S. Army regulations, infantry units were to carry two silk flags, each nearly six feet square: a national flag and a regimental flag. The national colors, the Stars and Stripes, were to have "13 horizontal stripes of equal breadth, alternately red and white, beginning with red. In the upper quarter, next the staff, is the Union, composed of a number of white stars, equal to the number of States, on a blue field, one-third the length of the flag, extending to the lower edge of the fourth red stripe from the top."

Applied to the 20-by-40-foot garrison flag or the 10-by-20-foot storm flag, these instructions resulted in a nearly square canton, or Union. Translated to smaller colors, however, the same rules produced a narrow rectangular canton. Some flag makers followed the awkward proportions; others ignored that part of the regulations.

No pattern was set for the stars. Although the practice of arranging them in rows had predominated in the navy and, to a lesser degree, in the army prior to the War, the design was not obligatory. Flag makers chose the star layout that best suited their needs.

Regulations called for embroidered white stars, and embroidered regimental designations on the center stripe of the national flag. The embroidery was to be in silver on infantry flags and in gold on artillery flags. Since the beginning of the 19th century, however, the army had been unable to find suitable embroiderers, and quartermasters consistently substituted silver and gold paint for the embroidered inscriptions and stars. Because it tended to tarnish, silver paint was abandoned in 1861 in favor of gold. Many local sewing circles and some commercial makers, however, did produce flags with embroidered or appliquéd white stars.

Regimental colors, a military unit's second flag, came in two basic patterns. Artillery units carried a yellow flag with two gold crossed cannons in its center. Infantry flags were dark blue and bore the coat of arms of the United States in the center. In both cases, a red scroll beneath the central device displayed the unit designation. Both artillery and infantry flags were fringed in yellow silk.

The patriotic groups that made flags for the departing volunteers in 1861 did their best to comply with these nebulous regulations, but the results were mixed. Likewise, many professional flag makers and mercantile houses dealing in military or other fancy goods tended to manufacture presentation colors according to their own interpretation of the regulations. These companies were scattered across the North and Midwest; and because they tended to serve a specific area, flags took on a regional look. The most important of these firms was Tiffany & Company of New York City, whose costly embroidered presentation colors surpassed all others and lifted the company from regional prominence to national celebrity.

Most of the volunteers who flocked to the Union cause in 1861 and early 1862 joined military units that were state sponsored. While the national government in Washington did expand the Regular Army and attempted to raise a number of units that transcended state boundaries, for the most part it relied upon the loyal states to provide troops in accordance with requested quotas. Until early 1862, the states were responsible not only for recruiting these regiments but also for supplying them, flags included.

A welter of colorful and creative patterns resulted. Some states furnished flags that conformed to U.S. Army regulations while others stuck to state motifs. Some combined the two. Pennsylvania, for instance, added the state's coat of arms to the Stars and Stripes. New Jersey followed suit, but offered the second flag, the regimental colors, in a pattern that followed federal regulations.

Connecticut also provided a pair of colors

for its regiments. The national flag bore both the stars and an eagle in its canton; the regimental flag was blue, and featured an eagle surmounting the combined coats of arms of the state and the nation.

Beginning in early 1862, the Federal government began assuming complete responsibility for supplying all units raised by the states for Union service. Before the War, the army's flags had been made at the U.S. Army clothing depot in Philadelphia, the Schuylkill Arsenal. Here cloth for flags was acquired, stored, cut, and then distributed to subcontractors for completion. For the two decades prior to the War, the Schuylkill Arsenal had relied solely on the Philadelphia craftsman Samuel Brewer to assemble and decorate the flags needed for the U.S. Army, and he had performed well. The influx of state volunteer units, however, overburdened Brewer and the arsenal, and so the U.S. Quartermaster's Department established additional depots at New York and Cincinnati.

Each of the depots adopted its own pattern, and the three varied significantly. National colors commissioned by the New York depot had square cantons with gold stars arranged in five horizontal rows. In contrast, Philadelphia depot national flags retained the narrow rectangular canton prescribed by regulations. The gold stars on these colors were arranged in two concentric rings, always with one star in each corner of the canton and usually with one star also in the center of the rings. The national colors supplied by the Cincinnati depot also incorporated the rectangular canton, but like the New York depot flags, their stars were arranged in rows.

The regimental flags supplied by the depots generally followed the pattern established in Philadelphia before the War. But there were slight variations involving the red scroll that bore the unit name on each flag.

Once the colors were issued, a regiment's commanding officer was responsible for inscribing the appropriate designation. The contractors to these three depots accounted for nearly 2,400 national flags and 2,350 regimental flags during the War—the bulk of the colors issued to the Union army.

By the winter of 1861-62, Union troops had begun marking their national and regimental flags with the names of battles in which they had fought. This practice, dating back to the 1830s in the Regular Army, was officially sanctioned by the War Department on February 22, 1862. A regiment's flag—especially when emblazoned with battle honors—was its most important symbol. But the colors also had a practical purpose: The rank and file aligned on them when in motion in battle or drill, and they also served as a rallying point for a unit that became disorganized, either in attack or in retreat.

Because a regimental flag was often the only trace of a unit visible in the smoke-choked field of battle, it drew an inordinate amount of enemy fire. Accordingly, casualties were thickest closest to the colors. To compensate for the expected losses, the color guard of a Union regiment—those responsible for keeping the flag aloft—was relatively large, consisting of from six to nine men, depending on the tactics manual employed by the unit commander.

The color guard of a cavalry regiment was significantly smaller, usually only a standard-bearer followed by a single corporal. Instead of the pair of flags borne by most infantry regiments, cavalry color guards carried only the regimental standard. This flag was similar to, but smaller than, the infantry regimental flag specified by regulations: approximately two and a quarter by two and a half feet.

In the saddle, at a walk or a gallop, each mounted company of the Army—whether dragoons, mounted rifles, cavalry, or light artillery—aligned its ranks on a swallow-tailed flag called a guidon. Initially these flags were divided into two horizontal bars, red over white. In January of 1862, however, the design was changed. Two flag-making firms from Philadelphia, Horstmann Brothers and Evans & Hassall, were given the unissued surplus of red-and-white guidons and commissioned to alter them to comply with the new regulations. They added stripes and a canton filled with concentric rings of stars, a design that echoed the pattern of the national colors produced by the Philadelphia depot. The design served as the model for 10,200 guidons supplied by the major depots throughout the War.

The order that changed the design of the guidons also affected the design of the camp colors. These small (18 by 18 inches) flags marked the borders of a military camp and at times were carried into combat to help with troop alignment. Originally, they were white for infantry and red for artillery, and bore the unit designation on one side. After January of 1862, however, camp colors were imprinted with the design of the Stars and Stripes, generally with the pattern of the national flag adopted by the New York depot.

Other functional flags evolved in the Union army during the course of the War that were not governed by Army regulations. These included hospital flags and guidons, which marked the way to ambulances and field hospitals. More widespread were the so-called designating flags, which identified the headquarters of the upper echelons—corps, divisions, and brigades—of a particular army. A system devised by General McClellan for the Army of the Potomac in 1862 used combinations of red flags, white flags, and blue flags, or flags divided into bars of those colors, to distinguish various higher headquarters. With numbers added, they identified the regiments of each brigade.

McClellan's elaborate system proved too confusing, and in 1863 the Army of the Potomac adopted a method that identified commands by the shape of the flag. A swallow-tailed flag marked a corps headquarters, a rectangular flag a division headquarters, and a triangular flag a brigade headquarters. Individual divisions were further differentiated by the use of the distinctive badges that had been adopted for enlisted men's uniforms earlier in 1863. A red badge on a white field distinguished the first division of a corps, a white badge on a blue field the second, and a blue badge on a white field the third. These color patterns were repeated on the flags of the brigades of each division.

Other Union armies experimented with their own distinguishing systems in 1862 and 1863, with varying degrees of success. Gradually, however, the highly practical model of the Army of the Potomac became the standard for armies in the East. The system was transported to the Western armies in late 1863, when the 11th and 12th Army Corps were sent to reinforce Grant at Chattanooga.

Unlike their Confederate counterparts, who were forced to surrender or destroy their flags, or secretly bear them home, the men of the Union army retired their colors in glory at the end of the conflict. In the victory parades through Washington in May of 1865, units marched with their worn and tattered colors or the replacements they had recently received. With the mustering out of the great volunteer armies during the summer of 1865, the War Department permitted the return of the unit flags to the states in which the regiments had originated. A number of states held formal ceremonies depositing the flags in their capitol buildings, where for many years to come their ripped and soiled folds were cared for by veterans who had risked their lives to defend the colors and all that they represented.

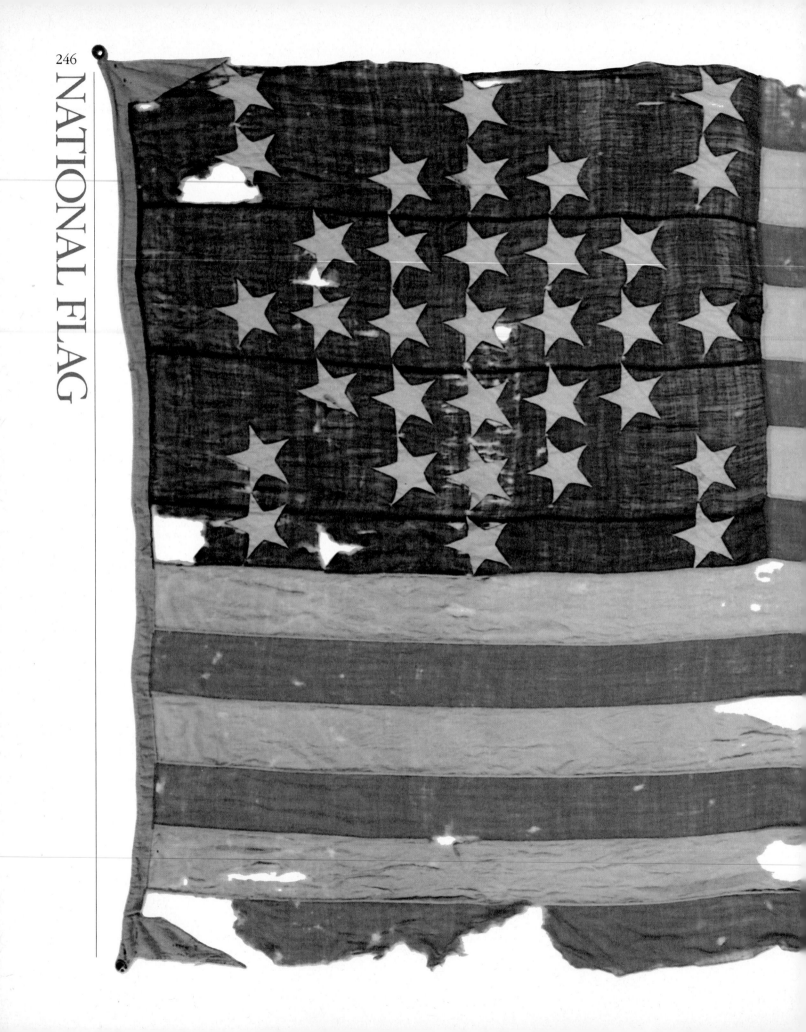

FORT SUMTER STARS AND STRIPES

This United States storm flag flew over Fort Sumter throughout most of the Confederate bombardment. After surrendering, Union Maj. Robert Anderson took the shot-torn banner with him, little suspecting that four years later he would return and once more raise that very flag over the fort.

2D MASSACHUSETTS INFANTRY REGIMENT

Presented to the 2d Massachusetts by a committee of Boston women on June 26, 1861, the national flag above was carried in all but one of the battles fought by the regiment. The regiment's color sergeant *(right)* holds the tattered flag on the steps of the Atlanta courthouse in 1864.

COLORBEARER OF THE 2D MASSACHUSETTS INFANTRY

20TH NEW YORK STATE MILITIA

The state coat of arms adorns this distinctive yellow regimental banner, presented to the unit on October 11, 1861, in Kingston, New York. It was carried in the Second Battle of Bull Run, where six standard-bearers were among the 279 casualties suffered by the regiment.

Special Colors for Volunteers

In the patriotic fervor that swept the North after the firing on Fort Sumter, many of the military units forming throughout the loyal states were given one or more special colors by the women of their community or by a local civic organization. Made in sewing circles or by the mothers, sisters, wives, and sweethearts of the new volunteers, the home-fashioned flags were usually presented in formal ceremonies just before the regiments departed the state. Impassioned speeches extolling the soldiers' sacrifice and inciting them to glorious deeds in defense of flag and Union accompanied the transfer of the treasured banners.

Later in the War, some regiments were given exceedingly fancy presentation flags, but these valuable colors were rarely carried into battle.

15TH KENTUCKY INFANTRY REGIMENT

At Perryville in October 1862, after Rebel fire broke the staff of this flag, Capt. James B. Forman rigged the fallen colors to a fence rail and held the shot-riddled folds aloft. The homemade flag was lettered by Hugh Wilkins of Louisville.

23D NEW JERSEY INFANTRY REGIMENT

Presentation flags were often embellished with mottoes and nicknames —such as this national flag donated in 1862 to the 23d regiment of New Jersey Volunteers, also known as the Yahoos. The unit was one of the nine-month regiments formed in September of 1862 in response to Lincoln's call for troops.

6TH CALIFORNIA INFANTRY REGIMENT

This regimental flag retains its bright colors because it was left safely behind in San Francisco while several companies of the unit fought Indians in northwest California and Nevada in 1864.

31ST PENNSYLVANIA INFANTRY REGIMENT

Later renumbered the 82d Infantry, the 31st Pennsylvania received the regimental colors shown here on October 23, 1861, at its Washington, D.C., camp. Donated by a group of Philadelphia friends, the flag bears the state coat of arms on one side (above) and the national arms on the other.

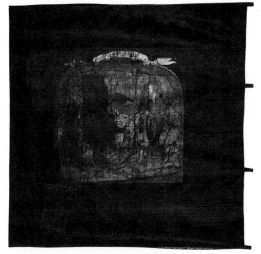

2D WISCONSIN INFANTRY REGIMENT

The Wisconsin coat of arms adorns the regimental flag above, which was made by the women of Madison and presented to the unit on August 2, 1861. The other side bears the U.S. coat of arms.

1ST KENTUCKY INFANTRY REGIMENT

An embroidered eagle graces the regimental colors made by John Shilleto of Cincinnati. Renumbered the 3d Kentucky not long after it was organized in October 1861, the regiment suffered 133 killed and wounded at the Battle of Stones River.

Tokens of Appreciation

Throughout the War, friends and benefactors of many regiments purchased special colors for presentation to the units. Well-heeled patrons of regiments from the Middle Atlantic and New England states often commissioned finely embroidered or painted flags from Paton & Company or Tiffany & Company of New York City. Horstmann Brothers and Evans & Hassall of Philadelphia and Sisco Brothers of Baltimore also provided presentation colors. Benefactors in the Midwest often turned to Baldwin's Fancy Bazaar of Indianapolis or John Shilleto of Cincinnati. Many of the late-War commercial presentation flags were given as tokens of appreciation to volunteer regiments when they reenlisted.

21ST MASSACHUSETTS INFANTRY REGIMENT

At Fredericksburg on December 13, 1862, this national flag—which was probably made by a Boston firm—was stained with the blood of its colorbearer, Thomas Plunkett *(right)*. A direct hit by a Rebel shell cost Plunkett one of his arms and part of the other.

COLOR SGT. THOMAS PLUNKETT

6TH MICHIGAN INFANTRY REGIMENT

The citizens of Kalamazoo commissioned this flag from Horstmann Brothers and presented it to the regiment in late 1861 or early 1862. The battle honors, added in 1863, signify the unit's service in Louisiana, where it was one of the first regiments to occupy New Orleans on May 2, 1862.

18TH MICHIGAN INFANTRY REGIMENT

Commissioned by a benefactor named Henry Waldron, the elegant national flag above was made by Tiffany & Company. The flag was dispatched to the 18th Michigan while it was in Toledo, en route south, in early September 1862. Two of its 34 embroidered stars were torn off in battle.

104TH NEW YORK INFANTRY REGIMENT

Tiffany & Company produced this silk regimental flag embroidered with the shields from the New York and United States coats of arms. The wife of Gen. James S. Wadsworth donated the colors to the unit on May 22, 1862.

2D MINNESOTA INFANTRY REGIMENT

Presented to the regiment after it helped win the Battle of Mill Springs, Kentucky, the colors above feature the light blue canton typical of its maker, Hugh Wilkins of Louisville. Its once-silver stars have tarnished to black.

Late-War Presentation Flags

51ST NEW YORK INFANTRY REGIMENT

This distinctive regimental flag was presented to the 51st New York by the city of New York, probably when the unit was in Manhattan on furlough in March and April of 1864. The banner features the coat of arms of New York State on one side *(right)* and the coat of arms of New York City on the reverse. During the siege of Petersburg, the regiment lost 21 killed and 73 wounded.

52D NEW YORK INFANTRY REGIMENT

Presented to the 52d New York—also known as the German Rangers—in 1863, this regimental banner honors the unit's service during the bloody battles of the Peninsular campaign, as well as at Antietam and Fredericksburg. A personification of Liberty astride an eagle adorns the flag, which was crafted by a New York embroiderer, Franceskca Klein.

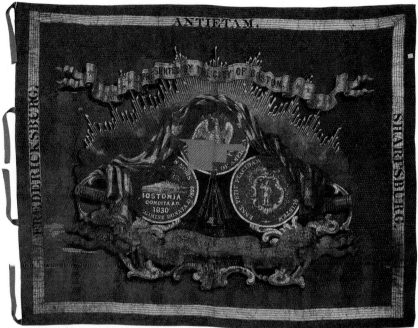

30TH MASSACHUSETTS INFANTRY REGIMENT

An eagle graces the canton of the national colors given to the 30th Massachusetts on May 3, 1864. The battle honors had been painted on before the presentation; the other honors were added later. At Cedar Creek, Virginia, the regiment lost 108 men.

28TH MASSACHUSETTS INFANTRY REGIMENT

The fourth Irish flag to be carried by the regiment during the War, this banner was presented to Col. Richard Byrnes by the city of Boston on May 5, 1864, one month before he was mortally wounded at Cold Harbor. The coats of arms of the United States, the commonwealth of Massachusetts, and the city of Boston adorn the colors. The honors of Sharpsburg and Antietam refer to the same action.

51ST PENNSYLVANIA INFANTRY REGIMENT

Replete with 11 battle honors, the colors above were presented to the 51st Pennsylvania on March 10, 1864. Just two months later, at Spotsylvania Courthouse, the flag, its bearer, and eight other members of the regiment were captured single-handedly by Pvt. Leonidas H. Deane of the 12th Virginia Infantry.

31ST PENNSYLVANIA INFANTRY (2D RESERVES)

Carried into battle at the Wilderness and Spotsylvania, this national flag was donated to the regiment on March 16, 1864, by the Cooper Shop Volunteer Refreshment Saloon, a civilian organization that provided food and drink to the troops.

Colorbearer John Thomas DeFevers of the 27th Kentucky Infantry poses with the national colors of his regiment. DeFevers saved the flag from capture by the Rebels during the siege of Knoxville on September 27, 1863, by tying it around two fence rails and swimming with it across the Tennessee River.

Furnished by the States

To furnish colors to the units raised within their borders, the states turned to local flag makers whenever possible. Massachusetts, for example, ordered its national and regimental flags from Charles O. Eaton of Boston. Because commercial flag makers were scarce in neighboring New Hampshire and Vermont, those two states turned to Eaton for some of the flags they supplied. The western states generally bought flags from local and regional makers. The state governments were erratic in providing flags, however. The only states that consistently issued colors to their regiments throughout the War were Pennsylvania and Massachusetts.

13TH KENTUCKY INFANTRY REGIMENT

Typical of the first regimental colors ordered by Kentucky, the flag at right features the state coat of arms in place of the national emblem specified by U.S. regulations. The flag, made by Hugh Wilkins of Louisville, was delivered to the regiment in February 1862 and carried in the Battle of Shiloh.

8TH WISCONSIN INFANTRY REGIMENT

Known as the Eagle Regiment because it carried a live American eagle perched on a staff beside the colors, the 8th Wisconsin received the national flag at far left in October 1861. It was made by Gilbert Hubbard of Chicago.

15TH WISCONSIN INFANTRY REGIMENT

The Wisconsin state motto, "Forward," surmounts the U.S. coat of arms on this regimental flag made by Gilbert Hubbard. Nicknamed the Scandinavian Regiment, the unit was composed mostly of Norwegian men from the upper Midwest who gathered in Madison to form the regiment.

3D CONNECTICUT INFANTRY REGIMENT

An eagle perches atop the combined shields of Connecticut and the United States on the flag at left, which is typical of the regimental colors furnished by the state. Mustered in April 1861 for three months' service, the 3d Connecticut fought under this banner at First Bull Run.

9TH CONNECTICUT INFANTRY REGIMENT

Received by the regiment in October of 1861, the Stars and Stripes at right is representative of the national colors purchased by Connecticut for its volunteer units during 1861 and 1862. The battle honor was added sometime after the regiment helped drive back the Rebel attack at Baton Rouge on August 5, 1862.

Colors from Pennsylvania and Massachusetts

61ST PENNSYLVANIA INFANTRY REGIMENT

Color Sergeant Joseph Fisher was awarded the Medal of Honor for advancing with this state flag through Confederate lines at Petersburg on April 2, 1865. Badly wounded, he carried the flag until he collapsed from loss of blood.

28TH PENNSYLVANIA INFANTRY REGIMENT

Made by Evans & Hassall, this flag was given to the regiment on May 23, 1865. The governor of the state had ordered the flag four months earlier after receiving a letter from Col. John Flynn, commander of the 28th. Flynn requested a replacement for the "shattered and battle-torn remains" of the "old pet" they had carried throughout the War.

SGT. REUBEN W. SCHELL

7TH PENNSYLVANIA INFANTRY RESERVES

While tending the state flag above, all the men of the regiment's color guard were either killed or severely wounded during the bloody engagement at White Oak Swamp in Virginia on June 30, 1862. After the battle, a private named Reuben W. Schell *(left)* was promoted to corporal and awarded the honor of carrying the colors. Later promoted to sergeant, Schell bore the colors at Antietam, where eight bullets riddled the banner but left him unharmed.

19TH MASSACHUSETTS INFANTRY REGIMENT

A bit smaller than U.S. regulation flags, these colors were issued to the regiment in March of 1864. The banner, carried at the Wilderness and Spotsylvania, was captured at Petersburg just three months after it was issued.

27TH MASSACHUSETTS INFANTRY REGIMENT

While campaigning on the coast of North Carolina in 1863, the regiment had the lower stripes of its national flag inscribed with the names and dates of four battles. The upper honors on the banner, which was purchased from Eaton by Massachusetts in September of 1861, were probably added earlier, after the regiment had helped capture New Bern, North Carolina, on March 14, 1862.

20TH MASSACHUSETTS INFANTRY REGIMENT

Issued to the 20th Massachusetts in October of 1862, this fancy state flag—made by Charles O. Eaton of Boston—was preserved by the regiment and was probably never used in the field. The hard-fighting unit lost 163 dead and wounded at Fredericksburg.

32D MASSACHUSETTS INFANTRY REGIMENT

Fighting under this flag at Petersburg on June 18, 1864, the 32d Massachusetts lost 103 killed or wounded out of 190 men. The regiment received the colors in early 1862.

33D MASSACHUSETTS INFANTRY REGIMENT

Typical of Massachusetts state colors, this flag, issued to the regiment in 1865, has a pine tree on one side *(above)* and the Indian-adorned state seal on the other.

Late-War State Issues

2D WISCONSIN INFANTRY REGIMENT

In August of 1863, the 2d Wisconsin received a new brace of silk colors: a national flag *(below, right)* and a state regimental flag on a new pattern *(below)*, both made by Gilbert Hubbard of Chicago. After fighting under the colors at the Wilderness and Spotsylvania, the unit was so reduced by casualties that it was assigned to provost-guard duty for the rest of its term.

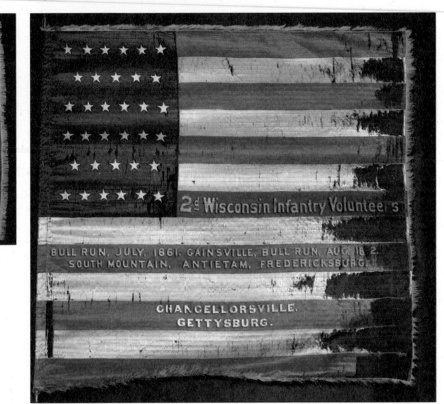

1ST DELAWARE INFANTRY REGIMENT

Fighting under the regimental colors *(above)* at Antietam on September 17, 1862, the 1st Delaware lost nearly one-third of its men, including the entire color guard. The flag was so damaged by the fierce combat that it was never again carried into battle. At right, a succeeding color guard of the veteran regiment proudly displays the war-torn relic.

5TH MINNESOTA INFANTRY REGIMENT

Made by Horstmann Brothers of Philadelphia, this silk regimental flag is painted with the Minnesota coat of arms. In December of 1864, the 5th Minnesota Infantry fought at the Battle of Nashville and lost 107 men.

14TH WEST VIRGINIA INFANTRY REGIMENT

The state coat of arms of West Virginia adorns this flag carried by the 14th Infantry. The unit sustained significant losses in hard fighting at the Battle of Cloyd's Mountain in West Virginia in May 1864 and at Carter's Farm in Virginia that July.

1ST MICHIGAN INFANTRY REGIMENT

The Michigan coat of arms appears on the colors carried by the 1st Michigan. In a letter written August 8, 1864, during the Petersburg campaign, the unit's commanding officer, Lt. Col. William A. Throop, praised his stalwart troops: "Long and fatiguing marches, severe and continued fighting, and all the vicissitudes of the campaign, have failed to dishearten the men."

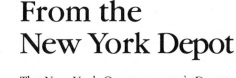

From the New York Depot

The New York Quartermaster's Depot was the first of the Federal army depots during the Civil War to commission independent contractors to manufacture national and regimental colors. The Philadelphia and Cincinnati depots followed this practice *(see pages 262-265)*.

For regimental colors, the contractors used a basic pre-War pattern. The central device was a large eagle beneath a double arc of stars. The eagle hovered above a scroll that was inscribed simply with *regiment* and *infantry,* leaving a blank space for the regimental number. National colors delivered by contract to the depots conformed to army regulations. However, the New York depot made the cantons square, whereas Philadelphia and Cincinnati maintained the rectangular shape.

22D WISCONSIN INFANTRY REGIMENT

In March of 1863, the 22d Wisconsin was ambushed by Gen. Nathan Bedford Forrest and his cavalry at Tompkinsville, Kentucky. Of the regiment's 363 men, 213 were killed, wounded, or captured. After the Confederates paroled the captives, the regiment received this 34-star national flag.

UNKNOWN U.S. REGULARS INFANTRY REGIMENT

A U.S. Regulars regiment lost this flag to Sgt. John F. Lovins of Company B, 3d Confederate Infantry, at Stones River. Hundreds of men from this brigade were killed or wounded near ground that by the end of the first day had been dubbed Hell's Half Acre.

2D U.S. REGULARS INFANTRY REGIMENT

The ornate 1848 colors at right served as the prototype for regimental flags commissioned by the New York depot during the War. For efficiency, however, many of the finer details found on this flag were eliminated.

His regimental colors billowing beside his tent, Col. James McMahon of the 164th New York enjoys a game of chess in the company of his visiting family.

104TH NEW YORK INFANTRY REGIMENT

The 104th New York was issued this replacement flag after losing its colors at the Battle of Weldon Railroad in Virginia in August of 1864. Weldon Railroad is included among the regiment's battle honors despite its having lost its flag there.

18TH NEW YORK INFANTRY REGIMENT

From the excellent condition of this regimental flag, it is obvious that it was never carried in combat. The banner was issued at the time of the regiment's mustering out in May of 1863.

123D INDIANA INFANTRY REGIMENT

The regiment's 35-star national flag reflects the whim of contractor William Scheible, who varied the usual horizontal arrangement of stars in the canton by placing them in five vertical rows instead.

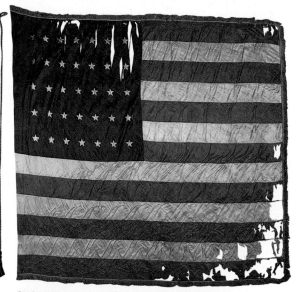

57TH PENNSYLVANIA INFANTRY REGIMENT

The flag maker Alexander Brandon was commissioned by the New York depot to manufacture this 35-star national banner. His name is imprinted on the flag's sleeve.

Philadelphia Depot Colors

36TH WISCONSIN INFANTRY REGIMENT

The regiment's 35-star national flag was manufactured by Evans & Hassall in 1864. It fell into the hands of the 44th North Carolina at the Battle of Reams' Station, Virginia, in August of that year.

3D WISCONSIN INFANTRY REGIMENT

The 3d Wisconsin was one of the few regiments to acquire colors that had been manufactured by Samuel Brewer, the sole pre-War flag contractor to the Philadelphia Quartermaster's Depot.

68TH PENNSYLVANIA INFANTRY REGIMENT

This unmarked national flag follows the 34-star pattern established by Horstmann Brothers and Evans & Hassall. They departed from custom by arranging the stars in a double oval pattern.

U.S. TREASURY GUARDS FLAG

A tear in the fly edge of this flag indicates where John Wilkes Booth's spur caught the banner when he leapt from Lincoln's box in Ford's Theatre after shooting the president.

81ST PENNSYLVANIA INFANTRY REGIMENT

A Horstmann Brothers creation, this regimental flag was carried from late 1863 through November 1864 and accompanied the unit through the carnage at Spotsylvania, where it was badly damaged.

7TH REGIMENT, U.S. QUARTERMASTER FORCES

William Scheible, who produced this 35-star national flag, varied the usual pattern by omitting the center star in the oval arrangement and adding a star to the outer ring.

84TH PENNSYLVANIA INFANTRY REGIMENT

Manufactured by Horstmann Brothers, the 84th's flag lacked the scrollwork of pre-War flags. It was inscribed with the unit's name by an artist commissioned by the regiment's commander.

76TH PENNSYLVANIA INFANTRY REGIMENT

The 76th Pennsylvania's regimental colors were manufactured by Evans & Hassall of Philadelphia, who followed the Horstmann Brothers pattern but inverted the curve of the scroll.

Cincinnati Depot Contract Flags

**1ST INFANTRY
REGIMENT
U.S. QUARTERMASTER
FORCES**

This national flag boasts
the honors the regi-
ment garnered for help-
ing in the defense of
Johnsonville and Nash-
ville in November and
December of 1864.

**1ST INFANTRY
REGIMENT
U.S. QUARTERMASTER
FORCES**

The 1st was composed
of civilians organized
to defend the quarter-
master's depots in the
Nashville garrison. Its
regimental colors were
manufactured by the
contractor John Shilleto
of Cincinnati.

18TH OHIO INFANTRY REGIMENT

The solitary battle honor on the regimental colors below, typical of those manufactured by Longly & Brother, provides a grim reminder of the carnage the regiment experienced at Stones River.

93D OHIO INFANTRY REGIMENT

This national flag, like the one at far left, was made by John Shilleto of Cincinnati, who left a space for a star in the lower right corner of the canton in anticipation of the Union's admitting a 35th state.

67TH INDIANA INFANTRY REGIMENT

Sergeant Charles Riley of Company I poses with his regiment's national colors. An Indiana regimental flag usually bore the unit name on the red stripe below the canton.

39TH KENTUCKY INFANTRY REGIMENT

This Longly & Brother flag was typical of those issued to Kentucky regiments late in the War. The 39th hailed from the Big Sandy Valley region of the state.

111TH OHIO INFANTRY REGIMENT

Less stylized than the eagles rendered by other flag contractors, this one fashioned by John Shilleto looks as if it might take wing should the heat of battle become too intense.

Heavy Artillery Flags

Heavy artillery regiments defended forts and garrisons with arsenals of big guns that were cumbersome to move. The companies of light artillery regiments maintained smaller, more mobile guns and were usually attached to infantry commands in the field.

The flags that artillery units carried predominantly featured the colors of gold and red. The stars and lettering on national colors were applied with gold thread or paint. Regimental colors were adorned with gold crossed cannons with a red scroll curling above and beneath. Since light artillery rarely operated as full regiments in the field, few regimental colors were issued in that service. Rather, light artillery companies flew guidons or specially designed flags.

3D U.S. HEAVY ARTILLERY

The regimental flag contracted by the New York depot displays a design change made around 1862 in flags from that source. The angle of the crossed cannons became narrower, and both the cannons and the scrolls took up more of the field. In other artillery colors, space for the cannons and scrolls was confined more to the center, as in the 3d Pennsylvania's flag on the facing page.

5TH REGIMENT, U.S. HEAVY ARTILLERY, "C"

The silk regimental colors at right were presented by the black citizens of Natchez, Mississippi, to a regiment that was known variously as the 9th Regiment, Louisiana Volunteers, a.d.; 1st Regiment, Mississippi Heavy Artillery, a.d.; and, finally, 5th Regiment, U.S. Heavy Artillery, "C." The *a.d.* stood for "African descent"; the *C* for "colored."

COMPANY OF THE 1ST MAINE HEAVY ARTILLERY

The 18th Maine Infantry became the 1st Maine Heavy Artillery after being trained to operate cannon while garrisoned at Washington, D.C. Here, a detachment of the 1st Maine drills at Fort Sumner, Maryland, during winter 1863. Many heavy artillery regiments carried Stars and Stripes guidons like this one as flank markers.

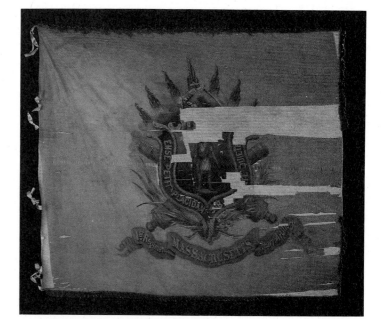

3D PENNSYLVANIA HEAVY ARTILLERY

A streamer bearing the Pennsylvania regiment's battle honors was attached to the staff of its regimental colors. Company I of the 3d Pennsylvania was present for Lee's surrender at Appomattox.

1ST MASSACHUSETTS HEAVY ARTILLERY

This flag bearing the state coat of arms of Massachusetts was made by the Boston contractor Charles O. Eaton and issued in 1863. At Sayler's Creek on April 6, 1865, it was torn by a 30-pound shell.

Light Artillery Flags

PENNSYLVANIA RINGGOLD LIGHT ARTILLERY

Three days after Lincoln issued his call to arms on April 15, 1861, Pennsylvania's Governor Andrew G. Curtin sent five companies to defend the nation's capital. Among them was the Ringgold Light Artillery, which bore this silk flag.

1ST KENTUCKY VETERAN INDEPENDENT LIGHT ARTILLERY

The flag at left was one of the last of those made by the contractor Hugh Wilkins for Kentucky troops. It was issued in 1864, when the battery was reorganized as a veteran unit under Capt. Daniel Glassie.

**BATTERY L
1ST U.S. ARTILLERY**

This unofficial pattern, with its laurel-wreath substitutions for the usual scrolls, proved popular with many artillery units. The flag here is made of scarlet silk and is trimmed in gold fringe. The crossed cannons, unit designation, and numerous battle honors are all embroidered in yellow thread.

**GUIDON BEARER, BATTERY H
1ST MICHIGAN LIGHT ARTILLERY**

SANDS' 11TH OHIO BATTERY

Battle honors on this early-War artillery guidon record the battery's presence at the siege of New Madrid and the capture of Island No. 10 in the Mississippi River in 1862. Capt. Frank C. Sands was the commander of the battery.

4TH BATTERY, MASSACHUSETTS LIGHT ARTILLERY

This national guidon was issued after the battery fought at Baton Rouge, Louisiana, where it helped the 9th Connecticut Infantry Regiment capture several enemy caissons filled with ammunition.

9TH BATTERY, MASSACHUSETTS LIGHT ARTILLERY

The topmost inscription on this 1864 guidon is the battle honor the 9th earned at Gettysburg for checking the advance of the 21st Mississippi. The battery's Capt. John Bigelow recalled Rebels "yelling like demons."

8TH NEW YORK CAVALRY REGIMENT

At Waynesboro, Virginia, on March 2, 1865, colorbearer John Kehoe was killed while carrying this standard, which had been given to the unit in May 1864. His replacement, Nathan Bowen, was killed just one month later at Five Forks.

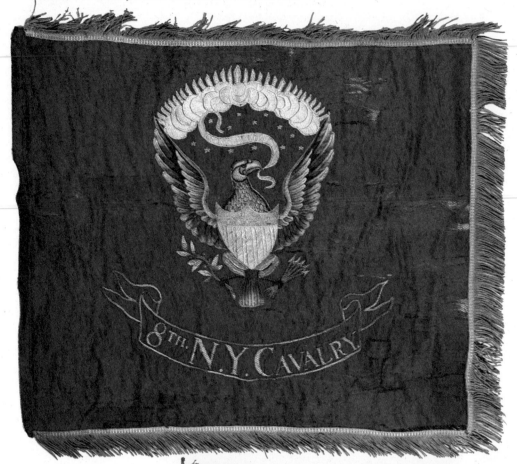

Regulation Cavalry Colors

The six-foot-square flag borne by the infantry would have been devilishly difficult to carry on a horse at a canter and impossible to manage at a gallop. Accordingly, cavalry regiments carried much smaller flags than foot units. Called standards, these compact colors measured roughly two feet by two and a half feet.

Federal regulations called for mounted regiments to carry only one silk standard. Like the infantry regimental colors, the cavalry standard featured the United States coat of arms on a blue field. Variations on the regulation flag were many, however, as different makers rendered the coat of arms in their own style. In addition to the regimental standard borne by a mounted unit, each company rode with its own guidon for identification. As with infantry units, cavalry regiments also carried a variety of nonregulation flags.

13TH NEW YORK CAVALRY REGIMENT

Storm clouds hover above the eagle on this standard borne by the 13th. Two companies of the unit served in the New York City draft riots of July 1863.

2D MINNESOTA CAVALRY REGIMENT

Two arcs of gold stars grace this presentation standard carried by the unit, which served in the Dakota Territory fighting the Sioux Indians.

2D U.S. CAVALRY REGIMENT

The regimental flag borne by the 2d is typical of the flags carried by the U.S. Cavalry before the War. It served as the basic model for regulation cavalry standards throughout the conflict.

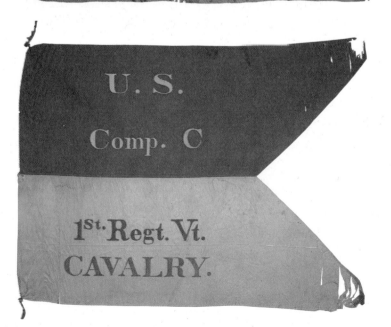

6TH PENNSYLVANIA CAVALRY REGIMENT

Carried by I Troop of the 6th Pennsylvania Cavalry, the silk guidon at left typifies the Stars and Stripes design called for by the regulations of January 1862. At Brandy Station, Virginia, on June 9, 1863, the tenacious 6th Pennsylvania fought and charged for more than 12 straight hours.

COMPANY A, "CALIFORNIA HUNDRED"
2D MASSACHUSETTS CAVALRY REGIMENT

A grizzly bear ornaments this silk guidon presented by the mayor of San Francisco to the company of California horsemen who fought with the 2d Massachusetts.

COMPANY C, 1ST VERMONT CAVALRY REGIMENT

This early-War regulation guidon was produced by the Philadelphia depot. At Gettysburg, the 1st fought with Elon Farnsworth's brigade, leading a gallant but disastrous charge against a large force of Rebel infantry. Farnsworth was killed, and the regiment sustained 65 losses.

Custom Flags for Mounted Units

20TH NEW YORK CAVALRY REGIMENT—"McCLELLAN CAVALRY"

The elaborately embroidered blue silk regimental standard above—which combines the shields from the New York State and the U.S. coats of arms—and the finely crafted national flag at left were both fashioned by Tiffany & Company of New York. Despite the fact that cavalry regiments were not authorized to carry a national flag, several units, the 20th New York Cavalry among them, were nonetheless presented with the Stars and Stripes by local patriotic groups.

1ST NEW YORK MOUNTED RIFLES

Columbia, the personification of America, decorates this regimental standard especially made for presentation to the 1st New York Mounted Rifles. The unit served primarily in North Carolina and southeastern Virginia.

2D MISSOURI CAVALRY REGIMENT—"MERRILL'S HORSE"

Under the command of Col. Lewis Merrill, the 2d Missouri Cavalry captured more than 400 prisoners while pursuing the Confederates at Little Rock in the summer of 1863. This Stars and Stripes carried by the regiment was made by Tiffany & Company.

The officers of the 16th Pennsylvania Cavalry Regiment pose at camp with their regimental standard—embellished with the state coat of arms—displayed behind them. A camp servant peeks from behind the tree at right in the photograph.

7TH PENNSYLVANIA CAVALRY REGIMENT

Made by Horstmann Brothers of Philadelphia, this state standard was likely carried by the 7th Cavalry on April 2, 1865, when the unit dismounted and joined the successful attack on the Rebel defenses of Selma, Alabama.

3D MASSACHUSETTS CAVALRY REGIMENT

On February 21, 1865, while the 3d Massachusetts Cavalry was in the field near Pleasant Valley, Maryland, it received this state standard inscribed with 13 battle honors. The flag was manufactured by Charles O. Eaton of Boston.

2D MASSACHUSETTS CAVALRY REGIMENT

The California coat of arms and a long list of battle honors grace this ornate standard. It was presented at the close of the War to the four companies of the so-called California Battalion, 2d Massachusetts Cavalry.

The 39th New York, with its contingent of Italian immigrants, called itself the Garibaldi Guard after Giuseppe Garibaldi, the great hero of Italian unification. The two officers of the 39th standing at center, Col. Frederic D'Utassy and Lt. Col. Alex Repetti, reaped no such glory; both ended their careers in the U.S. Army in disgrace.

15TH WISCONSIN INFANTRY REGIMENT

This national flag, presented to the Norwegian men of the midwestern regiment, bears a slogan that translates "For God and our land." It features a shield with the royal lion of Norway in the blue silk canton.

17TH WISCONSIN INFANTRY REGIMENT

Company B of the regiment was presented with this Irish flag before leaving the state in 1862 to campaign with Grant. Colonel John Doran described the reception that the unit got as it arrived on the battlefield of Corinth: "The regiment was greeted with as hearty a cheer as was ever raised for the sons of Erin."

Flags of Ethnic Regiments

Hundreds of thousands of volunteers who flocked to support the Union cause were first-generation Americans who had migrated to the United States in the 1840s and settled in the North. As an inducement to these immigrants to enlist, President Lincoln gave general's commissions to well-known European political expatriates and placed them in command of ethnic troops.

More than 200,000 Germans served in the Union armies, and scores of regiments had German majorities. The Irish alone constituted the majority of at least 20 Federal regiments. The 55th New York was manned entirely by French residents of New York City and bore the name La Garde Lafayette. The 79th New York, principally Scotsmen, wore kilts for full-dress ceremonies and tartan trousers in the field. The flags of the ethnic regiments, adorned with exotic symbols and foreign inscriptions, were as colorful as the accented speech of the rank and file.

69TH REGIMENT, NEW YORK STATE MILITIA

This Irish banner came to be known ironically as the Prince of Wales flag. The regiment became famous for refusing to take part in a parade for the Prince of Wales on October 11, 1860, when the prince was visiting the United States.

9TH CONNECTICUT INFANTRY REGIMENT

This regimental flag shows an eagle perched above the joined symbols of Ireland and the United States. The 9th's Capt. R. S. Davis acknowledged the regiment's Irish heritage by stating that Connecticut was "represented by the sons of the ever-green shamrock."

9TH MASSACHUSETTS INFANTRY REGIMENT

This presentation regimental flag was borne by the 9th Massachusetts at Gaines' Mill on June 27, 1862. Ten bearers of the unit's national colors were either killed or wounded that day; yet, as though charmed, the colorbearer of this Irish flag was never hit. A motto on the reverse reads: "As aliens and strangers thou didst us befriend. As sons and patriots we do thee defend."

**22D REGIMENT
U.S. COLORED TROOPS**

The black artist David Bowser painted the regimental colors for all 11 regiments of U.S. Colored Troops from Pennsylvania. Allegories about the liberation of the slaves were depicted on the obverse, as shown on the 22d's colors at right. The reverse was painted with the United States seal.

Banners for Black Regiments

After President Lincoln issued the Emancipation Proclamation in 1863, several Northern states organized regiments of black troops who carried flags that were either issued by state authorities or presented by benefactors. Beginning in 1864, when blacks volunteered in great numbers, they were mustered directly into the U.S. Army, rather than into state regiments. At its peak, the United States Colored Troops included well over a hundred regiments of infantry, cavalry, and heavy artillery, and several companies of light artillery.

Altogether, 178,892 blacks served in the Union army, and 32,369, or more than a sixth of their number, died in uniform—a slightly higher proportion than among their white comrades in arms. The Federal government awarded at least 21 black soldiers its newly created Medal of Honor.

26TH REGIMENT, U.S. COLORED TROOPS

Organized in February of 1864 at Rikers Island, the regiment was ordered to the Department of the South, where it remained through the War. Before leaving New York, the unit was presented with two embroidered flags *(above and right).*

After observing the 26th Regiment during the Federal advance on Johns and James islands outside Charleston, South Carolina, Maj. Gen. John G. Foster recanted his earlier misgivings about the military aptitude of black regiments: "I am now relieved of apprehension as to this class of troops, and believe with active service and drill, they can be made thorough soldiers."

54TH MASSACHUSETTS INFANTRY REGIMENT

After the bearer of this flag fell storming the ramparts of Fort Wagner in South Carolina, Pvt. Thomas Ampey took it up and continued the charge. At daybreak his body was found near that of this regiment's Col. Robert Gould Shaw. The colors had been captured.

54TH MASSACHUSETTS INFANTRY REGIMENT

For valiantly protecting this flag during the assault on Fort Wagner, Sgt. William Carney became the first black soldier to win the Medal of Honor. He was wounded while returning to his regiment.

5TH REGIMENT CORPS D'AFRIQUE

General Nathaniel Banks probably ordered national colors like this one from Boston for each of the units of the Corps d'Afrique, which he organized in New Orleans in 1863.

UNIDENTIFIED COLOR SERGEANT OF THE 108TH U.S. COLORED TROOPS

84TH INFANTRY REGIMENT, U.S. COLORED TROOPS

Organized in April of 1864 from the 12th Infantry, Corps d'Afrique, these troops served in the Department of the Gulf, as the battle honors on their national flag proudly attest.

278

13TH CONNECTICUT INFANTRY REGIMENT

Throughout most of the War, this regiment served in the Department of the Gulf as part of Gen. Cuvier Grover's 2d division. In August of 1864, the division became part of Sheridan's army in the Shenandoah Valley, and the 13th Connecticut went on to win battle honors for its performance at Port Hudson and Cedar Creek, among other citations adorning this handsomely embroidered regimental flag.

Colors by Tiffany

The prestigious New York City firm of Tiffany & Company, known by 1848 for its exquisite jewelry, turned its attention in 1861 to War-related products, including swords, medals, and flags. Colors embroidered by Tiffany & Company were among the most desirable and costly honors a regiment could receive. National colors by Tiffany were entirely embroidered. Regimental colors were usually embroidered with the state coat of arms or painted with allegorical scenes.

IRON BRIGADE

The intrepid Iron Brigade included the 2d, 6th, and 7th Wisconsin; the 19th Indiana; and the 24th Michigan infantry regiments. After the Battle of Gettysburg, and on the anniversary of Antietam, a group of citizens from the three states presented the brigade with this embroidered blue silk banner.

13TH INDIANA INFANTRY REGIMENT

The central device on this embroidered regimental flag combines the Indiana state seal and the shield of the United States. The battle honor on the bottom scroll attests to the regiment's valiant conduct at Rich Mountain, West Virginia, in July of 1861. It also distinguished itself at Winchester the following year.

63D NEW YORK INFANTRY REGIMENT

Framed by the regiment's colors, Gen. William Brady *(seated at right)* and his officers pose for this 1865 photograph. The 63d's history as part of the hallowed Irish Brigade is revealed in the long list of battle honors that crowd the field of the embroidered colors below. Irish symbols on the flag include a sunburst illuminating a harp and a cluster of shamrocks.

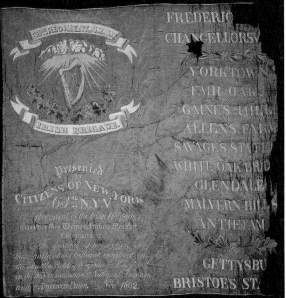

69TH NEW YORK INFANTRY REGIMENT

Temporarily without their flags, Capt. Thomas F. Meagher and his men maintained their unity at Fredericksburg on December 13, 1862, by wearing sprigs of green boxwood in their caps. This Irish flag reached the regiment two days later. In 1963, President John Kennedy gave the flag to the government of Ireland.

Tiffany-embroidered marker of the 69th New York Volunteers, captured by Kershaw's South Carolina Brigade at Fredericksburg.

A Record of Battle Honors

56TH MASSACHUSETTS INFANTRY REGIMENT

This national flag, issued to the regiment in 1865, was carried in the Grand Review, the parade of troops in Washington, D.C., at the end of the War. It bears the battle honor the regiment earned at the Wilderness, where the regiment's colonel was "shot dead through the jugular vein" while attempting to rally the men.

6TH WISCONSIN INFANTRY REGIMENT

This was the last national flag issued to the 6th Wisconsin, one of the famed Iron Brigade regiments, which distinguished itself on the battlefields of Antietam and Gettysburg.

37TH NEW YORK INFANTRY REGIMENT

Laden with the Irish symbols of harp and shamrock, this banner was presented to the regiment, the so-called Irish Rifles, by the city of New York in 1863. The men carried the flag in the Battle of Chancellorsville.

18TH U.S. INFANTRY REGIMENT, 1ST BATTALION

Among the many citations on this regimental flag is one for the Battle of Stones River, where 102 of the regiment's 603 men were killed.

18TH U.S. INFANTRY REGIMENT, 1ST BATTALION

This regiment's national flag was issued in 1864. In his report of the Atlanta campaign, the 1st's commander commended his color sergeants for valor.

50TH PENNSYLVANIA INFANTRY REGIMENT

Bearing a complete list of battle honors, the regimental colors below were issued to be carried in the Grand Review. An earlier flag had been badly damaged at Spotsylvania, where one colorbearer had been killed and two others wounded saving it from capture.

7TH KENTUCKY INFANTRY REGIMENT

This national flag was carried by veterans from the 7th, 19th, and 22d Kentucky regiments who joined in 1864 to form a new unit. It was named for the 7th Kentucky because that unit had contributed the most men.

DESIGNATING FLAGS

Army of the Potomac 1862-63

Colonel Alexander Hays and the men of the 63d Pennsylvania assemble with their 3d Regiment flag.

3D REGIMENT
1ST BRIGADE
1ST DIVISION

Using the national colors of red, white, and blue in patterns of vertical or horizontal bands, Gen. George McClellan devised an elaborate system of headquarters flags in 1862. On the flag above, the combination of red and white indicates the 1st Brigade, 1st Division. The number refers to the regiment.

11TH PENNSYLVANIA INFANTRY REGIMENT

Private William H. West carried this flag into battle at Second Bull Run. The banner's number and its pattern of blue, white, and blue bands designated the 11th Pennsylvania as the 4th Regiment, 3d Brigade, 2d Division. The Pennsylvanians were part of the III Army Corps of the Army of Virginia. General McClellan's overly complex designating system was abolished in early 1863.

3D DIVISION, VI ARMY CORPS

Below is the headquarters flag of Brig. Gen. J. B. Ricketts, who commanded the 3d Division of the VI Corps from April of 1864 through the end of the War. The rectangular shape of the flag indicates a division; blue was the color of the 3d Division. The Saint Andrew's Cross is the symbol of the VI Corps. Battle honors were rarely applied to headquarters flags, as is the case here.

XI ARMY CORPS HEADQUARTERS

After he replaced Ambrose Burnside as commander of the Army of the Potomac in 1863, Joseph Hooker adopted this style of headquarters flag as part of a new system of designating flags. He prescribed a blue swallow-tailed flag with a white cross botonée bearing the corps' number in red.

2D BRIGADE, 1ST DIVISION, XII CORPS

General Joseph Hooker adopted this triangular brigade flag. It bears the five-pointed star of the XII Corps and the red-on-white colors of the 1st Division. The blue stripe along the lance edge identifies the 2d Brigade. Three of this brigade's regiments were from Maryland; the fourth was from New York.

Army of the Potomac 1864-65

V CORPS HEADQUARTERS

Major General Gouverneur K. Warren stands with his staff and their swallow-tailed headquarters flag, which bears the Maltese cross *(inset)* of the V Corps. Headquarters flags were essential to messengers trying to locate commanders in the confusion of a battlefield. In August of 1864, the same month the Maltese cross was adopted by the V Corps, Warren's troops confounded the efforts of Maj. Gen. Henry Heth's Confederate brigades to retake the Weldon Railroad.

3D BRIGADE, 3D DIVISION, V CORPS

Colonel J. W. Hoffman adopted this flag while commanding the 3d Brigade, V Corps. After Gettysburg, the I Corps, decimated in the battle, merged with the V Corps. This flag reflects their joint insignia of central disk and Maltese cross, respectively.

MEADE'S HEADQUARTERS FLAG

In May of 1864, Gen. George Meade adopted this elaborate banner as the general headquarters flag for the Army of the Potomac. Its ornate design, with an eagle in a wreath of laurel leaves, prompted General Grant to exclaim, "What's this!—Is Imperial Caesar anywhere about here?"

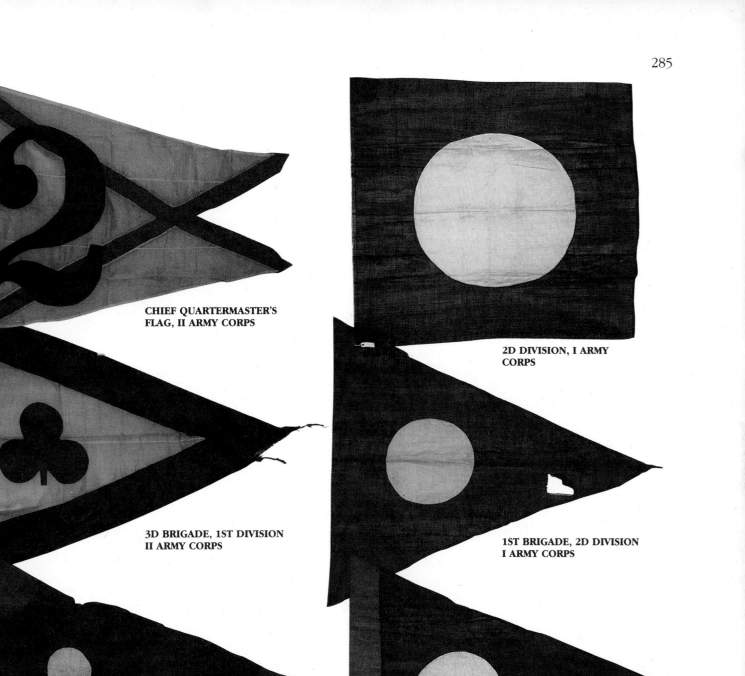

CHIEF QUARTERMASTER'S
FLAG, II ARMY CORPS

2D DIVISION, I ARMY
CORPS

3D BRIGADE, 1ST DIVISION
II ARMY CORPS

1ST BRIGADE, 2D DIVISION
I ARMY CORPS

4TH BRIGADE, 2D DIVISION
II ARMY CORPS

2D BRIGADE, 2D DIVISION
I ARMY CORPS

At Antietam, the II Corps suffered double the casualties of any other corps on the battlefield. In March of 1863, the trefoil, or three-leaf clover, was adopted as their corps badge and used on their flags. The men referred to the insignia as clubs for its resemblance to the playing-card suit. Upon rushing into battle they were said to cry out, "Clubs are trumps!"

The disk or "full moon" became the insignia of the I Corps troops in March of 1863. After they merged with the V Corps, they were allowed to continue using the I Corps emblem that by then defined them.

Eastern Armies 1864-65

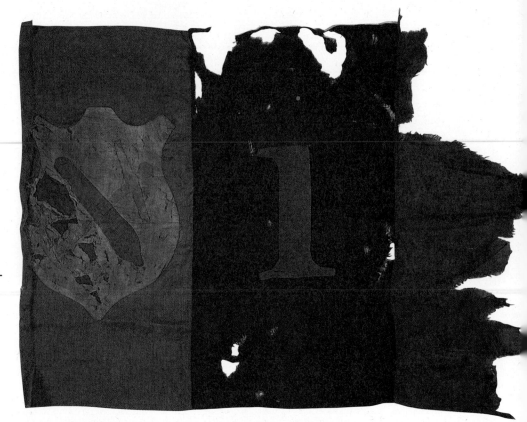

HEADQUARTERS FLAG 1ST BRIGADE, 4TH DIVISION, IX CORPS

This tattered banner, ripped by fire during the Battle of the Crater at Petersburg, bears witness to the devastating losses suffered by the black troops of Gen. Ambrose Burnside's independent command, who carried the flag. One Confederate recalled, "The whole floor of the trench was strewn with the dead bodies of Negroes."

2D DIVISION, IX CORPS

The IX Corps rejoined the Army of the Potomac in May of 1864 after having been part of Gen. Ambrose Burnside's independent command. The new flags received by the corps in November of 1864 displayed the corps badge, a crossed cannon and anchor overlaying a shield. The emblem was a reminder of the IX Corps' earlier amphibious duties along the Atlantic coast.

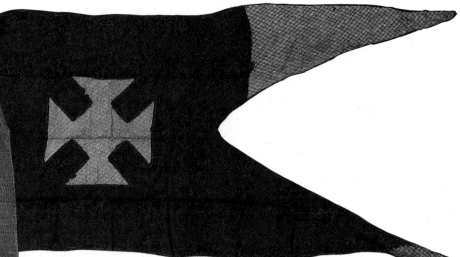

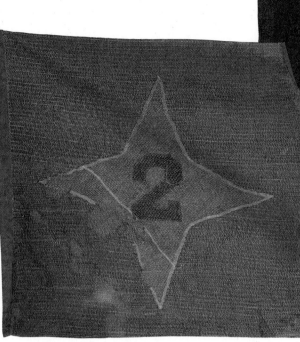

HEADQUARTERS FLAG, XIX CORPS

After November of 1864, this corps abandoned the square shape and four-pointed star device that distinguished the flags they had carried since February of 1863 and adopted a swallow-tailed banner that was confusingly similar to the headquarters flag of the Army of the Potomac's V Corps. Both corps displayed Maltese crosses, although the XIX Corps did not include its number on the cross.

2D DIVISION, XIX CORPS FLAG

His X Corps headquarters flag hanging behind him, Maj. Gen. Alfred Howe Terry sits surrounded by his devoted staff.

Colors of Cavalry Commands

ARMY OF THE POTOMAC, CAVALRY CORPS 3D DIVISION

Two crossed blue sabers, the symbol of the cavalry, decorate this rectangular division headquarters flag. The designating flags furnished to the cavalry corps of the Army of the Potomac were of the same shape, size, and color pattern as those of the infantry.

ARMY OF THE POTOMAC, CAVALRY CORPS 1ST DIVISION, 3D (RESERVE) BRIGADE

This regulation triangular flag identified a brigade headquarters. The crossed sabers in the center served as corps badges for all cavalry corps in the Union armies.

ARMY OF THE POTOMAC, HORSE ARTILLERY BRIGADE

The Horse Artillery Brigade adopted this blue-and-white designating flag adorned with red crossed cannons in October of 1864. At that time the brigade was composed of seven units: six regular army batteries and the 6th New York Independent Battery.

MILITARY DIVISION OF THE MISSISSIPPI CAVALRY CORPS, 4TH DIVISION, 2D BRIGADE

In a system adopted in November 1864, a red-and-white forked flag designated the 1st Brigade, and a red-and-blue flag the 2d *(below)*. All the flags bore a division number above and below crossed sabers.

PERSONAL GUIDON OF MAJ. GEN. GEORGE A. CUSTER

Like many cavalry leaders, Custer preferred to identify his command with a swallow-tailed flag rather than with the Army of the Potomac regulation flag. He carried this guidon of red-and-blue bunting into battle as he led the 3d Cavalry Division in the Shenandoah Valley in 1864 and 1865.

The distinctive yellow guidon flying over the mounted troops below identifies them as the 1st Brigade of Gen. William Averell's cavalry division. The scene depicts the brigade's victorious charge against Confederate earthworks outside Winchester, Virginia, in September of 1864.

Garrisoned in Washington, D.C., to be trained in the newly formed Signal Corps, these Pennsylvania volunteers pose with the flags of their service. Each signal officer in the Union army was issued a set of seven such flags in red, white, and black, each bearing a contrasting center square.

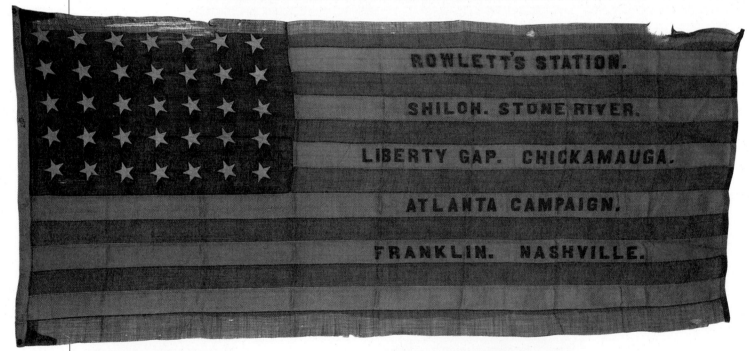

RECRUITING FLAG, 32D INDIANA INFANTRY REGIMENT

It was standard practice in the Union army that during slack periods in the fighting, an officer of the regiment would be detailed to go back to his state to recruit men to fill the depleted ranks. Recruiting banners usually were not inscribed with battle honors, although the familiar, glorious names on this flag may have served as an additional enticement to join up.

FISHER'S SIGNAL CORPS FLAG

As of March 1862, any Signal Corps officer who distinguished himself in battle was allowed to replace the center squares on his flags with stars on which he could list his battle honors, as did Lt. Benjamin F. Fisher on the flag at left.

20TH NEW YORK VETERAN CAVALRY

This marker, embroidered by Tiffany & Company, was carried by the regiment while it campaigned in North Carolina in the summer of 1864. The hospitable reception that the men received from the civilians there prompted Col. Newton B. Lord, the regimental commander, to remark, "There is a deep Union feeling among at least three-fifths of the people."

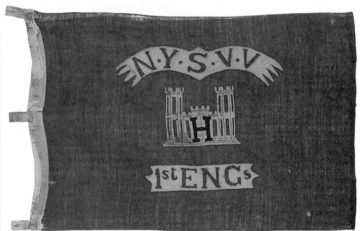

1ST REGIMENT, NEW YORK ENGINEERS

In 1864, this regiment reenlisted and was sent to serve with the Army of the James operating in the area around Petersburg and Richmond. At that time, Company H was issued this marker bearing the castle that symbolized the engineer branch of service.

A sergeant of the 23d Massachusetts holds a marker flag in the muzzle of his weapon.

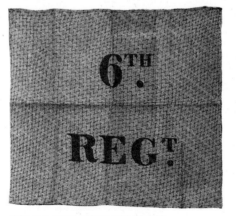

6TH U.S. INFANTRY REGIMENT

Camp flags were used to mark the limits of a camp. This one, of white bunting and 18 inches square, was probably first used during the Mexican War.

2D U.S. ARTILLERY REGIMENT

Artillery camp colors were of red bunting with white lettering. The paint would bleed through the fabric so that the designation read correctly on the obverse but backward on the reverse.

Hospital Flags

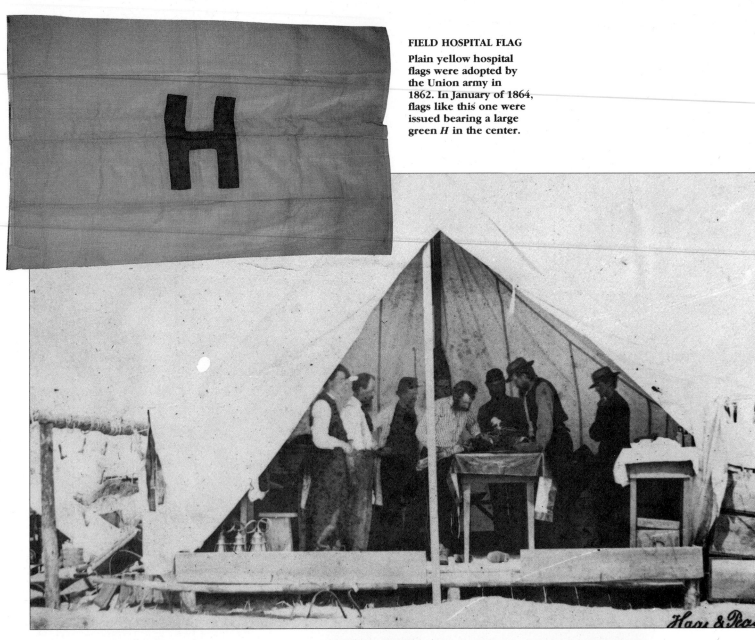

FIELD HOSPITAL FLAG
Plain yellow hospital flags were adopted by the Union army in 1862. In January of 1864, flags like this one were issued bearing a large green *H* in the center.

Surgeons in a Federal hospital tent operate on a soldier whose leg was injured in the siege of Charleston in 1863. In an era of primitive surgical techniques, the horrors of life for the wounded rivaled the terrors of the battlefield.

AMBULANCE GUIDON
These green-bordered, yellow banners marked the way for ambulances carrying the sick and wounded to hospitals. They were issued in the final year of the War.

Navy Flags

Flags flown by Union ships during the Civil War fell into several categories. A ship's large Stars and Stripes was called an ensign and was carried by every U.S. Navy ship. Depending on the occasion, it would be hoisted at different positions on the vessel. There were nine sizes of ensigns depending on the ship's class. Five sizes of boat flags patterned after the Stars and Stripes flew from the ships' launches. Secondary navy flags included commission pennants, jacks, signal flags, and designating flags.

34-STAR ENSIGN, U.S.S. MONITOR

This ensign was draped on the coffin of naval architect John Ericsson, designer of the ironclad *Monitor*, when he died in 1889. The *Monitor* battled the Confederate *Virginia* at Hampton Roads, Virginia, on March 9, 1862.

16-STAR BOAT FLAG, U.S.S. CUMBERLAND

The *Cumberland* was rammed and sunk by the *Virginia* at Hampton Roads in 1862. The *Virginia*'s chief engineer likened his ship's iron ram to "the stinger of a wasp."

13-STAR BOAT FLAG, U.S.S. VARUNA

On April 24, 1862, the *Varuna* took part in the attempt under Adm. David G. Farragut to capture New Orleans. The ship's career ended after it was rammed by the enemy.

The *Onandaga*'s national ensign waves from its bow as the ironclad lies at anchor in the James River in the summer of 1864.

The Banners
of Victory

118TH NEW YORK INFANTRY REGIMENT

At six feet six inches tall, Color Sgt. Joseph A. Hastings stands head and shoulders above his comrades. This photo was taken in Plattsburgh, New York, after the regiment was mustered out on June 13, 1865. After the War, Union regiments throughout the country began relinquishing their colors to their state repositories. The 118th turned its three flags over to the Bureau of Military Statistics in Albany. Two of the colors were badly war-torn; the other was new and listed all of the regiment's battle honors, including Richmond. The new flag *(above)* was ringed in black crepe in mourning for President Lincoln's assassination.

"There is one thing that our government does that suits me to a dot," wrote a Union soldier of modest schooling to his mother in 1863. "That is, we fight mostly with artillery. The rebels fight mostly with infantry. They fight as though a man's life was not worth one cent or in other words with desperation; or like General Lafeyet said to Washington, there is more dogs where them come from. Our Generals are careful of there men." However biased the soldier's observation, one thing was certain: From the beginning of the War, the Federal artillery was the Union army's most formidable asset. According to Colonel Charles Wainwright, chief of artillery of the I Corps, the same battle scene repeatedly played itself out: The Confederate infantry would press forward, against the Federal infantry, advancing steadily through pastures and woodlands; then the Federal cannon would maneuver into position and begin raining case shot and canister on the Rebel troops, breaking their charge. And so it went: Time and again, the Yankee artillery delivered Union forces from defeat at Shiloh, Malvern Hill, Fredericksburg, and other battles.

This ability was in part due to the North's industrial might. Northern soil claimed most of the nation's technicians and machine shops. "While the South had at the beginning of the War the better raw material for infantry and cavalry," said General Henry Hunt, chief of artillery for the Army of the Potomac, "the North had the best for artillery. A battery requires many mechanics with their tools and stores, and also what are called handy men. No country furnishes better men for the artillery proper than our Northern, and particularly our New England, states."

With the onset of the Civil War, the Union's foundries worked around the clock casting Northern metal into Federal cannon—chiefly 12-pounder smoothbore Napoleons and three-inch ordnance rifles, the backbone of the Yankee artillery. The three-inch ordnance rifles, wrought-iron pieces with flowing, graceful curves that eliminated stress points, combined reliability with deadly accuracy. "The Yankee three-inch rifle was a dead shot at any distance under a mile," recalled a Confederate gunner. "They could hit the end of a flour barrel more often than miss." Northern foundries produced more than a thousand ordnance rifles during the War. But for sheer killing power, the bronze 12-pounder howitzer, named the Napoleon for its patron, Napoleon III, led the field. These 4.62-inch smoothbores fired heavy projectiles and were the primary defensive and close-range artillery weapon in the Federal service.

Other contributions to the Union war effort included the Parrott guns manufactured at the West Point Foundry. These weapons were produced in 10- and 20-pounder field versions and in larger sizes for laying siege or defending forts. The big, cast-iron Parrotts, which fired 100- and 200-pound projectiles, were loathed by the men in the ranks for their tendency to explode when fired repeatedly. They were inexpensive, however, and were turned out in such numbers that one Yankee quipped that the parrot should replace the eagle as the national symbol.

A further boon to the army was the legacy of the small but well-trained U.S. Regular Army artillery. This elite corps became the nucleus of the new volunteer artillery, providing expert guidance in the art of gunnery and in battlefield tactics. The old-line artillerists proved invaluable in battle after battle. Brigadier General John Gibbon commanded the crack Iron Brigade during the

Battle of Antietam on September 17, 1862. Charged with spearheading the assault of Federal troops through the Cornfield that morning, Gibbon posted the six Napoleons of Battery B, 4th U.S. Artillery, on a nearby knoll to protect his right flank. It was not long before the exposed battery came under withering fire, and soon 40 of its 100 men had fallen to Confederate bullets. Gibbon watched as the battery's guns belched canister toward the Rebels rattling through the corn—but to no avail; the gunners had unwittingly aimed their muzzles too high and were overshooting the enemy. As Confederate troops charged the Federal battery, Gibbon jumped off his horse, ran to one of the guns, and adjusted the elevating screw to depress the muzzle. Then, at the general's order, the crew fired several rounds more, blasting away a section of the Cornfield fence—and with it the onrushing Confederates. Gibbon's aplomb probably saved Battery B from being overrun.

For all the skill and daring of such devoted artillerists, however, most Union commanders—initially at least—had little feel for the tactical use of artillery. Under George McClellan, artillery batteries in the Army of the Potomac were assigned to divisions, with each division relinquishing two batteries to form a corps reserve. Control of the guns was inconsistent. Some divisions retained direct management of the batteries while others surrendered control to the corps. In still other commands, authority to direct the artillery was divided. In battle, this jumble of authority often meant confused and countermanded orders. As a consequence, the artillery was not always well used.

In 1863, thanks largely to the perseverance and keen abilities of Chief of Artillery Henry Hunt, the artillery of the Army of the Potomac was reorganized and its command centralized. Artillery batteries were grouped into brigades and placed under the leadership of a corps chief of artillery. In addition, the Artillery Reserve, a body of 100 guns including the horse artillery and siege cannon, was reorganized into five artillery brigades. Under Hunt's able command, the Reserve could be dispatched piecemeal or collectively to reinforce flagging batteries.

Throughout the War, when Yankee artillery succeeded in massing in the right place at the right time, the effect was truly devastating. Such demolition happened first at Malvern Hill in 1862. At this, the last of the Seven Days' Battles, nearly the entire artillery arm of McClellan's retreating army—some 250 cannon—was poised on a bluff flanking the James River as Lee's pursuing Confederate forces attacked. "Our batteries," said James Cooper Miller of the 2d Delaware, "literally cut lanes through their ranks." Said the Confederate general D. H. Hill, "It was not war, it was murder."

Federal guns were massed again at Antietam and yet again to cover the assault on Fredericksburg. At the grim and bloody repulse of Pickett's charge at Gettysburg, as many as 180 Federal cannon were massed hub to hub on Cemetery Ridge. Never had the Union artillery been so effectively managed nor the Confederate ranks so irretrievably broken. In Tennessee, at the Battle of Stones River, Major John Mendenhall, chief of artillery in Major General Thomas L. Crittenden's corps, clustered 58 guns to break up a key Confederate attack on the battle's second day. At Nashville, in December 1864, converging Federal artillery fire unhinged the attack of General John Bell Hood.

Whether it was field artillery saving the day in battle or massive siege guns bombarding Charleston and Petersburg to rubble, the Federal artillery earned its place in military lore. According to D. H. Hill's assessment, it need have feared no enemy in the world.

FIELD ARTILLERY

**12-POUNDER NAPOLEON
1ST RHODE ISLAND ARTILLERY**

At Gettysburg on the afternoon of July 3, 1863, this 12-pounder Napoleon was damaged by an exploding shell that killed two of the gunners. When the survivors tried to load the piece, the round became stuck in the dented muzzle and could not be extracted. Named after Emperor Napoleon III of France who adopted it for use in his army, the Napoleon proved deadliest in wooded country where engagements occurred within its 1,680-yard range.

Firing a Civil War cannon was a team effort requiring all the precision of polished drill on a parade ground. Experienced gunners working together *(next page)* could load and fire a fieldpiece every 30 seconds—even when enemy fire was bursting about them. The teamwork involved in the process kindled a fierce sense of comradeship among the gunners and an unswerving loyalty to the gun.

Above all else, the artillerist was expected to protect his gun. As one veteran cannoneer put it: "The gun is the rallying point of the detachment, its point of honor. It is that to which men look, by which they stand, with and for which they fight, by and for which they fall. As long as the gun is theirs, they are unconquered; when the gun is lost, all is lost."

When the War started, bronze-barreled smoothbore cannon dominated the North's artillery. Most were guns firing 6-pound ammunition on a relatively low trajectory and howitzers capable of lofting 12-pound projectiles on an arcing trajectory. Soon, however, the Ordnance Department began producing more effective weapons—chiefly the highly accurate rifles—for the Union arsenal.

Rifles and Smoothbores

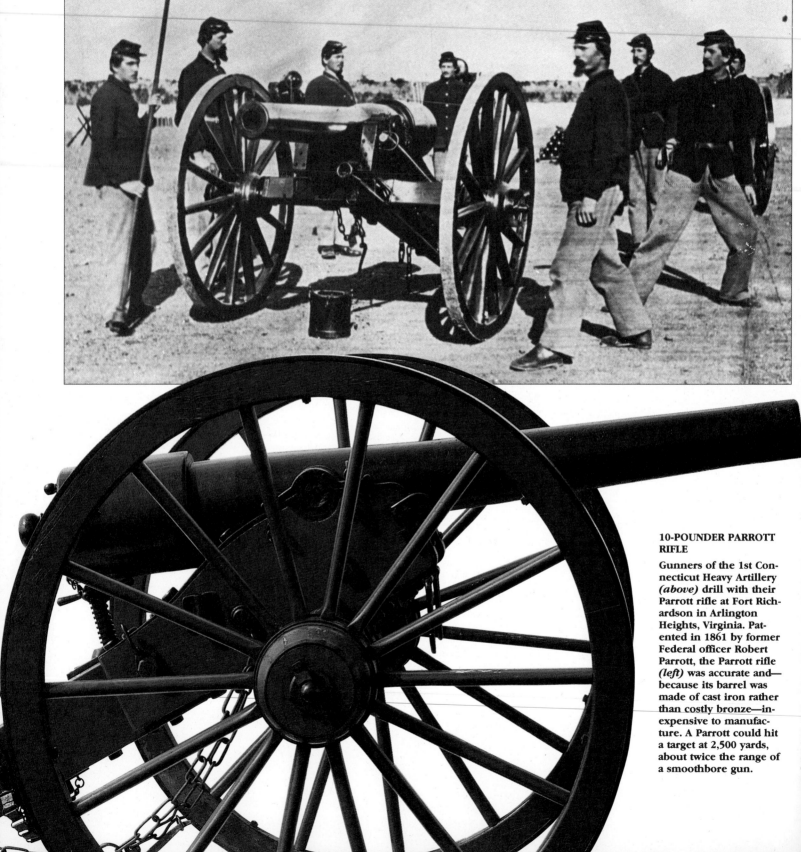

10-POUNDER PARROTT RIFLE

Gunners of the 1st Connecticut Heavy Artillery *(above)* drill with their Parrott rifle at Fort Richardson in Arlington Heights, Virginia. Patented in 1861 by former Federal officer Robert Parrott, the Parrott rifle *(left)* was accurate and—because its barrel was made of cast iron rather than costly bronze—inexpensive to manufacture. A Parrott could hit a target at 2,500 yards, about twice the range of a smoothbore gun.

MODEL 1841 6-POUNDER GUN

Used early in the War, the 6-pounder fired projectiles only 3.67 inches in diameter and was thought to lack sufficient power and range.

12-POUNDER HOWITZER

These smoothbore cannon could lob 12-pound projectiles along high, curved trajectories and over friendly forces into massed enemy or fortifications.

3-INCH ORDNANCE RIFLE

The 3-inch ordnance rifle was a highly accurate weapon, and since it was crafted of tough wrought iron, there was no need for breech reinforcement.

14-POUNDER JAMES RIFLE

General Charles T. James, a self-educated carpenter and mechanic, styled his bronze 14-pounder rifle on the sleek lines of iron ordnance rifles of his day.

The Tools of a Well-Drilled Team

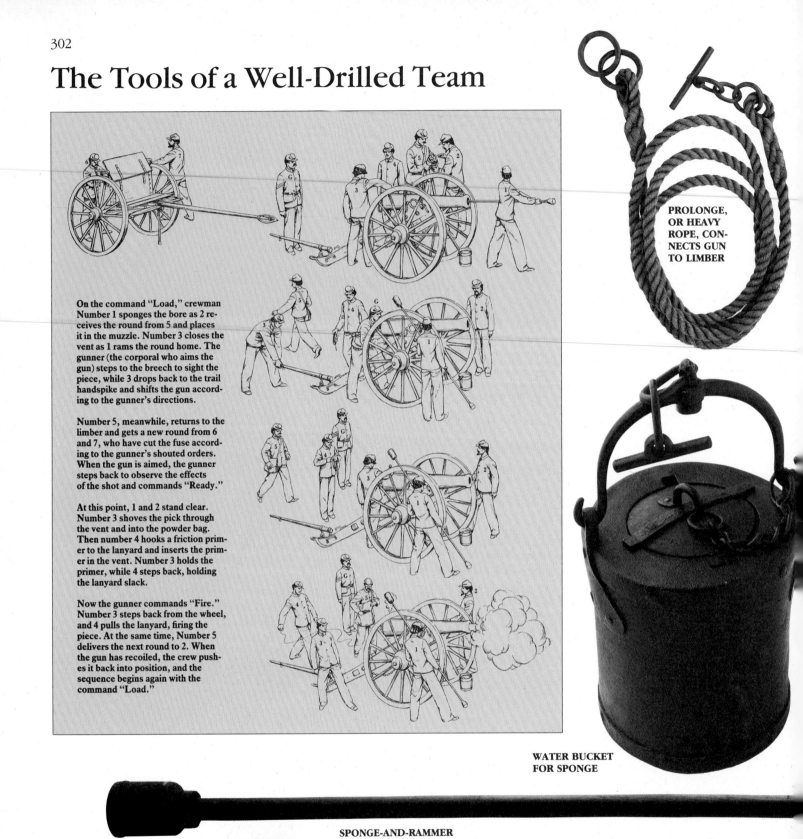

On the command "Load," crewman Number 1 sponges the bore as 2 receives the round from 5 and places it in the muzzle. Number 3 closes the vent as 1 rams the round home. The gunner (the corporal who aims the gun) steps to the breech to sight the piece, while 3 drops back to the trail handspike and shifts the gun according to the gunner's directions.

Number 5, meanwhile, returns to the limber and gets a new round from 6 and 7, who have cut the fuse according to the gunner's shouted orders. When the gun is aimed, the gunner steps back to observe the effects of the shot and commands "Ready."

At this point, 1 and 2 stand clear. Number 3 shoves the pick through the vent and into the powder bag. Then number 4 hooks a friction primer to the lanyard and inserts the primer in the vent. Number 3 holds the primer, while 4 steps back, holding the lanyard slack.

Now the gunner commands "Fire." Number 3 steps back from the wheel, and 4 pulls the lanyard, firing the piece. At the same time, Number 5 delivers the next round to 2. When the gun has recoiled, the crew pushes it back into position, and the sequence begins again with the command "Load."

PROLONGE, OR HEAVY ROPE, CONNECTS GUN TO LIMBER

WATER BUCKET FOR SPONGE

SPONGE-AND-RAMMER

WORM-AND-BRUSH FOR CLEANING BARREL

TRAIL HANDSPIKE

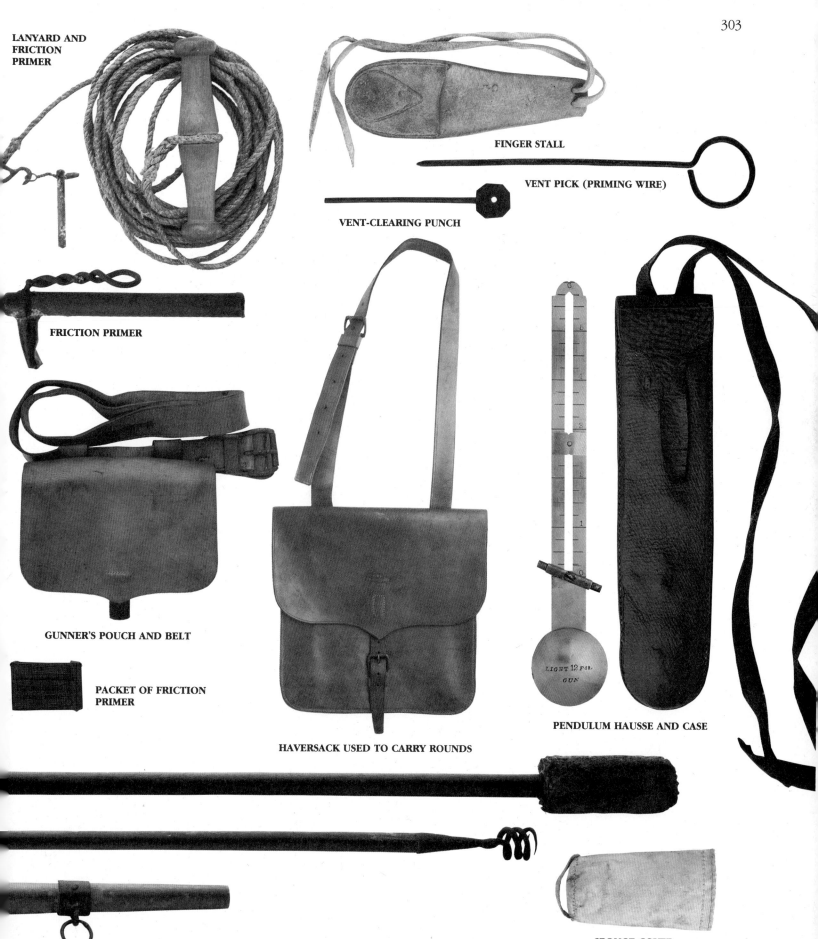

LANYARD AND
FRICTION
PRIMER

FINGER STALL

VENT PICK (PRIMING WIRE)

VENT-CLEARING PUNCH

FRICTION PRIMER

GUNNER'S POUCH AND BELT

PACKET OF FRICTION
PRIMER

HAVERSACK USED TO CARRY ROUNDS

PENDULUM HAUSSE AND CASE

SPONGE COVER

An Array of Lethal Ammunition

WOODEN FUSEPLUG
AUGER

PAPER TIME
FUSES

FUSE-CUTTING
GUIDE

AMMUNITION CRATE

GUNNER'S CALIPERS USED TO
MEASURE AMMUNITION SIZE

TOW HOOK USED TO OPEN AMMO CRATE AND UNPACK SHELLS

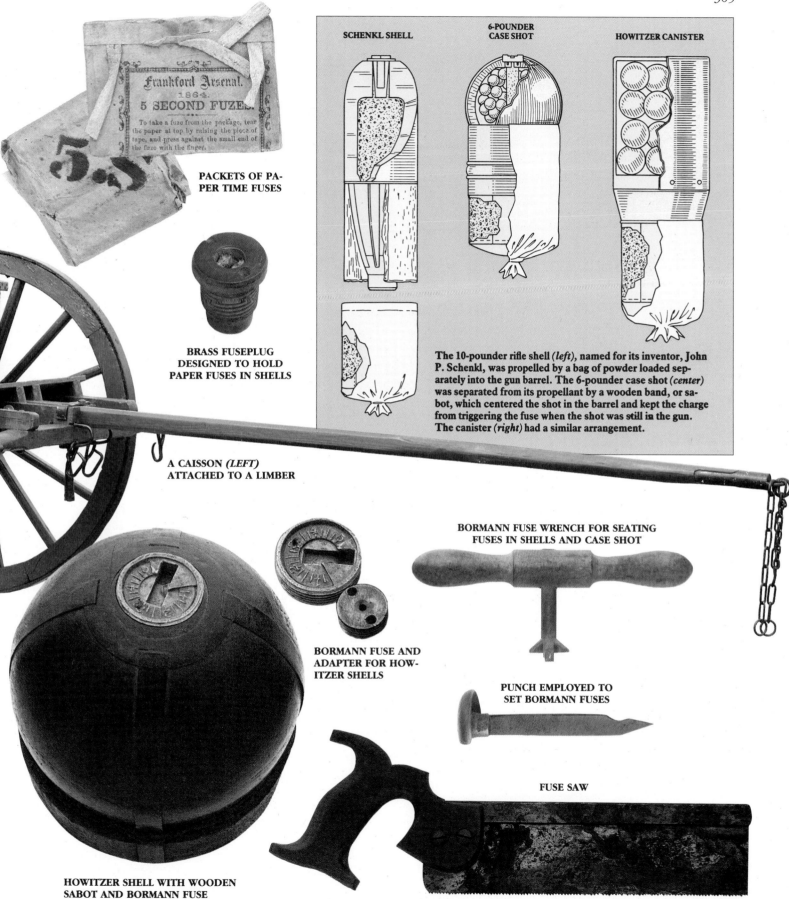

PACKETS OF PA-PER TIME FUSES

BRASS FUSEPLUG DESIGNED TO HOLD PAPER FUSES IN SHELLS

SCHENKL SHELL

6-POUNDER CASE SHOT

HOWITZER CANISTER

The 10-pounder rifle shell (*left*), named for its inventor, John P. Schenkl, was propelled by a bag of powder loaded separately into the gun barrel. The 6-pounder case shot (*center*) was separated from its propellant by a wooden band, or sabot, which centered the shot in the barrel and kept the charge from triggering the fuse when the shot was still in the gun. The canister (*right*) had a similar arrangement.

A CAISSON (*LEFT*) ATTACHED TO A LIMBER

BORMANN FUSE WRENCH FOR SEATING FUSES IN SHELLS AND CASE SHOT

BORMANN FUSE AND ADAPTER FOR HOW-ITZER SHELLS

PUNCH EMPLOYED TO SET BORMANN FUSES

FUSE SAW

HOWITZER SHELL WITH WOODEN SABOT AND BORMANN FUSE

COASTAL ARTILLERY

Members of the 1st Connecticut Heavy Artillery drill with 4.5-inch siege rifles at Arlington Heights on the Virginia side of the Potomac River.

Inside Fort Totten near Washington, D.C., on the northeast perimeter of the city, officers of the 3d Massachusetts Heavy Artillery show off a rifled Parrott gun that could hurl 100-pound shells six miles.

JAMES SHELL

When this 7-inch, 84-pound James shell was fired, gases entered the projectile's base, passed through its ribs, and expanded a lead sabot into the barrel's rifling, which made the shell rotate.

HOTCHKISS SHOT FOR PARROTT RIFLE

This 6.4-inch shot had a bottle-shaped top with a rod of iron and a bottom that expanded a lead sabot *(missing)* into the rifling, imparting spin.

SCHENKL SHELL

Before it was fired, the bottom of this Federal Schenkl shell was encased in a papier-mâché sabot. The sabots were subject to moisture damage that made them swell and sometimes prevented loading.

Crew members surround the 11-inch Dahlgren shell gun aboard their steam sloop. Designed by Admiral John A. Dahlgren, who commanded the South Atlantic Blockading Squadron from 1863 to 1865, the 11-inch Dahlgren could hurl 170-pound shot at enemy ironclads.

NAVAL SHELL WITH THREE TIME FUSES

The Shipboard Behemoths

The battles for control of Southern coastal forts were dominated by artillery duels between the most powerful weapons of the Civil War—heavy, large-caliber naval guns with bores 6 to 15 inches in diameter. These big guns employed a wide range of highly destructive ammunition, such as the massive 11-inch, 121-pound shell at left. Ammunition for the smooth-bores was generally spherical, and for the rifled guns, conical.

By the start of the War, the shell appeared to have established its superiority over the old-fashioned cannonball by virtue of its explosive force. But the invention of ironclad vessels revived the use of solid shot, which, when fired from mighty rifled cannon, was capable of piercing the ships' armor.

An overlapping system of rails allowed gunners of the U.S.S. *Wabash* to move this 150-pounder Parrott rifle from one side of the screw steamer to the other. The 16,000-pound pivot gun was mounted on a carriage that recoiled along the tracks.

PARROTT RIFLE SIGHT

"Old Abe," the 13-inch mortar aboard the U.S.S. *Para*, could loft 218-pound exploding shells over the walls of Confederate forts.

ACKNOWLEDGMENTS

The editors wish to thank the following individuals and institutions for their valuable assistance in the preparation of this volume:

Connecticut: Hartford—Dean Nelson, Museum of Connecticut History. Southbury—Don Troiani.

Massachusetts: Boston—Steve Hill. Cambridge—James Stametelos, Tony Stametelos.

New Jersey: Cherry Hill—C. Paul Loane.

New York: Albany—Thomas C. Duclos, New York State Division of Military and Naval Affairs; Robert E. Mulligan, Jr., New York State Museum.

Ohio: Dayton—Larry Strayer.

Pennsylvania: Gettysburg—Bill Brown III, Lawrence H. Eckert, Jr., Gettysburg National Military Park. Philadelphia—Russ Pritchard, War Library and Museum.

Washington, D.C.: Harry Hunter, Don Kloster, National Museum of American History, Smithsonian Institution.

PICTURE CREDITS

The sources for the illustrations in this volume are listed below. Credits from left to right are separated by semicolons, from top to bottom are separated by dashes. Photographs taken on assignment for Echoes of Glory by Larry Sherer, assisted by Andrew Patilla, are followed by an asterisk (*).

3: Pennsylvania Capitol Preservation Committee's *Advance the Colors!* 5: Quantico Marine Base, Quantico, Va., photographed by Larry Sherer; courtesy State Historical Society of Wisconsin—courtesy Don Troiani Collection, photographed by Al Freni; California State Capitol Museum, Sacramento, photographed by Robert DiFranco—Fort Ward Museum, City of Alexandria, Va., photographed by Larry Sherer—Manassas National Battlefield Park, photographed by Larry Sherer. 6, 7: Painting by Julian Scott, Smithsonian Institution, Washington, D.C., No. CT 80-1290. 8: L. M. Strayer Collection, copied by Brian Blauser. 10, 11: Courtesy of the Burton Historical Collection of the Detroit Public Library, copied by Nemo Warr. 13: Courtesy Dean E. Nelson*. 14, 15: Massachusetts Commandery of the Military Order of the Loyal Legion and U.S. Army Military History Institute (Mass./MOLLUS/USAMHI), copied by Robert Walch. 17: Hayes Presidential Center, Fremont, Ohio. 18, 19: Western Reserve Historical Society, Cleveland. 21: Library of Congress No. B8171 3310. 22: U.S. Marine Corps Museum, Quantico, photographed by Larry Sherer. 28, 29: Library of Congress No. B8171 7143—Smithsonian Institution, National Museum of American History, Washington, D.C.* 30, 31: Gettysburg National Military Park Museum*; courtesy Dean S. Thomas Collection*—Gettysburg National Military Park Museum*—courtesy Don Troiani Collection* (2)—Fort Ward Museum, City of Alexandria, Va., photographed by Henry Beville—courtesy Dean S. Thomas Collection; Richard F. Carlile Collection, photographed by Bill Patterson; courtesy Don Troiani Collection* (2)—courtesy Paul Davies Collection*. 32, 33: Smithsonian Institution, National Museum of American History, Washington, D.C.*—courtesy Dean S. Thomas Collection—Gettysburg National Military Park Museum*—courtesy Don Troiani Collection*—Gettysburg National Military Park Museum*—courtesy Dean S. Thomas Collection*; courtesy Don Troiani Collection* (2). 34, 35: Smithsonian Institution, National Museum of American History, Washington, D.C.* (3)—courtesy Don Troiani Collection*—Earl J. Hess Collection at U.S. Army Military History Institute, photographed by A. Pierce Bounds. 36, 37: Richard F. Carlile Collection, photographed by Bill Patterson (2)—Gettysburg National Military Park Museum*—courtesy Don Troiani Collection* (4). 38, 39: Courtesy Don Troiani Collection*—courtesy Dean E. Nelson Collection* (2); Library of Congress—courtesy Harris Andrews, photographed by Fil Hunter—courtesy Don Troiani Collection*—Gettysburg National Military Park Museum*—courtesy Dean S. Thomas Collection*; courtesy Don Troiani Collection* (2). 40, 41: Courtesy

Larry Beyer, photographed by Larry Sherer (2)—First City Regiment*—courtesy Dean S. Thomas Collection* (2); Collection of the Lehigh County Historical Society. 42-43: Smithsonian Institution, National Museum of American History, Washington, D.C.* 44, 45: Courtesy Don Troiani Collection* (2)—West Point Museum Collections, photographed by Henry Groskinsky—courtesy Jerry Coates Collection* (2)—Richard F. Carlile Collection; Jerry Coates Collection*. 46, 47: Cincinnati Historical Society—The War Library and Museum, MOLLUS, photographed by Larry Sherer—Fort Ward Museum, City of Alexandria, Va., photographed by Henry Beville—courtesy Dean S. Thomas Collection* (2); courtesy Stamatelos Brothers Collection, Cambridge*; Richard F. Carlile Collection. 48, 49: Courtesy Collection of C. Paul Loane, photographed by Arthur Soll—War Library and Museum, MOLLUS, photographed by Larry Sherer—Smithsonian Institution, National Museum of American History, Washington, D.C.*—courtesy Dean S. Thomas Collection* (2); Illinois State Historical Library, Springfield. 50, 51: U.S. Marine Corps Museum, Quantico, photographed by Larry Sherer—Quantico Marine Base, Quantico, Va., photographed by Larry Sherer—Henry and Nettie Daidone Collection* (3). 52, 53: Sketch by Alfred R. Waud, Library of Congress; Smithsonian Institution, National Museum of American History, Washington, D.C.*—Richard F. Carlile Collection, photographed by Bill Patterson; courtesy John N. Ockerbloom—courtesy Dean S. Thomas Collection* (2)—Gettysburg National Military Park Museum*—courtesy Dean S. Thomas Collection. 54, 55: Gettysburg National Military Park Museum* (2)—courtesy Jerry Coates Collection*—Gettysburg National Military Park Museum* (2). 56, 57: Courtesy Arthur O'Leary; Gettysburg National Military Park Museum*—U.S. Marine Corps Museum, Quantico, photographed by Michael Latil—courtesy Dean S. Thomas Collection*—U.S. Marine Corps Museum, Quantico, photographed by Michael Latil—Museum of the Confederacy, Richmond, Va.*; Gettysburg National Military Park Museum*. 58, 59: Gettysburg National Military Park Museum*; courtesy Dean S. Thomas Collection*—courtesy Stamatelos Brothers Collection, Cambridge*—U.S. Marine Corps Museum, Quantico, photographed by Michael Latil—courtesy Stamatelos Brothers Collection, Cambridge*—courtesy John D. McAulay Collection*—Fort Ward Museum, City of Alexandria, Va., photographed by Gordon Kurzweil; Museum of the Confederacy, Richmond, Va.* (2). 60, 61: U.S. Marine Corps Museum, Quantico, Virginia photographed by Michael Latil—Gettysburg National Military Park Museum*—Museum of the Confederacy, Richmond, Va.*; Richard F. Carlile Collection—Gettysburg National Military Park Museum*. 62, 63: Gettysburg National Military Park Museum*—courtesy John D. McAulay Collection*—courtesy Dean S. Thomas Collection*—courtesy Herb Peck, Jr.; courtesy John D. McAulay Collection*. 64, 65: U.S. Army Center of Military History, Washington, D.C., photographed

by Larry Sherer—Library of Congress No. B8184 10164; Gettysburg National Military Park Museum*; courtesy Frank and Marie-T. Wood Print Collections; U.S. Marine Corps Museum, Quantico, photographed by Larry Sherer; State Historical Society of Wisconsin Neg No. WHi (x32) 6306. 66, 67: National Rifle Association, photographed by Leon Dishman—Gettysburg National Military Park Museum*; Richard F. Carlile Collection, photographed by Bill Patterson—courtesy Herb Peck, Jr.; Gettysburg National Military Park Museum* (2)—courtesy Dean S. Thomas Collection*; Museum of the Confederacy, Richmond, Va.* 68, 69: Ohio Historical Society, photographed by David R. Barker—Gettysburg National Military Park Museum*; courtesy John A. Hess—Gettysburg National Military Park Museum*; courtesy Jerry Coates Collection*. 70, 71: National Archives Neg. No. 111-B-4405—courtesy Don Troiani Collection* (2). 72: Gettysburg National Military Park Museum* (2)—Library of Congress—Civil War Library and Museum, Philadelphia* (2)—Gettysburg National Military Park Museum*—Library of Congress; Gettysburg National Military Park Museum. 74, 75: Gettysburg National Military Park Museum*. Portrait courtesy William B. Styple Collection*. 76, 77: Courtesy Chris Nelson Collection, photographed by Michael Latil; Richard F. Carlile Collection; Library of Congress No. LCB8171 7091—courtesy H. L. Woodlief* (2)—Gettysburg National Military Park Museum* (2). 78, 79: Museum of the Confederacy, Richmond, Va., photographed by Ronald H. Jennings—courtesy Stamatelos Brothers Collection, Cambridge*; courtesy Herb Peck, Jr.—courtesy Collection of C. Paul Loane*—Western Reserve Historical Society, Cleveland—Fort Ward Museum, City of Alexandria, Va., photographed by Henry Beville. 80, 81: Gettysburg National Military Park Museum*—Richard F. Carlile Collection; Fort Ward Museum, City of Alexandria, Va., photographed by Henry Beville—Fort Ward Museum, City of Alexandria, Va., photographed by Henry Beville; West Point Museum, photographed by Henry Groskinsky. 82: Courtesy D. Mark Katz; Civil War Library and Museum, Philadelphia* (2); Mass./MOLLUS/USAMHI, copied by A. Pierce Bounds; courtesy New York State Museum, Albany, N.Y.* 83: First Regiment Infantry Armory, Philadelphia* (3); Mass./MOLLUS/USAMHI, copied by A. Pierce Bounds; Gettysburg National Military Park Museum* (2). 84, 85: New York State Division of Military and Naval Affairs, Military History Collection* (4)—First Regiment Infantry Armory, Philadelphia* (2)—New York State Division of Military and Naval Affairs, Military History Collection* (2). 86, 87: Courtesy Will Gorgas, New Bern, N.C.* (2)—Civil War Library and Museum, Philadelphia* (2)—Western Reserve Historical Society, Cleveland; courtesy Stamatelos Brothers Collection, Cambridge* (4). 88: Courtesy Don Troiani Collection, photographed by Al Freni. 92: Courtesy Michael McAfee—courtesy Collection of C. Paul Loane*. 93: West Point Museum Collections, U.S. Military Academy (USMA)*. 94: New York State Division of

Military and Naval Affairs, Military History Collection*; Atlanta Historical Society, Atlanta, Ga.*—portrait courtesy Michael McAfee*—New York State Division of Military and Naval Affairs, Military History Collection* (2). 95: Courtesy New York State Museum, Albany, N.Y.*; courtesy Michael McAfee*; courtesy New York State Museum, Albany, N.Y.*—West Point Museum Collections, USMA* (2). 96: Courtesy Dean E. Nelson Collection*—courtesy New York State Museum, Albany, N.Y.* (2); portrait courtesy Michael McAfee*. 97: Courtesy Don Troiani Collection* (3), except top right portrait courtesy Michael McAfee*. 98: Portrait Library of Congress No. B8184-B-29. Civil War Library and Museum, Philadelphia* (3); New York State Division of Military and Naval Affairs, Military History Collection*. 99: Library of Congress No. B8184-7371; Custer Battlefield National Monument, Crow Agency, Montana, photographed by Dennis Sanders; courtesy William B. Styple Collection*—courtesy Don Troiani Collection*; Gettysburg National Military Park Museum*; bottom portrait courtesy Brian Pohanka. 100: Courtesy John N. Ockerbloom Collection* (3), except portrait Mass./MOLLUS/USAMHI, photographed by A. Pierce Bounds. 101: First button courtesy Chris Nelson, photographed by Philip Brandt George; remainder Vernon Floyd Moss III, Wilson, N.C.*; clothes courtesy Collection of C. Paul Loane*. 102: Courtesy Dr. and Mrs. Bruce English, Ashland, Va.—courtesy Don Troiani Collection*; Civil War Library and Museum, Philadelphia*. 103: Courtesy Seward R. Osborne, copied and photographed by Henry Groskinsky 104: Massachusetts Historical Society, Boston—courtesy Chris Nelson Collection* (3). 105: 1st City Troop, Pennsylvania National Guard*—courtesy Stamatelos Brothers Collection, Cambridge*; West Point Museum Collections, USMA* (2). Portrait courtesy Michael McAfee*. 106: Courtesy Stamatelos Brothers Collection, Cambridge* (4), except bottom hat courtesy Don Troiani Collection*, portrait Richard F. Carlile Collection, photographed by Bill Patterson. 107: Courtesy Stamatelos Brothers Collection, Cambridge* (4)—Smithsonian Institution, National Museum of American History, Washington, D.C.*; courtesy Collection of C. Paul Loane*; Smithsonian Institution, National Museum of American History, Washington, D.C.* 108: Kean Wilcox—courtesy Stamatelos Brothers Collection, Cambridge* (3). 109: Courtesy John W. Kuhl; courtesy Don Troiani Collection, photographed by Al Freni—West Point Museum Collections, USMA*; courtesy Michael McAfee*; West Point Museum Collections, USMA*; courtesy Henry Deeks*. 110: Western Reserve Historical Society—courtesy Michael McAfee*; West Point Museum Collections, USMA*. 111: Civil War Library and Museum, Philadelphia* (2); Richard F. Carlile Collection—courtesy Don Troiani Collection* (3). 112: Courtesy Collection of C. Paul Loane* (3)—Western Reserve Historical Society, Cleveland. 113: Courtesy Stamatelos Brothers Collection, Cambridge* (3)—courtesy Robert G. Borrell Sr., photographed by Michael Latil (2). Right portrait courtesy Michael McAfee*. 114: Chicago Historical Society No. ICHi-08204—courtesy Don Troiani Collection* (2). 115: Courtesy Collection of C. Paul Loane*, except sash and trousers, courtesy Don Troiani Collection*. 116: Civil War Library and Museum, Philadelphia* (3), except top right courtesy Don Troiani Collection*. 117: Courtesy Don Troiani Collection* (3)—courtesy of the Rhode Island Historical Society. 118: Courtesy Vermont Historical Society—courtesy Don Troiani Collection* (3). 119: Civil War Library and Museum, Philadelphia* (2); courtesy Don Troiani Collection*—West

Point Museum Collections, USMA* (2); courtesy Collection of C. Paul Loane*. 120: U.S. Army Center of Military History; courtesy Dennis Reem, Frederick, Md., photographed by Larry Sherer—Mass./MOLLUS/USAMHI, copied by A. Pierce Bounds. 121: Courtesy Stamatelos Brothers Collection, Cambridge*; Smithsonian Institution, National Museum of American History, Washington, D.C.*; courtesy Dennis Reem, Frederick, Md., photographed by Larry Sherer. 122: Courtesy Don Troiani Collection*; Terence P. O'Leary—courtesy Collection of C. Paul Loane*; courtesy Don Troiani Collection*. 123: Courtesy Stamatelos Brothers Collection, Cambridge* (3)—courtesy D. Mark Katz. 124: Courtesy T. Scott Sanders. 125: Smithsonian Institution, National Museum of American History, Washington, D.C.* (2); courtesy Stamatelos Brothers Collection, Cambridge*—New York State Division of Military and Naval Affairs, Military History Collection*; courtesy Stamatelos Brothers Collection, Cambridge*—L. M. Strayer Collection; courtesy John N. Ockerbloom Collection*; courtesy Stamatelos Brothers Collection, Cambridge*. 126: Smithsonian Institution, National Museum of American History, Washington, D.C.*; courtesy Don Troiani Collection, photographed by Henry Groskinsky—courtesy Stamatelos Brothers Collection, Cambridge* (2); Kean Wilcox; courtesy Don Troiani Collection, photographed by Henry Groskinsky. 127: Courtesy Stamatelos Brothers Collection, Cambridge*; courtesy Don Troiani Collection*—courtesy Stamatelos Brothers Collection, Cambridge* (2); Smithsonian Institution, National Museum of American History, Washington, D.C.* 128: Gettysburg National Military Park Museum*; courtesy Michael McAfee*—courtesy Stamatelos Brothers Collection, Cambridge* (2); courtesy Collection of C. Paul Loane*—courtesy Don Troiani Collection*; courtesy Collection of C. Paul Loane*. 129: Gettysburg National Military Park Museum*; courtesy Michael McAfee*—courtesy Les Jensen Collection*—courtesy Collection of C. Paul Loane*. 130: Courtesy Collection of C. Paul Loane*; courtesy Don Troiani Collection* (4)—bottom kepi, West Point Museum Collections, USMA*. 131: New York State Division of Military and Naval Affairs, Military History Collection, photographed by Henry Groskinsky; courtesy Collection of C. Paul Loane*—Smithsonian Institution, National Museum of American History, Washington, D.C.* (2); courtesy Michael McAfee*. 132: Courtesy Michael McAfee* (2)—Museum of the Confederacy, Richmond, Va.*—Library of Congress No. B8184 4376. 133: Smithsonian Institution, National Museum of American History, Washington, D.C.* (2), except portrait courtesy Michael McAfee*. 134: New York State Division of Military and Naval Affairs, Military History Collection*; courtesy Michael McAfee*—courtesy Don Troiani Collection*; Smithsonian Institution, National Museum of American History, Washington, D.C.*—Western Reserve Historical Society, Cleveland. 135: Courtesy New York State Museum, Albany, N.Y.* 136: From the *Album of the Second Battalion Duryée Zouaves: One Hundred and Sixty-Fifth Regiment New York Volunteer Infantry, 1906,* courtesy Brian Pohanka; Smithsonian Institution, National Museum of American History, Washington, D.C.*—courtesy Don Troiani Collection, photographed by Henry Groskinsky. 137: NSDAR, Hendrick Hudson Chapter, Hudson, N.Y., photographed by Al Freni; Rochester Museum & Science Center, Rochester, N.Y., photographed by Al Freni (2). 138: Courtesy Don Troiani Collection*; Smithsonian Institution, National Museum of American History, Washington, D.C.*; courtesy Michael McAfee*—courtesy Don Troiani

Collection* (2). 139: Smithsonian Institution, National Museum of American History, Washington, D.C.* (2)—West Point Library, photographed by Henry Groskinsky. 140: Courtesy Don Troiani Collection* (3)—Library of Congress No. B817 7348. 141: Military Images Collection; Smithsonian Institution, National Museum of American History, Washington, D.C.* (2). 142: State Museum of Pennsylvania/Pennsylvania Historical and Museum Commission, copied by A. Pierce Bounds; Smithsonian Institution, National Museum of American History, Washington, D.C., photographed by Dane Penland—courtesy Don Troiani Collection* (5). 143: Smithsonian Institution, National Museum of American History, Washington, D.C.* (2)—Hendrick Hudson Chapter, NSDAR, Inc., Hudson, N.Y., photographed by Al Freni—Rochester Museum & Science Center, Rochester, N.Y., photographed by Al Freni—from the Photographic Collection of the Rochester Historical Society. 144: West Point Museum Collections, USMA*; courtesy Collection of C. Paul Loane*—courtesy Michael McAfee*; courtesy Collection of C. Paul Loane; New York State Division of Military and Naval Affairs, Military History Collection*. 145: West Point Museum Collections, USMA*; courtesy Michael McAfee* (3). 146: Smithsonian Institution, National Museum of American History, Washington, D.C.*; courtesy Michael McAfee*—Smithsonian Institution, National Museum of American History, Washington, D.C.* (2). 147: Courtesy Don Troiani Collection*; Smithsonian Institution, National Museum of American History, Washington, D.C.*—Bill Turner Collection. 148: Courtesy Michael McAfee*—New York State Division of Military and Naval Affairs, Military History Collection* (4). 149: Courtesy Collection of C. Paul Loane* (3)—courtesy Don Troiani Collection*. 150: Courtesy Michael McAfee*; Smithsonian Institution, National Museum of American History, Washington, D.C.*—New York State Division of Military and Naval Affairs, Military History Collection*; Vernon Floyd Moss III, Wilson, N.C.*; New York State Division of Military and Naval Affairs, Military History Collection*. 151: New York State Division of Military and Naval Affairs, Military History Collection*; courtesy Michael McAfee*; Smithsonian Institution, National Museum of American History, Washington, D.C.*—Western Reserve Historical Society, Cleveland. 152: First Regiment Infantry Armory, Philadelphia*—First Regiment, Pennsylvania National Guard* (3). 153: First Regiment Infantry Armory, Philadelphia* (2); courtesy Collection of C. Paul Loane*—West Point Museum Collections, USMA* (3), portrait courtesy Michael McAfee*. 154: West Point Museum Collections, USMA* (3)—courtesy Michael McAfee*. 155: Western Reserve Historical Society, Cleveland—Smithsonian Institution, National Museum of American History, Washington, D.C.* 156: Left trousers, Smithsonian Institution, National Museum of American History, Washington, D.C.*; courtesy Stamatelos Brothers Collection, Cambridge* (4). 157: Courtesy Stamatelos Brothers Collection, Cambridge* (3)—courtesy Michael McAfee*; Gettysburg National Military Park Museum*. 158: Courtesy Stamatelos Brothers Collection, Cambridge* (3), except portrait courtesy Richard K. Tibbals. 159: Western Reserve Historical Society, Cleveland; courtesy Don Troiani Collection*—Smithsonian Institution, National Museum of American History, Washington, D.C.*; Mass./MOLLUS/USAMHI, copied by A. Pierce Bounds. 160: Vernon Floyd Moss III, Wilson, N.C.*; courtesy Michael McAfee*—Smithsonian Institution, National Museum of American History, Washington, D.C.; courtesy Confederate Relic Room, Columbia, S.C.*—Gettysburg National Military

Park Museum*. 161: Library of Congress No. B8171-7890—courtesy Michael McAfee*—courtesy Stamatelos Brothers Collection, Cambridge*. 162: Atlanta Historical Society, Atlanta, Ga.* (2)—Mass./MOLLUS/USAMHI, copied by A. Pierce Bounds. 163: Atlanta Historical Society, Atlanta, Ga.*; Civil War Library and Museum, Philadelphia* (2)—Atlanta Historical Society, Atlanta, Ga.* (2). 164: Courtesy Stamatelos Brothers Collection, Cambridge*. 165: National Archives—courtesy Stamatelos Brothers Collection, Cambridge* (2). 166: Courtesy Stamatelos Brothers Collection, Cambridge*. 167: Western Reserve Historical Society, Cleveland—courtesy Stamatelos Brothers Collection, Cambridge* (3). Close-up shirt, Atlanta Historical Society, Atlanta, Ga.* 168: Courtesy Tom Buckner, photographed by David M. Sullivan; courtesy Stamatelos Brothers Collection, Cambridge* (3). 169: Courtesy Stamatelos Brothers Collection, Cambridge* (3), except portraits courtesy Michael McAfee*. 170: Courtesy New York State Museum, Albany, N.Y.* (2)—Smithsonian Institution, National Numismatic Collections, Washington, D.C. (2)—courtesy William B. Styple Collection* (2); courtesy Stamatelos Brothers Collection, Cambridge*. 171: Courtesy Stamatelos Brothers Collection, Cambridge* (4)—Western Reserve Historical Society, Cleveland. 172: Courtesy Stamatelos Brothers Collection, Cambridge*; courtesy Collection of C. Paul Loane*; courtesy Stamatelos Brothers Collection, Cambridge* (2)—Civil War Library and Museum, Philadelphia* (2); courtesy Collection of C. Paul Loane—Civil War Library and Museum, Philadelphia* (3). Box: Art by Time-Life Books. 173: Civil War Library and Museum, Philadelphia*; courtesy Beverly M. Dubose III*; Civil War Library and Museum, Philadelphia*—courtesy Stamatelos Brothers Collection, Cambridge*; Civil War Library and Museum*—courtesy Stamatelos Brothers Collection, Cambridge*; courtesy Collection of C. Paul Loane*; courtesy Barry Kluck, Hershey, Pa., photographed by Larry Sherer—courtesy Collection of C. Paul Loane*—courtesy Collection of C. Paul Loane*; Civil War Library and Museum, Philadelphia; courtesy Stamatelos Brothers Collection, Cambridge* (2). Box: courtesy Don Troiani Collection (4)—courtesy Stamatelos Brothers Collection, Cambridge*. 174: Courtesy collection of C. Paul Loane*; New York State Division of Military and Naval Affairs, Military History Collection*—courtesy Collection of C. Paul Loane* (2); courtesy Don Troiani Collection*—courtesy Collection C. Paul Loane* (2)—courtesy Don Troiani Collection* (2). Box: Vernon Floyd Moss III, Winston, N.C.* 175: Courtesy Don Troiani Collection*; courtesy William B. Styple Collection* (3)—courtesy Don Troiani Collection; courtesy Collection of C. Paul Loane*—New York State Division of Military and Naval Affairs, Military History Collection* (3); courtesy Don Troiani Collection*. 176: Courtesy Collection of C. Paul Loane*—New York State Division of Military and Naval Affairs, Military History Collection*—courtesy Collection of C. Paul Loane*; Richard F. Carlile Collection, copied by Bill Patterson. 177: Courtesy Don Troiani Collection*; First Regiment Infantry Armory, Philadelphia*—courtesy Will Gorgas, New Bern, N.C.*—courtesy Collection of C. Paul Loane* (2). 178: Courtesy Don Troiani Collection*—courtesy Chris Nelson Collection*—New York State Division of Military and Naval Affairs, Military History Collection* (2)—courtesy Will Gorgas, New Bern, N.C.* 179: West Point Museum Collections, USMA*—courtesy

Collection of C. Paul Loane*—Gettysburg National Military Park Museum*—courtesy Collection of C. Paul Loane*. 180: Courtesy Stamatelos Brothers Collection, Cambridge*—New York State Division of Military and Naval Affairs, Military History Collection*—courtesy Collection of C. Paul Loane*. 181: Illinois Historic Preservation Agency, courtesy A. W. Mueller Collection, Galena, Ill.; courtesy Collection of C. Paul Loane* (2)—New York State Division of Military and Naval Affairs, Military History Collection*. 182: Courtesy Don Troiani Collection*—courtesy Collection of C. Paul Loane* (2)—courtesy James C. Frasca, Croton, Ohio, photographed by Andy Cifranic. 183: U.S. Army Military History Institute (USAMHI), copied by A. Pierce Bounds; courtesy Chris Nelson Collection*—courtesy Don Troiani Collection*—courtesy Collection of C. Paul Loane* (2). 184: Gettysburg National Military Park Museum*; courtesy Alan T. Nolan—courtesy Ronn Palm; courtesy Don Troiani Collection, photographed by Al Freni. 185: West Point Museum Collections, USMA*—courtesy Collection of C. Paul Loane*—New York State Division of Military and Naval Affairs, Military History Collection*—James C. Frasca, Croton, Ohio, photographed by Andy Cifranic. 186: Courtesy Collection of C. Paul Loane, photographed by Arthur Soll; Gettysburg National Military Park Museum*—courtesy Stamatelos Brothers Collection, Cambridge*—courtesy William B. Styple Collection*. 187: West Point Museum Collections, USMA*; Richard F. Carlile Collection, copied by Bill Patterson—courtesy Michael McAfee*. 188: New York State Division of Military and Naval Affairs, Military History Collection*; courtesy Don Troiani Collection*; courtesy Stamatelos Brothers Collection, Cambridge*—courtesy Collection of C. Paul Loane*—Gettysburg National Military Park Museum*. 189: Courtesy Stamatelos Brothers Collection, Cambridge*; courtesy Collection of C. Paul Loane* (2)—Western Reserve Historical Society, Cleveland—courtesy Don Troiani Collection*; courtesy Stamatelos Brothers Collection, Cambridge*. 190: Courtesy Don Troiani Collection*; Richard F. Carlile Collection, photographed by Bill Patterson—New York State Division of Military and Naval Affairs, Military History Collection*—courtesy Don Troiani Collection*. 191: Courtesy Stamatelos Brothers Collection, Cambridge* (3)—courtesy Don Troiani Collection*; courtesy Dean E. Nelson Collection*. 192: Richard F. Carlile Collection; courtesy Stamatelos Brothers Collection, Cambridge*; courtesy Don Troiani Collection*—courtesy Stamatelos Brothers Collection, Cambridge* (4). 193: Courtesy Stamatelos Brothers Collection, Cambridge* (2)—courtesy Don Troiani Collection*; New York State Division of Military and Naval Affairs, Military History Collection*—courtesy Chris Nelson Collection*; Civil War Library and Museum, Philadelphia*. 194: Fort Ward Museum, City of Alexandria, Va., photographed by Larry Sherer. 198, 199: Courtesy Stamatelos Brothers Collection, Cambridge*—Museum of the Confederacy, Richmond, Va.*—Kean Wilcox; courtesy Collection of C. Paul Loane*; courtesy Don Troiani Collection*. 200: Civil War Library and Museum, Philadelphia* (2)—courtesy Don Troiani Collection, photographed by Al Freni—courtesy Michael McAfee*. 201: Courtesy Collection of C. Paul Loane* (2); courtesy Chris Nelson Collection*—courtesy Don Troiani Collection*; courtesy Chris Nelson Collection*. 202: Courtesy Don Troiani Collection* (3)—courtesy Collection of C. Paul Loane*—courtesy Don Troiani Collection* (2). 203: Courtesy Don Troiani Collection* (2)—courtesy James C. Frasca, Croton, Ohio; First Regi-

ment Infantry Armory, Philadelphia*; courtesy Don Troiani Collection—New York State Division of Military and Naval Affairs, Military History Collection*; courtesy Don Troiani Collection*. 204, 205: Richard F. Carlile Collection; Atlanta Historical Society, Atlanta, Ga.* (2); courtesy Stamatelos Brothers Collection, Cambridge* (5)—Atlanta Historical Society, Atlanta, Ga.* (2)—courtesy Don Troiani Collection*—courtesy Stamatelos Brothers Collection, Cambridge*; Cavalry Museum, Fort Riley, Kansas; Atlanta Historical Society, Atlanta, Ga.*—bottom left courtesy Chris Nelson Collection*. 206: Museum of the Confederacy, Richmond, Va.*; courtesy Ronn Palm—courtesy Don Troiani Collection*. 207: Courtesy Don Troiani Collection*; courtesy Collection of C. Paul Loane*; First Regiment Infantry Armory, Philadelphia*. 208: Courtesy Stamatelos Brothers Collection, Cambridge*—courtesy Don Troiani Collection*—courtesy Collection of C. Paul Loane* (2). 209: courtesy Stamatelos Brothers Collection, Cambridge*. 210: Courtesy Ronn Palm—courtesy Collection of C. Paul Loane*; New York State Division of Military and Naval Affairs, Military History Collection*. 211: Courtesy Collection of C. Paul Loane* (2), except top right courtesy Don Troiani Collection*. 212: Courtesy Don Troiani Collection* (2); Kean Wilcox—courtesy Collection of C. Paul Loane*; courtesy Don Troiani Collection*. 213: Courtesy Don Troiani Collection* (2); courtesy Stamatelos Brothers Collection, Cambridge*—courtesy Don Troiani Collection* (2)—courtesy Stamatelos Brothers Collection, Cambridge*; courtesy Don Troiani Collection*. 214: Courtesy Stamatelos Brothers Collection, Cambridge* (2)—courtesy Don Troiani, photographed by Henry Groskinsky; Civil War Library and Museum, Philadelphia*; courtesy Collection of C. Paul Loane*. 215: West Point Library, photographed by Henry Groskinsky; courtesy Stamatelos Brothers Collection, Cambridge*—Museum of the Confederacy, Richmond, Va.*; courtesy Stamatelos Brothers Collection, Cambridge*. Bottom portrait courtesy Ronn Palm. 216: Courtesy Stamatelos Brothers Collection, Cambridge*. 217: Courtesy Stamatelos Brothers Collection, Cambridge* (3); courtesy John N. Ockerbloom Collection*—Museum of the Confederacy, Richmond, Va.* 218: Courtesy Ronn Palm—U.S. Army Center of Military History, Washington, D.C., photographed by Larry Sherer (2)—courtesy Chris Nelson Collection*. 219: U.S. Army Center of Military History, Washington, D.C., photographed by Larry Sherer; courtesy Don Troiani Collection*. 220: Courtesy Don Troiani Collection*—courtesy John A. Hess. 221: Courtesy Don Troiani Collection*. 222: Courtesy Collection of C. Paul Loane*; courtesy Chris Nelson Collection* (2); courtesy Stamatelos Brothers Collection, Cambridge* (2)—courtesy Chris Nelson Collection*—courtesy Stamatelos Brothers Collection, Cambridge* (6). 223: Courtesy Stamatelos Brothers Collection, Cambridge* (12); courtesy Beverly M. Dubose III, Atlanta, Ga.*—courtesy Chris Nelson Collection*. 224: Courtesy Don Troiani Collection* (6)—courtesy James C. Frasca, Croton, Ohio. 225: Courtesy Collection of C. Paul Loane*; courtesy Don Troiani Collection, photographed by Henry Groskinsky—courtesy Don Troiani Collection*; courtesy Chris Nelson Collection* (2)—courtesy Collection of C. Paul Loane*—Atlanta Historical Society, Atlanta, Ga.*; courtesy Stamatelos Brothers Collection, Cambridge*. 226, 227: Smithsonian Institution, National Museum of American History, Washington, D.C., photographed by Steve Tuttle; Smithsonian Institution, National Museum of American History, Washington, D.C., photographed by Dane Penland; National Archives—Smithsonian

Institution, National Museum of American History, Washington, D.C., photographed by Dane Penland; Museum of the Confederacy, Richmond, Va., photographed by Larry Sherer (2). 228: State Historical Society of Wisconsin. 230, 231: Gettysburg National Military Park Museum*; Library of Congress—Mark A. Elrod Collection; Kentucky Historical Society-Military History Museum. 232, 233: Courtesy Ronn Palm; Library of Congress No. B817 7611—courtesy Mark A. Elrod Collection*; Gettysburg National Military Park Museum*. 234: California Citizen Soldier Museum—Gettysburg National Military Park Museum*. 235: Courtesy Don Troiani Collection*. 236: Courtesy Stamatelos Brothers Collection, Cambridge*; Library of Congress; Michael J. McAfee—Atlanta Historical Society, Atlanta, Ga.* 238: Courtesy Ronn Palm; courtesy Don Troiani Collection* (2)—courtesy Stamatelos Brothers Collection, Cambridge* (2). 240: Courtesy Don Troiani Collection*—Milwaukee Public Museum, photographed by David Busch; Smithsonian Institution, National Museum of American History, Washington, D.C.* 241: New York State Division of Military and Naval Affairs, Military History Collection*; courtesy William B. Styple Collection*—courtesy Don Troiani Collection, photographed by Al Freni. 242: Courtesy California State Capitol Museum, Sacramento, Calif., photographed by Robert DiFranco. 246, 247: National Park Service/HFC, Washington, D.C. 248: Massachusetts State House Flag Project, Bureau of State Office Buildings, Commonwealth of Massachusetts, photographed by Douglas Christian; Michael J. Hammerson, London—New York State Division of Military and Naval Affairs, Military History Collection, photographed by Henry Groskinsky. 249: Kentucky Historical Society-Military History Museum; courtesy Howard Michael Madaus—California State Capitol Museum, Sacramento, Calif., photographed by Robert DiFranco—Pennsylvania Capitol Preservation Committee's *Advance the Colors!*; Wisconsin Veterans Museum, Madison. 250: Kentucky Historical Society-Military History Museum—Massachusetts State House Flag Project, Bureau of State Office Buildings, Commonwealth of Massachusetts, photographed by Douglas Christian; courtesy William Gladstone Collection. 251: Michigan Capitol Committee, photography by Peter Glendinning (2)—New York State Division of Military and Naval Affairs, Military History Collection*; Military Historical Society of Minnesota. 252: New York State Division of Military and Naval Affairs, Military History Collection, photographed by Henry Groskinsky. 253: Massachusetts State House Flag Project, Bureau of State Office Buildings, Commonwealth of Massachusetts, photographed by Douglas Christian (2)—Pennsylvania Capitol Preservation Committee's *Advance the Colors!* (2). 254: Kentucky Historical Society-Military History Museum. 255: Wisconsin Veterans Museum, Madison (2)—State of Connecticut General Assembly, Joint Committee on Legislative Management, photographed by Gus Johnson (2). 256: Pennsylvania Capitol Preservation Committee's *Advance the Colors!* (3)—courtesy Robert Schell Ulrich. 257: Massachusetts State House Flag Project, Bureau of State Office Buildings, Commonwealth of Massachusetts, photographed by Douglas Christian—Massachusetts State House Flag Project, Bureau of State Office Buildings, Commonwealth of Massachusetts, photographed by Jack Leonard (2)—Massachusetts State House Flag Project, Bureau of State Office Buildings, Commonwealth of Massachusetts, photographed by Douglas Christian (2). 258: Wisconsin Veterans Museum, Madison (2)—Historical Society of Delaware, Wilmington (2). 259: Military Historical Society of Minnesota; West Virginia

State Museum, photographed by Michael Keller—Michigan Capitol Committee, photography by Peter Glendinning. 260: Wisconsin Veterans Museum, Madison—West Point Museum, USMA, photographed by Henry Groskinsky; Milwaukee Public Museum, photographed by Leo Johnson. 261: U.S. Signal Corps photo, No. 111-B-259 (Brady Collection) National Archives—New York State Division of Military and Naval Affairs, Military History Collection*—courtesy Howard Michael Madaus, photographed by Leo Johnson—Pennsylvania Capitol Preservation Committee's *Advance the Colors!*—Indiana War Memorial, Indianapolis, photographed by Tom Pierson. 262: Wisconsin Veterans Museum, Madison (2)—Pennsylvania Capitol Preservation Committee's *Advance the Colors!*; National Park Service-Ford's Theatre, NHS. 263: Pennsylvania Capitol Preservation Committee's *Advance the Colors!*; West Point Museum Collections, USMA*—Pennsylvania Capitol Preservation Committee's *Advance the Colors!* (2). 264: West Point Museum Collections, USMA*. 265: Ohio Historical Society (2)—courtesy Michael McAfee; Kentucky Historical Society-Military History Museum; courtesy Ohio Historical Society, photographed by David R. Barker. 266: Tom Tracy, courtesy Presidio Army Museum Collection, San Francisco—West Point Museum Collections, USMA*. 267: Maine State Museum, photographed by Gregory Hart—from *Armies and Leaders*, Vol. 10, "The Photographic History of the Civil War," edited by Francis Trevelyan Miller, published by The Review of Review Co., New York, 1912—Pennsylvania Capitol Preservation Committee's *Advance the Colors!*; Massachusetts State House Flag Project, Bureau of State Office Buildings, Commonwealth of Massachusetts, photographed by Douglas Christian. 268: Kentucky Historical Society-Military History Museum; State Museum of Pennsylvania/Pennsylvania Historical and Museum Commission—West Point Museum Collections, USMA*. 269: Courtesy Ronn Palm; courtesy Howard Michael Madaus, photographed by Leo Johnson—Massachusetts State House Flag Project, Bureau of State Office Buildings, Commonwealth of Massachusetts, photographed by Douglas Christian (2). 270: New York State Division of Military and Naval Affairs, Military History Collection, photographed by Henry Groskinsky—New York State Division of Military and Naval Affairs, Military History Collection*; Military Historical Society of Minnesota. 271: West Point Museum Collections, USMA*—War Library and Museum, MOLLUS, photographed by Larry Sherer; California State Capitol Museum, Sacramento, Calif., photographed by Robert DiFranco—Vermont Historical Society, photographed by Andrew Kline. 272: New York State Division of Military and Naval Affairs, Military History Collection* (3); Civil War Library and Museum, Philadelphia*. 273: U.S. Signal Corps photo, No. 111-B-2191 (Brady Collection) National Archives; Pennsylvania Capitol Preservation Committee's *Advance the Colors!*—Massachusetts State House Flag Project, Bureau of State Office Buildings, Commonwealth of Massachusetts, photographed by Douglas Christian; California State Capitol Museum, Sacramento, Calif., photographed by Robert DiFranco. 274: Western Reserve Historical Society, Cleveland—Vesterheim, Norwegian-American Museum, Decorah, Iowa—Wisconsin Veterans Museum, Madison. 275: Kenneth H. Powers; State of Connecticut General Assembly, Joint Committee on Legislative Management, photographed by Gus Johnson—Massachusetts State House Flag Project, Bureau of State Office Buildings, Commonwealth of Massachusetts, photographed by Douglas Christian. 276: Photography Collections, Uni-

versity of Maryland, Baltimore County—New York State Division of Military and Naval Affairs, Military History Collection* (2). 277: Massachusetts State House Flag Project, Bureau of State Office Buildings, Commonwealth of Massachusetts, photographed by Douglas Christian (2)—Milwaukee Public Museum, photographed by Leo Johnson; courtesy Michael McAfee*; Smithsonian Institution, Washington, D.C. 278: State of Connecticut General Assembly, Joint Committee on Legislative Management, photographed by Gus Johnson—Wisconsin Veterans Museum, Madison; Indiana War Memorial, Indianapolis, photographed by Tom Pierson. 279: Courtesy Jack O'Brien, Irish Cultural Society; Notre Dame University, photographed by Kevin B. Knepp—Kenneth H. Powers; New York State Division of Military and Naval Affairs, Military History Collection*. 280: Massachusetts State House Flag Project, Bureau of State Office Buildings, Commonwealth of Massachusetts, photographed by Douglas Christian—Wisconsin Veterans Museum, Madison; New York State Division of Military and Naval Affairs, Military History Collection, photographed by Henry Groskinsky. 281: West Point Museum Collections, USMA* (2)—Kentucky Historical Society-Military History Museum; Pennsylvania Capitol Preservation Committee's *Advance the Colors!* 282: Smithsonian Institution, Division of Armed Forces History, Washington, D.C.—Milwaukee Public Museum—Pennsylvania Capitol Preservation Committee's *Advance the Colors!* 283: Smithsonian Institution, Division of Armed Forces History, Washington, D.C. 284: West Point Museum Collections, USMA*—National Archives Neg. No. 111-B-37—Civil War Library and Museum, Philadelphia*; War Library and Museum/MOLLUS, photographed by Larry Sherer. 285: Smithsonian Institution, Division of Armed Forces History, Washington, D.C. 286: Milwaukee Public Museum—Smithsonian Institution, Division of Armed Forces History, Washington, D.C. 287: West Point Museum Collections, USMA* (2)—Library of Congress. 288: Smithsonian Institution, Division of Armed Forces History, Washington, D.C. 289: Courtesy Howard Michael Madaus, photographed by Leo Johnson; courtesy Butterfield & Butterfield, Auctioneers Corp.—painting by Thure de Thulstrup, Soldiers and Sailor's Memorial Hall, Pittsburgh, photographed by Herbert K. Barnett. 290: Western Reserve Historical Society, Cleveland—courtesy Howard Michael Madaus, photographed by Leo Johnson—Civil War Library and Museum, Philadelphia*. 291: New York State Division of Military and Naval Affairs, Military History Collection*—courtesy Michael McAfee*; courtesy Howard Michael Madaus, photographed by Leo Johnson—West Point Museum Collections, USMA* (2). 292: Smithsonian Institution, Division of Armed Forces History, Washington, D.C.—Mass./MOLLUS/USAMHI—Smithsonian Institution, Division of Armed Forces History, Washington, D.C. 293: Smithsonian Institution, Washington, D.C.—Milwaukee Public Museum, photographed by Leo Johnson—Smithsonian Institution, Washington, D.C.—Mass./MOLLUS/USAMHI, copied by Robert Walch. 294, 295: Courtesy Michael McAfee*; New York State Division of Military and Naval Affairs, Military History Collection*. 296: Manassas National Battlefield Park, National Park Service, photographed by Larry Sherer. 298, 299: Courtesy of the Rhode Island State House, Providence, photographed by Mark Sexton. 300: Courtesy Philip Brandt George—Manassas National Battlefield Park, photographed by Larry Sherer. 301: Gettysburg National Military Park Museum*. 302, 303: Artwork by Donna J. Neary; Gettysburg National Military Park Museum*; Richard Katter Collection, photographed by Larry Sherer (4)—Atlanta Historical Society, Atlanta, Ga.*—Fort Ward Museum, City of Alexandria, Va., photographed by Larry Sherer (5)—Gettysburg National Military Park Museum*—Fort Ward Museum, City of Alexandria, Va., photographed by Larry Sherer (2)—Richard Katter Collection, photographed by Larry Sherer (2). 304, 305: Gettysburg National Military Park Museum*; Fort Ward Museum, City of Alexandria, Va., photographed by Larry Sherer (2); Gettysburg National Military Park Museum*;

Fort Ward Museum, City of Alexandria, Va., photographed by Larry Sherer; Richard Katter Collection, photographed by Larry Sherer—Homer Babcock Collection, photographed by Larry Sherer; artwork by William J. Hennessy, Jr.—Manassas National Battlefield Park, photographed by Larry Sherer—courtesy Will Gorgas, New Bern, N.C.*; Eagle Head Arsenal, Manassas, Va., photographed by Larry Sherer; Richard Katter Collection, photographed by Larry Sherer (4)—Gettysburg National Military Park Museum*; Eagle Head Ar-

senal, Manassas, Va., photographed by Larry Sherer. 306: Library of Congress No. B8184 4547A—Library of Congress No. B8171 7249. 307: Atlanta Historical Society, Atlanta, Ga., photographed by Michael W. Thomas. 308: Mass./MOLLUS/USAMHI, copied by A. Pierce Bounds—Atlanta Historical Society, Atlanta, Ga., photographed by Michael Thomas. 309: USAMHI, copied by A. Pierce Bounds (2). Parrott sight, Fort Ward Museum, City of Alexandria, Va., photographed by Larry Sherer.

BIBLIOGRAPHY

BOOKS

Adams, George Worthington, *Doctors in Blue*. New York: Henry Schuman, 1952.

Albert, Alphaeus H., *Record of American Uniform and Historical Buttons*. Boyertown, Pa.: Boyertown Publishing, 1976.

Anderson, Bern, *By Sea and by River: The Naval History of the Civil War*. New York: Alfred A. Knopf, 1962.

Beatty, John, *The Citizen-Soldier*. Cincinnati: Wilstach, Baldwin & Co., 1879.

Boatner, Mark Mayo, III, *The Civil War Dictionary*. New York: David McKay, 1959.

Bryant, Carolyn, *And the Band Played On, 1776-1976*. Washington, D.C.: Smithsonian Institution Press, 1975.

Chamberlain, Joshua Lawrence, *The Passing of the Armies*. Dayton: Press of Morningside Bookshop, 1981.

Coates, Earl J., and Dean S. Thomas, *An Introduction to Civil War Small Arms*. Gettysburg, Pa.: Thomas Publications, 1990.

Coggins, Jack, *Arms and Equipment of the Civil War*. New York: The Fairfax Press, 1983.

Davis, Carl L., *Arming the Union: Small Arms in the Civil War*. Port Washington, N.Y.: Kennikat Press, 1973.

Davis, William C. (Ed.), *Touched by Fire: A Photographic Portrait of the Civil War* (Vol. 1). Boston: Little, Brown, 1985.

De Forest, John William, *A Volunteer's Adventures: A Union Captain's Record of the Civil War*. New Haven: Yale University Press, 1946.

Dickey, Thomas S., and Peter C. George, *Field Artillery Projectiles of the American Civil War*. Atlanta: Arsenal Press, 1980.

D'Otrange Mastai, Boleslaw, and Marie-Louise D'Otrange Mastai, *The Stars and the Stripes*. New York: Alfred A. Knopf, 1973.

Dunlop, W. S., *Lee's Sharpshooters: The Forefront of Battle*. Dayton: Press of Morningside Bookshop, 1982.

Dyer, Frederick H., *A Compendium of the War of the Rebellion* (Vols. 1 and 2). Dayton: Press of Morningside Bookshop, 1979 (reprint of 1908 edition).

Editors of Time-Life Books, The Civil War series. Alexandria, Va.: Time-Life Books, 1987.

Edwards, William B., *Civil War Guns*. Secaucus, N.J.: Castle Books, 1978.

Elting, John R., *Military Uniforms in America* (Vol. 3). Novato, Calif.: Presidio Press, 1982.

Elting, John R., and Michael J. McAfee (Eds.), *Military Uniforms in America* (Vol. 3). Novato, Calif.: Presidio Press, 1982.

Flayderman, Norm, *Flayderman's Guide to Antique American Firearms*. Northfield, Ill.: DBI Books, 1980 (second edition).

Garofalo, Robert, and Mark Elrod, *A Pictorial History of Civil War Era Musical Instruments and Military Bands*. Charleston, W.Va.: Pictorial Histories Publishing, 1985.

Goss, Warren Lee, *Recollections of a Private*. New York: Thomas Y. Crowell, 1890.

Hazen, Margaret Hindle, and Robert M. Hazen, *The Music Men*. Washington, D.C.: Smithsonian Institution Press, 1987.

Hazlett, James C., Edwin Olmstead, and M. Hume Parks, *Field Artillery Weapons of the Civil War*. Newark: University of Delaware Press, 1983.

Hitchcock, Frederick L., *War from the Inside*. Philadelphia: J. B. Lippincott, 1904.

Hogg, Ian V., *Weapons of the Civil War*. New York: Military Press, 1987.

Holmes, Oliver Wendell, Jr., *Touched with Fire: Civil War Letters and Diary*. Cambridge: Harvard University Press, 1946.

Johnson, Robert Underwood, and Clarence Clough Buel (Eds.), *Battles and Leaders of the Civil War* (Vol. 4). New York: Century, 1888.

Lewis, Berkeley R., *Small Arms and Ammunition in the United States Service 1776-1865*. Washington, D.C.: Smithsonian Institution Press, 1968.

Long, E. B., with Barbara Long, *The Civil War Day by Day: An Almanac, 1861-1865*. Garden City, N.Y.: Doubleday, 1971.

Lord, Francis A.:
Civil War Collector's Encyclopedia (Vol. 1). Secaucus, N.J.: Castle Books, 1965.

Lord, Francis A., and Arthur Wise, *Bands and Drummer Boys of the Civil War*. South Brunswick, N.J.: Thomas Yoseloff, 1966.

Lyman, Theodore, *Meade's Headquarters 1863-1865: Letters of Colonel Theodore Lyman*. Ed. by George Agassi. Boston: Atlantic Monthly Press, 1922.

McAulay, John D.:
Carbines of the Civil War 1861-1865. Union City, Tenn.: Pioneer Press, 1981.
Civil War Breech Loading Rifles. Lincoln, R.I.: Andrew Mowbray, 1987.

Madaus, H. Michael, *The Warner Collector's Guide to American Longarms*. New York: Main Street Press, 1981.

Murfin, James V., *Battlefields of the Civil War*. New York: Portland House, 1988.

Olson, Kenneth E., *Music and Musket: Bands and Bandsmen of the American Civil War*. Westport, Conn.: Greenwood Press, 1981.

Peterson, Harold L., *The American Sword, 1775-1945*. Philadelphia: Ray Riling Arms Books, 1965.

Porter, Horace, *Campaigning with Grant*. Alexandria, Va.: Time-Life Books, 1981 (reprint of 1897 edition).

Reilly, Robert M., *United States Military Small Arms, 1816-1865*. Baton Rouge, La.: Eagle Press, 1970.

Ripley, Warren, *Artillery and Ammunition of the Civil War*. New York: Promontory Press, 1970.

Sauers, Richard A., *Advance the Colors! Pennsylvania Civil War Battle Flags*. Harrisburg, Pa.: Pennsylvania Capitol Preservation Committee, 1987.

Stevens, George T., *Three Years in the Sixth Corps*. Alexandria, Va.: Time-Life Books, 1984 (reprint of 1866 edition).

Stockwell, Elisha, Jr., *Private Elisha Stockwell, Jr., Sees the Civil War*. Ed. by Byron R. Abernethy. Norman: University of Oklahoma Press, 1958.

Sword, Wiley, *Firepower from Abroad: The Confederate Enfield and the Le Mat Revolver, 1861-1863*. Lincoln, R.I.: Andrew Mowbray, 1986.

Sylvia, Stephen W., and Michael J. O'Donnell:
Civil War Canteens. Orange, Va.: Moss Publications, 1990.
The Illustrated History of American Civil War Relics. Orange, Va.: Moss Publications, 1978.

Todd, Frederick P.:
American Military Equipage, 1851-1872 (Vol. 1). New York: Charles Scribner's Sons, 1978.
American Military Equipage, 1851-1872, State Forces (Vol. 2). New York: Chatham Square Press, 1983.

Tucker, Glenn, *Chickamauga: Bloody Battle in the West*. Indianapolis: Bobbs-Merrill, 1961.

United States Navy, Naval History Division, *Civil War Naval Chronology, 1861-1865*. Washington, D.C.: United States Department of the Navy, 1971.

United States War Department, *War of the Rebellion: A Compilation of the Official Records of the Union and Confederate Armies* (Series 1-3). Washington, D.C.: Government Printing Office, 1889.

Warner, Ezra J., *Generals in Blue*. Baton Rouge: Louisiana State University Press, 1977 (reprint of 1964 edition).

Wasson, R. Gordon, *The Hall Carbine Affair*. New York: Pandick Press, 1948.

Wiley, Bell Irvin, *The Life of Billy Yank: The Common Soldier of the Union*. Baton Rouge: Louisiana State University Press, 1981.

Wilson, R. L., *The Colt Heritage*. New York: Simon and Schuster, 1939.

PERIODICALS

Borrell, Robert, Sr., "U.S. Army Uniforms of the Civil War." *Military Images,* November-December 1981.

Haarmann, Albert W., "The Blue and the Gray." *Military Images,* May-June 1985.

Katcher, Philip, "Naval Uniforms of the Civil War." *Military Images,* November-December 1979.

McAfee, Michael J.:
"U.S. Army Uniforms of the Civil War. Part I: The Frock Coat." *Military Images,* January-February 1981.

"U.S. Army Uniforms of the Civil War. Part II: The Sack Coat." *Military Images,* July-August 1981.

"U.S. Army Uniforms of the Civil War. Part IV: The Jacket." *Military Images,* May-June 1982.

"U.S. Army Uniforms of the Civil War. Part V: The Overcoat." *Military Images,* September-October 1982.

"U.S. Army Uniforms of the Civil War. Part VI: Zouaves and Chasseurs." *Military Images,* November-December 1982.

"U.S. Sharpshooters: Army Uniforms of the Civil War. Part VII." *Military Images,* March-April 1984.

"What Is a Zouave?" *Military Images,* September-October 1979.

Madaus, Howard Michael:

"The Flags of the Iron Brigade. Part I: Into the Fray." *Wisconsin Magazine of History,* Autumn 1985.

"McClellan's System of Designating Flags, Spring-Fall 1862." *Military Collector and Historian,* Spring 1965.

Schoenfeld, Martin, "The 14th Brooklyn." *Military Images,* September-October 1987.

Stacey, John, "Naval Uniforms of the Civil War. Part II: U.S. Naval Engineers." *Military Images,* January-February 1980.

Stacey, John, and Paul DeHaan, "Naval Uniforms of the Civil War. Part IV: Enlisted Men of the U.S. Navy." *Military Images,* May-June 1980.

Styple, William, "The Kearny Medal." *Military Images,* November-December 1987.

Winey, Michael J., "Pennsylvanians in Gray." *Military Images,* July-August 1982.

OTHER SOURCES

Fox, William F., "Regimental Losses in the American Civil War, 1861-1865." Albany, N.Y.: Albany Publishing, 1893.

Hill, Steven, and Martha Richardson, "Military Flags of Massachusetts." Unpublished manuscript.

Madaus, Howard Michael:

"Camp Colors, General Guide Flags, and Flank Markers in the U.S. Army, 1861-1865." Unpublished manuscript.

"The Conservation of Civil War Flags: The Military Historian's Perspective." Paper presented at Flag Symposium, Harrisburg, Pa.: Pennsylvania Capitol Preservation Committee, October 29-30, 1987.

Nelson, Chris, "Those Funny Looking Shoes." *Military Images,* November-December 1984.

Peterson, Harold L., "The British Infantry Musket, 1702-1783." *Military Collector and Historian,* December 1951.

Powers, Kenneth H., "Raise the Colors and Follow Me: The Irish Brigade at the Battle of Antietam." New York: Sixty-Ninth Regiment Armory.

INDEX